financial

freedom

FOR

WOMEN

Personal Finance Series

financial

freedom

FOR

WOMEN

Bruce Cameron

ZEBRA

Published by Zebra Press
an imprint of Struik Publishers
(a division of New Holland Publishing (South Africa) (Pty) Ltd)
PO Box 1144, Cape Town, 8000
New Holland Publishing is a member of the Johnnic Publishing Group

First published 2002

1 3 5 7 9 10 8 6 4 2

Publication © Zebra Press 2002
Text © Bruce Cameron 2002

Cover photographs © Photo Access (front) and Independent Newspapers (back)

Publishing manager: Marlene Fryer
Managing editor: Robert Plummer
Editor: Martha Evans
Cover & text designer: Natascha Adendorff
Typesetter: Natascha Adendorff
Photo researcher: Colette Stott

Reproduction by Hirt & Carter Cape
Printed and bound by CTP Book Printers

ISBN 1 86872 347 X

www.zebrapress.co.za

Log on to our photographic website www.imagesofafrica.co.za for an African experience.

The information in this book is current as at March 2002; is given in good faith; and has been
derived from sources believed to be accurate. While every effort has been made by the author
to ensure accuracy, neither the author nor the publisher give a warranty for reliability or
accuracy and cannot be held responsible for any errors, omissions or changes in the financial
environment which will affect the accuracy. The material is not intended as individual
professional advice, and we recommend that you consult a financial adviser before making
any investment or other financial decision.

Contents

Acknowledgements   vii
Introduction   ix

1   Know Yourself   1
2   Your Financial Plan   11
3   Debt – Your Achilles Heel   20
4   Saving   27
5   Banking   31
6   Spending Wisely   40
7   Women in the Workplace   48
8   Tax   52
9   Buying a Car   66
10   Your Own Home   74
11   Timeshare   91
12   Love and Marriage   98
13   The Cost of Children   110
14   Life Assurance   114
15   Health Assurance   130
16   Protecting What You Own   140
17   Choosing an Adviser   152
18   Rules of Investment   158
19   Investment Made Simple   166
20   Foreign Investment   197
21   Retirement   202
22   Estate Planning   233

Select bibliography   243
Contact details   244
Index   245

For the important women in my life: Lynne, Nikki, Kate, Ali and Tatum

Also to my late mother, Mollie, who showed me by example that women need not be dependent

Acknowledgements

Being editor of the *Personal Finance* publications of Independent Newspapers (South Africa) has placed me in a very advantageous position. This book and others I have written are based primarily on questions and concerns raised by readers of the publications. Through the female readers (who make up a significant proportion of the *Personal Finance* readers) I became increasingly aware that, even in a society that proclaims it aims at being discrimination-free, there is a need for this book.

It is not only that there is still discrimination against women in various areas; there is also the simple fact that, for various reason, women often have different needs from men in managing their finances.

So, in writing this book, I have drawn on the many questions and problems I have dealt with over the past six years and acknowledge this assistance in arriving at what issues to deal with.

Though there is a bibliography at the end of the book, much more of the research has come in the form of advice and assistance from a great many individuals in the wider financial services industry. They are too numerous to name, but there are a few I would like to mention. They are Dave Hudson, Di Turpin and Stephen Bowey at Old Mutual, Hendrik du Toit and Jeremy Gardiner at Investec, George Rudman (now retired) and François Marais at Sanlam, and Adrian Gore at Discovery. The others know who they are and I thank them for their patience and assistance.

Then there are also the financial services companies that have provided information over the years. Predominant have been Discovery, Investec, Liberty Life, Old Mutual and Sanlam. My thanks to Sanlam, too, for sponsoring this book.

There are a number of people at Independent Newspapers I would like to thank: Ivan Fallon, the chief executive, who agreed with me that there was the need for a personal finance publication and provided tremendous support. Without *Personal Finance* this book would never have been written. To my current and former colleagues, particularly Alide Dasnois, Esann de Kock, Charlene Clayton, Laura du Preez, Theresa Smith, Carol Hobday, Jackie Cameron and Charlotte Matthews (women all), on whose experience, research and work I have drawn in writing this book.

I also want to thank people who have been more directly involved with the book, namely my wife, Lynne, who helped check the draft script and asked questions that needed to be answered; my personal assistant, Theresa Smith; and the publishers, Zebra, a subsidiary of Struik. In particular at Zebra I would like to mention editor Martha Evans, who is one of the most professional people with whom I have worked, as well as Marlene Fryer, Georgina Hatch, Robert Plummer and Natascha Adendorff.

Introduction

Why a finance book for women, you may ask. One rand earned, saved or spent by a woman is the same as one rand earned, spent or saved by a man. But take a closer look and you'll find that it is not quite so.

In the United States of America 75 percent of people living below the poverty level are women, and they are mainly elderly women. We don't have similar data available in South Africa, but we can expect the figures to be similar, if not worse. The main reason is that women tend to live longer than men, and they often run out of money before they die.

There are many reasons why one rand to a woman is not the same as one rand to a man. This guide will tell you where the disparities lie and how to overcome them. The book is designed to give you practical advice in the four main areas of proper control of financial affairs: how to design successful financial plans; how to accumulate wealth; how to protect your wealth; and how to spend wisely.

Women are increasingly taking control of their financial affairs, and are contributing more, sometimes the most, to the income of the family unit. Since the days when women were considered chattels of men, and marriage was a contract of near slavery, great strides have been made legally, but women are not yet out of the woods. From the day a girl child is born until the day a woman dies, her financial independence is undermined – psychologically, structurally and demographically.

This book will tell you:

- why the odds are against women;
- how to get square; and
- most important of all, how to make your money work for you.

Let's look at some of the reasons why women still have the odds stacked against them. There are four main 'battlefields' in which the odds are against them: in childhood, in adult relationships, in the workplace and finally in the retirement years.

Childhood

'Once upon a time, a beautiful girl was born in a far-off land. When she grew up, she ventured one day into a forest, where she was captured by an evil witch, but she was rescued by a handsome prince. They married and lived happily ever after in a golden castle.'

If you believe the syrup of romantic fairy tales you will never be financially independent. Yet, this myth, in one form or another, is the basis of many childhood stories and even the attitude of parents to their daughters.

Neither fairy tales nor marriage will assure girls of financial security. Kissing frogs is more likely to result in warts, or, put another way, in a lifelong, dangerous and unwanted dependency.

All children, not only boys, should be taught to reach for the stars, and that the only way they will pluck diamonds out of the sky is by their own hard work – by taking responsibility for themselves.

Young girls are seldom taught financial skills, either in the home or at school. How many parents would suggest to their daughters that they become doctors or lawyers, and that their sons marry a doctor or lawyer? But many parents sustain the 'happily ever after' myth for their daughters.

Little girls would grow up in the most wonderful way if their ambition (and that of the erring parent) was not to marry a doctor but to be one.

Adult relationships

Women grow up with society impressing on them that their role in life is to be good daughters and then mothers, so that they will be able to depend on their fathers and then husbands to sustain them financially. The truth is that more than one in four marriages end in divorce.

Women often enter marriage believing that the basic marriage contract will ensure future financial security. It seldom does. Anyone who has to depend on another for financial survival will never be free to make decisions in their own best interests.

How many women do you know who are in jeopardy of an unwanted relationship, who desperately want to escape, but don't have the power of financial independence?

Divorce figures would probably be even higher, but many women are economically trapped in unhappy marriages because they are financially dependent on their husbands. This dependency is frequently made worse because they have children for whom they would have to take responsibility if they divorced. Many women don't believe they can survive financially without their husbands. All women need to ensure that they have the confidence and qualifications to be free of entrapment.

Men often assume, incorrectly, that women are economic idiots who are unable to balance the family budget. And they sometimes see interference in the family budget as an attack on their manliness. Women take the route of least resistance. Many of them don't know how much their husbands earn, whether the family budget balances or the extent of family debt – and few of them ask. All too often, when they realise they need to take a hand, they are faced with a nightmare.

Some women also make the mistake of seeing the balancing of the household budget as managing the family finances. The household budget is a comparatively small, although important, part of the overall family finances.

Women also often accept that the money they earn is 'pin' or play money, while the money earned by their husbands is the real money that pays the bills. Even women who build their own nest egg during marriage find that their savings are the first to be plundered when things go wrong. The savings of women are used to bail out a wonky business venture, to pay for living expenses when income fails to meet expenditure, or to pay for the education of children.

Financial sales people often approach and deal only with the male member of the family, and worse still many women take the attitude that 'my husband deals with the finances'.

Lack of financial knowledge frequently leaves women afraid to make financial decisions, and as a result they are often the soft targets of unscrupulous financial sales people.

The workplace

Women are also often psyched into making the wrong job choices. Although many of them have solid grades at school, when it comes to a tertiary education they slip back into society-determined post-school education and career choices.

Society should ask why so many lesser-paid positions are filled by women. These include secretarial, nursing and shop counter-assistant jobs. It's not that these jobs are not important – the question is why certain jobs should be dominated by women.

The glass ceiling is probably the single biggest issue that prevents women from becoming financially independent. Women, despite anti-discrimination legislation, still earn less than their male counterparts and are often overlooked for promotion. The glass ceiling allows them to look through to the upper levels, but it seldom lets them through to the top jobs and salaries.

> **The glass ceiling allows them to look through to the upper levels, but it seldom lets them through to the top jobs and salaries.**

Women have greater spending pressures in the workplace than men. For example, men are not expected to arrive at work dressed like Versace models. Professional women are often pressurised into spending a far greater proportion of their income on appearance than men, leaving them with much less disposable income, which in turn limits their ability to make sound financial plans.

Also, because the income of a woman is not considered the main source of the family's wealth, they often accept lower-paid jobs and do not actively argue for more job responsibility and higher pay.

Women who go out on their own sometimes discover that they are not seen as entrepreneurs. Apart from not being encouraged to set up their own businesses, even when they show they have the same entrepreneurship as men, they come up against a multitude of barriers. Getting finance is often difficult. For example, banks often require husbands to stand surity for female entrepreneurs, but seldom the reverse.

The retirement years

The fact that women live on average seven years longer than men has an enormous impact on their financial security in the retirement years. Many women live in total poverty in old age because the 'gift' of longevity is not added into their financial calculations.

Longevity means that women need more money at retirement than men; yet they seldom have separate retirement plans. Separate retirement plans are not only essential because of the extra retirement years, but also because of things such as divorce and early widowhood.

The consequences of longevity also affect health plans. Because they live longer, women are frequently underinsured for health. Husbands tend to die earlier – often after a period of financially sapping illness. And women who divorce later in life also suddenly find that they are without a health insurance plan.

SOLUTIONS

Education is the key to real financial freedom for women (and men for that matter) – and education of the right type. No number of anti-discrimination laws will provide true freedom of choice for women if they are not empowered by the right influences and education to exploit that legal protection.

Education is not only about what children learn at school and then at technikon or university; you need to start influencing children from a young age so that they can visualise themselves in empowering roles, such as owning and managing their own business, being a senior executive and possibly supporting a husband, rather than being dependent on someone else. A girl's best friend is a commerce degree – not a diamond engagement ring!

A girl's best friend is a commerce degree – not a diamond engagement ring!

All women have to take sole responsibility for their financial decisions at some stage, often at times when they are extremely vulnerable, for example after divorce or the death of a spouse. If you don't provide the right grounding, it is you, as the parent, who is morally responsible when things go wrong.

The chapters in *Financial Freedom for Women* outline the general principles of keeping personal finances in order, with special emphasis on areas where women need to take care.

In short, these are the solutions for a secure financial future:

- You have to take ownership of your life.
- You must make your own financial decisions.
- You must plan on being single.
- You must do all you can not to be dependent on anyone else to survive.
- Accept that you are quite capable of handling money.
- You must have financial goals.
- You must start mapping out your financial future today.

1

Know Yourself

The first step to becoming financially independent and wealthy is to know yourself. Many people, including women, do not get ahead financially because they keep making the same mistakes. The reason for this is that they don't know themselves, and they don't have a sound financial plan.

Score yourself

Answer these questions to see how you fare in knowing yourself financially.

In Part One give yourself one point for every 'No' answer.

In Part Two give yourself one point for every 'Yes' answer.

1 Question	Yes	No
Do you avoid taking financial decisions?		
Are you afraid of making financial decisions?		
Do you doubt your ability to take financial decisions?		
Do you allow others to make your financial decisions?		
Do you feel that you are always in debt?		
Do you believe that your financial future will take care of itself?		
Do you believe that having money is materialistic?		
Do you rely on someone else for the money you have?		
Do you feel your financial position never improves?		
Do you depend on others to provide for you financially?		
Subtotal		

2 Question	Yes	No
Do you feel that you are financially successful?		
Are you in control of your money?		
Are you in control of your spending?		
Do you save money?		
Do you have a savings plan?		
Do you know the value of what you own?		
Do you know how much you owe?		
Do you invest in unit trusts?		
Do you understand the power of compound interest?		
Do you have a retirement plan?		
Subtotal		
TOTAL POINTS		

0 to 9 points

You are clearly locked into a dependency cycle, or your finances are in a chaotic state from which you need to break free. You are probably in severe debt and do not know how to get out of it. You desperately need to read this book and get yourself on course. You must take charge of your own finances.

Start by assessing all your strengths. (Forget about what you presume to be your weaknesses.) Tell yourself that you can succeed. If you can multiply five by five you can take control of your finances. Give yourself the power to change your life. By educating yourself about money, budgeting and investments you will increase your self-confidence. Start today by following the simple rules in this book, and you will be surprised at how quickly you will get it right.

9 to 15 points

You have a hit-and-miss approach to your finances. You know you have to do certain things, but you do not have a real plan to bring everything together. You need to learn how to structure your financial plans properly and how to avoid spending impetuously. You also need to be a bit more assertive about your financial plans.

16 to 19 points

You are well on your way to controlling your financial future. You already have the confidence and basic knowledge. You probably need only to have a bit more structure to your plans.

20 points

Congratulations! You are in control of your life. The only reason you are reading this book is to see if there are any additional hints you can pick up to strengthen your position. Hopefully, you will find a few tips.

Plan to succeed

Most people don't plan to fail; they fail to plan. Financial failure is not caused only by stupidity. Look at nearly every financial failure and almost without doubt you will find that the cause is a lack of realistic and proper planning. This applies as much to an individual as it does to a business venture. If you have a well-constructed plan you are more likely to succeed.

People who do not have proper plans face the following problems:

- They do not know where they are financially.
- They do not know how to budget.
- They do not have short- and long-term financial goals.
- They do not have consistent savings plans.
- They do not know about investments.
- They lack the confidence or self-discipline to make decisions.
- They are afraid of making mistakes and depend on others.
- They are never sure who to trust because they have done no homework for themselves.
- They do not know how to get help.
- They are not realistic. They dream about what life will be like but do little to make the dream come true.
- They procrastinate – leaving everything until tomorrow.

GETTING TO KNOW YOURSELF

So before deciding on how you are going to select the investment that is going to turn you into a millionaire overnight, you first need to get to know yourself financially. Once you know yourself financially, you can develop a plan to make yourself financially independent.

You must know where you are financially at any given moment to ensure that your plan to be wealthy will work. There are six key questions you need to ask about your finances: How much do you earn? How much do you pay out? How much are you owed? How much do you owe? How much do you own? What are your financial goals?

The first five questions form the basis for sound financial control, whether for an individual or a company. They make up what are called an income statement and a balance sheet. An income statement tells you how much money is coming in and how much money is going out. A balance sheet tells you how much you own and are owed (your assets) against how much you owe (your liabilities).

Your budget

A budget is not only a plan on how you will spend your money; it is also a record of how you have spent your money. Preparing a budget is fairly simple, particularly if you can use a computer spreadsheet. It is a list of your income (what you earn or receive from any source) and what you spend (the money you need to survive, to take holidays, to pay debts, etc.).

These are the advantages of budgeting correctly:

- It keeps you aware of where you money is going.
- It shows you where you went wrong in the past.
- It forces you to make considered choices (for example, the decision to buy something should not be made on the shop floor but within a properly considered plan).
- It helps you plan for the future.
- It tells you whether your plans are realistic.

There are three fundamental rules to correct budgeting:

- Keep your budget realistic: Budgeting will not help you control your finances if you aren't realistic. If there are to be any exaggerations then underestimate your income and overestimate your spending. If you do the opposite you will get yourself into trouble. To keep your budget realistic you should always have two columns of figures. The first column is what you have budgeted; the second column is what actually happened. This will help you to make adjustments to your budget and to establish where you are going wrong. It becomes far easier to identify where you may be overspending and putting your finances out of kilter.
- Income must always exceed spending: If you are budgeting correctly, your income will always exceed your spending. If not, you are digging yourself

into a debt trap that will strangle any chance of becoming wealthy. Always work on having a surplus of income over spending. Don't budget to spend every cent you have. Leave a margin if you possibly can of about 5 percent. It is a good idea to budget for luxuries, such as a night on the town, out of any surplus from the previous month. It gives you a reward for getting it right.

- Get your priorities right: The best place to start is to understand the difference between a need and a want. A need is basic food to survive; a want is caviar and champagne at the best restaurant in town. You must budget for needs first and leave wants until last. For example, I believe that the first thing on anyone's budget should be the repayment of debt (more on debt later). The second, surprisingly, is savings. You must see savings as part of spending, but the good thing about savings is that it is spending on yourself and your future security. In saying this, you should not be putting an inordinate amount of money into one area at the cost of another. This will only make budgeting more difficult.

An emergency fund

You must accept that you won't always get it right and that the unexpected happens. However, there are ways to deal with the unexpected so that you do not blow your budget to smithereens. The best way is to build up an emergency fund. Ideally, an emergency fund should equal at least three months' income. Make sure you understand the meaning of emergency. It is for when your car breaks down or in the event that you lose your job – not for the impulsive purchase of luxuries that are not included in your budget. Incidentally, a good emergency fund against the loss of your job is to build up accumulated leave. Most employers allow you to accumulate a certain number of days every year. If you lose your job, you have the security of an income for the period of leave you have accumulated. For this reason, it is also a good idea to take leave at the end, rather than at the beginning, of a leave cycle. If you have taken your annual leave at the start of the year and you leave your job after six months, you will have the pay you would have received for the number of days' leave to which you were not entitled deducted from you final cheque.

On the next two pages is an example of a budget:

MY BUDGET

Date _____

Expenditure (spending)	Budgeted	Actual
Repayment of debt		
Credit card	R	R
Overdraft	R	R
Home loan	R	R
Car lease	R	R
Other	R	R
Savings		
Savings for short-term goals	R	R
Savings for long-term goals	R	R
Assurance policies	R	R
Retirement funds	R	R
Unit trusts	R	R
Shares	R	R
Needs (items on which you must spend money)		
Transport	R	R
Food	R	R
Rent	R	R
Electricity and water	R	R
Wages	R	R
Essential clothing	R	R
School fees	R	R
Toiletries	R	R
Car insurance	R	R
Household insurance	R	R
Other	R	R
Wants (items that are not necessities)		
Entertainment	R	R
Clothing	R	R
Other	R	R
TOTAL SPENDING	R	R

Net income	Budgeted	Actual
Source	R	R
TOTAL INCOME	R	R
Total income		R
− Spending		R
= Surplus/deficit		R

Your balance sheet

A balance sheet is very easy to compile. It is a list of your assets (everything you own and are owed) and your liabilities (everything you owe). Always strive to have a minimum of liabilities and a maximum of assets. Having a balance sheet will help you avoid another fundamental mistake made by many people, namely confusing high income with wealth. People earning high salaries can be extremely poor because they have high debt; while someone earning a low income can be quite wealthy because they have built up their assets. The true measure of wealth is the extent by which the value of your assets is greater than your debts. Your balance sheet will provide you with warning signals about your financial health.

Monitor these warning signs:

• If you have more liabilities than assets you can be considered bankrupt and sequestrated by the people to whom you owe money – not a good thing.
• If your liabilities exceed your assets, or your liabilities are equal to more than three-quarters of your assets, you are in desperate trouble. The amount you pay in interest every month will make it impossible to get ahead. This situation is known as a debt trap. You will have to reduce your standard of living substantially and consider selling assets to reduce your debt load. You cannot put off taking hard and difficult decisions for another moment.
• If you are building up debt to pay for your current living expenses like rent, food or clothing, you are getting yourself into trouble.

You should work towards having no liabilities. Always try to keep your liabilities below half the value of your assets. When you are younger, this is obviously more difficult, as you have not had time to build up your assets.

On the next two pages is an example of a balance sheet:

MY BALANCE SHEET

My assets

Asset	Value

Short-term assets

Money owed to me
Owed by .... R
Owed by .... R

Bank savings accounts
Account no.................................... Bank............................... R
Motor vehicle (trade-in value) .... R

Other short-term assets (reflect only saleable value)
Asset.. R
Asset.. R

SUBTOTAL   R

Long-term assets

Unit trust funds
Unit trust account no .... Fund .... R
Unit trust account no .... Fund .... R

Life assurance policies (investments only)
Policy no .... Company .... R
Policy no .... Company .... R

Shares
Company .... R
Company .... R

Retirement Savings
Retirement fund .... R
Retirement annuity.. R

Property .... R
Other property .... R

SUBTOTAL   R

TOTAL ASSETS   R

My liabilities

Liability	Value
Short-term liabilities	
Bank	
Overdraft..	R
Credit card	R
Store cards	
Company	R
Company ...:......................................	R
Hire purchase	
Contract one....................................	R
Contract two....................................	R
Motor vehicle	
Lease contract	R
Loan...	R
Accounts	
Overdue electricity and water accounts.................................	R
Other short-term liabilities	
Debt to	R
Debt to	R
TOTAL SHORT-TERM LIABILITIES	R
Long-term liabilities	
Property	
First outstanding home loan......................................	R
Second outstanding home loan......................................	R
Other long-term liabilities	
Debt to	R
Debt to	R
TOTAL LONG-TERM LIABILITIES	R
TOTAL LIABILITIES	R
My net worth	
Total assets	R
− Total liabilities	R
= Net worth	R

Now that you know yourself financially you will be able to construct a comprehensive plan:

- to make or keep yourself financially stable;
- to meet the unexpected without being left destitute; and
- to achieve your financial goals.

2

Your
Financial Plan

Once you know your financial self you need to draw up a plan to secure your current and future financial well-being. Here women must plan on being single, whether they are married or not. You may be lucky enough to have a spouse who is loyal, loving and hardworking, but you can never tell what tomorrow holds. You are not a fortune-teller. No one can reliably predict the future, so plan for a financial scenario in which you will always be single, or are likely to become single, even if you are married. Remember that divorce is not the only reason why you could become single again. Death unfortunately comes without choice.

SEPARATING FINANCIAL AFFAIRS

By planning on being financially single you will not only take account of the unpredictable future, you will also make any relationship easier in the long run. Keeping your financial affairs separate does not imply distrust. It doesn't mean that you or your husband need to quietly hive off the family earnings into some secret trust that the other knows nothing about. That would imply something else. Separating financial affairs is just plain good sense and can prevent a lot of problems.

Keeping your financial affairs separate does not imply distrust.

Obviously, in a relationship it is impossible to separate financial affairs totally. For example, it can make good sense to have a joint bank account to manage household expenses. But you need to keep the main thrust of your financial affairs separate, particularly when it comes to ownership of assets. Separation of financial affairs covers everything, from separate bank accounts to savings plans, investments and retirement plans.

There are a number of practical reasons why you should keep both your assets and your liabilities in your own name:

- If either one of you goes bankrupt the assets of the other cannot be claimed by the other's creditors, unless of course you stood surety for your spouse's debts. This is particularly important if one or other partner is running a business of some sort.
- In the event of a divorce it can prevent messy conflict over what is rightfully yours.
- In the event of death your assets will not be tied up while an estate is wound up.
- It allows you to establish your own credit record. A sound credit record is important. If your partner owns a business that goes bankrupt, it may be important for you to have access to credit (or visa versa if you have your own business). Keeping your affairs separate does not mean that you cannot come to each other's aid in times of need. The important issue is to ensure that you structure the arrangements properly, as if you were conducting any other financial transaction.

Here are important ways to separate your financial affairs:

- If you are helping out a partner, for example in funding a business, make it a repayable loan rather than a gift. Make sure that a proper acknowledgement of debt is signed.
- Secure major assets. If your partner runs his own business, ensure that major assets, such as your home and motor vehicle, are in your name or in the name of an inter vivos trust of which you are also a trustee and beneficiary. You need to do this to ensure that creditors cannot attach the asset/s if the business venture falls apart. For the same reason, an inter vivos trust is also a good idea if you are running your own business. (For more information on trusts, see p. 237 in Chapter 22.)
- Having your own financial adviser rather than a joint financial adviser means that your interests will be put first. You can also compare notes with your partner on what is being advised.
- Don't turn yourself into a pumpkin. Don't take the attitude 'I am bad with figures. I let my husband do all those things for me.' Stay fully involved

in all your family finances. On the death of a husband or after a divorce, many women are left stranded and at the mercy of unscrupulous people because they know nothing about money. You don't have to spend your days studying economic tomes, but there are many newspaper publications, like *Personal Finance* appearing in all the Saturday newspapers of the Independent Newspaper group, which will help keep you informed in understandable language.

* Maintain a separate source of income. Many single women, or women in the early years of marriage, hold down successful jobs, and are later faced with a conflict of interest when they have children. Do they give up their jobs and devote their lives to their children, or do they keep their careers going? The answer is a matter of individual choice. However, you should find some alternative source of income as soon as possible so that you can at least keep your savings and investment plans on track. Employers are becoming increasingly more sensitive to motherhood by allowing for half-day employment and even having crèches on the premises. Many professional women manage their own businesses from home. Keeping your hand in will make it easier to fit back into the work force when you need to.

SETTING YOUR GOALS

Before you can draw up a financial plan you need to know your goals. This is as important as knowing your financial self. Not having financial goals is like taking a holiday without knowing where you are going.

Your goals must also be attainable. It is pointless setting goals that you have no chance of achieving. This will only result in giving up and not achieving any goals.

> **Not having financial goals is like taking a holiday without knowing where you are going.**

You should have short-, medium- and long-term goals, which must be an integral part of your budget. You need to understand the differences between these types of goals because you will use different financial structures and products to achieve them.

Short-term goals

Short-term goals are those that you wish to achieve within 12 to 36 months. They include:

- building up an emergency fund;
- paying off debt;
- further education for yourself;
- a deposit on a home;
- an overseas holiday; and/or
- buying a new car.

Most short-term saving is done through interest-earning investments such as a bank savings account, bank term (fixed) deposits, bank money market accounts or unit trust money market funds. The reason for this is that most longer-term savings have costs attached to them. If you withdraw money in medium- to longer-term savings vehicles such as unit trust equity funds you will not have allowed sufficient time for the recovery of costs. (See p.186 in Chapter 19 for more information on unit trusts.)

Medium-term goals

Medium-term goals cover a three- to twenty-year period. They include:

- paying off the mortgage bond on your home;
- saving for the education of children; and/or
- saving to start a business.

You would use mainly capital growth investments, such as shares or equity unit trusts, for medium- to long-term financial goals.

Long-term goals

There is essentially only one long-term goal: to have sufficient money for retirement. In setting this goal you also need to decide on the age at which you want to retire. You must start saving today if you want a financially secure retirement. You would use mainly capital growth investments, such as bonds and investments in the share market, to achieve long-term goals.

You need to list your goals. Here is a basic list.

	Amount	Period
Short-term goals		
Outstanding debt		
Credit card	R	
Clothing account	R	
Other debt	R	
New purchases		
Motor vehicle	R	
New stove	R	
Other purchases	R	
Holiday trip	R	
Other	R	
Medium-term goals		
Mortgage bond	R	
Education of children	R	
New business	R	
Long-term goals		
Retirement	R	

You will probably discover that you don't know all the answers. For example, if you are 25, how do you know how much money you will need for retirement or even when you will be able to retire? The point of this exercise is to help you identify not only what you already know but also what you might not know. It is good to know what you want or need in the future. The next question is whether you can afford your goals.

STRUCTURING YOUR FINANCIAL PLAN

Now that you know how much money you have and how much money you want and need, try to pull it all together. The key to the success of any financial plan is to know what you need and how much you can afford. The affordability of any plan is essential. If proper priority is not given to your different needs and wants in terms of affordability, your whole plan may well crash. You need to balance your needs with your income and assets.

Life is a balancing act of many risks. Financially, the main risk for everyone is not having enough money to meet needs when they occur. Some risks, such as having sufficient money to pay for the education of children while you are alive, you can meet on your own; and some you need to share with others, such as what happens if you die before you have saved enough for the education of children. To take care of the unexpected, such as death or disability, you need life assurance.

There is no single plan that will suit everyone, as there are five independent factors that affect everyone's financial needs. These are your wealth, your income, your health, your dependants and your goals.

Many people make the mistake of simply guessing at a savings plan and how much life and disability assurance they need – and to make matters worse they think they need to guess only once or twice in a lifetime. The result is that your financial plan can be totally out of line with what you need. For example, you may have too much life assurance, but too little disability assurance, and your savings plans may be nowhere near adequate for important things such as paying for the education of children or retirement.

The key to constructing a cohesive and affordable plan lies in what is called a financial needs analysis (preferably done with the assistance of a good financial adviser).

A financial needs analysis

A financial needs analysis is not something you do only once in the hope of finding all the solutions to your problems. You need to have it done on a regular basis, particularly when your circumstances change. The most important occasions to service your financial position with a financial needs analysis include:

- if you have not had an analysis done in the past five years;
- if you marry;
- if you have children;
- if you divorce;
- if you lose a spouse;
- if you are about to retire; or
- if you start your own business.

The best place to start is with a good financial adviser. You need to take time with an adviser to establish what you do and don't need. An adviser should use a computer program (of which there are many) to do a financial needs analysis. You can do the analysis yourself nowadays if you have access to the Internet. Many financial services companies have programs available to the public. However, unless you have real expertise, you will still need the services of a financial adviser to get advice on the correct financial products for your purposes.

A financial needs analysis, also known as a fact find, will identify:

- your destination (what you need to achieve);
- your travelling kit (what you already have in assets); and
- your financial route map (what you can afford and how to use your financial resources to the best advantage).

Most people need the following:

- risk assurance or income protection against dying or disability;
- a goal saving plan that will include all your financial goals, whether short- or long-term;
- a retirement saving plan that should be treated separately from other financial goals because of its importance; and
- health assurance. (Your medical scheme and things such as hospital and chronic disease assurance must be measured to see if they continue to meet your needs.)

The question you need to ask is how much you can allocate to goal saving, retirement saving, life assurance and healthcare, and how much you can afford for each category. The best place to start is with how much risk assurance you need against dying and disability. If you are single and have no children you could very well argue that you do not need life assurance because you have no dependants, but you will probably need assurance against being disabled and unable to work again.

In deciding how much risk assurance you need you must take the following into account:

- Do you have dependants? If so, how many, and what will their needs be if you die or become disabled?
- What will you need if you become disabled?
- What are your assets? The more you have in assets, the less you need in assurance. If you are wealthy you do not need as much risk assurance as someone with low accumulated wealth but high income.
- What are your liabilities? What will happen to your debts if you die or are disabled? The more money you owe, the more risk assurance you will

17

probably need, and the greater the necessity for a properly constructed and targeted savings and investment plan.

- What is your income and how much do you spend? Your current and future income and spending will determine the design of your financial plan, allowing you to decide on risk and/or investment priorities that you can leave until later when you are earning more. A computer-based program will allow you to make changes to see what will happen under different scenarios.
- How is your health? If you are healthy you can take a greater chance of meeting risk through income than if you are unhealthy.
- What is your current risk assurance? Your current assurance for both life and disability must be assessed to see if you have too much or too little. Include any benefits you will receive from a retirement savings plan in this assessment, whether it is employer-sponsored or attached to a retirement annuity.
- For what time period do you need assurance? You need to break your risk assurance into different periods. For example, you don't need life assurance to cover the education of children until you are 70.

Remember that in deciding on your life assurance needs you should work on the basis of leaving your dependants an adequate amount of money. Don't plan on leaving them immensely wealthy. Rather use as much as possible to improve your own wealth, particularly for your retirement. (See p. 117 in Chapter 14 for a worksheet that will provide you with a rough indication of how much life assurance you need.)

Once you have assessed your life assurance and disability needs, the following priorities should follow:

- Healthcare: Many people forget about healthcare cover until they fall ill or have a major accident. By then it is often too late.
- Retirement saving: You must never underestimate or leave your retirement savings plans out of any financial needs analysis. You need to check whether your investments are keeping you on track to meet your retirement targets at the age you have targeted. You will find, because of variations in inflation and investment performance, that your retirement plans need constant adjustment.
- Goal saving for needs, such as the education of children.
- Goal saving for wants, such as an overseas skiing trip.

Finally, remember that planning your finances is like cutting a diamond. It is a multifaceted affair in which every facet must balance and blend with the others to get a brilliant finish.

3

Debt – Your Achilles Heel

The one thing, more than any other, that makes financial plans go badly awry is debt. As long as you have debt you will not be able to build up wealth. You must make debt repayment a priority. Many people believe that it is not a problem to have debt, but this is the wrong attitude. The main reason for this is that you are renting someone else's money and have to pay interest. It is better to have someone paying you interest.

THERE IS GOOD DEBT

This is not to say you should not borrow money at all. There is some good debt. If you borrow money to buy what is called an appreciating asset, which you can normally expect to go up in value, you can strengthen your position. An appreciating asset is any asset that gains value while you own it. A home is a good example. Most homes, over time, improve in value. You would have to spend many years saving and paying rent before you would be able to buy a home or property of your own for cash. The only option is to borrow money. But again you should repay the debt as quickly as possible.

Don't see borrowing to invest on a stock exchange as good debt. While, historically, assets on a stock exchange have improved in value faster than other assets, they are also extremely volatile. You may find yourself in a financial squeeze if interest rates on your loan soar, while prices on the stock exchange crash – not an unusual occurrence.

MOST DEBT IS BAD DEBT

Avoid borrowing to buy any asset that depreciates in value, such as furniture and even motor vehicles. Interest charged on depreciating assets such as hire purchase on furniture tends to be much higher than interest charged on appreciating assets like a home loan.

The very worst type of debt is money borrowed to buy consumables, like food, clothes or entertainment. These are things that have little or no resale value. If you are borrowing to pay for things that you consume, you are in serious financial trouble. Many people don't realise that they are borrowing to pay for what they consume when they use a store card, a credit card and even a shop account and don't pay back all the money owed every month. After a month, in most cases, you will be paying interest on an outstanding balance. Once you have to pay interest or cannot pay an account in one month, this is debt.

If you are borrowing to pay for things that you consume, you are in serious financial trouble.

The problem with debt is that it is often just too easy to borrow. Switch on a television set, open a newspaper, read the junk mail that clutters your mailbox, go window shopping, look at letters from your bank: everywhere people want to lend you money. But remember that they also want it back, usually with interest.

There are eight major warning signs for being too deeply in debt. These are:

1. You have negative net worth. In other words, you owe more than you own. (Check your balance sheet.)
2. Your spending exceeds your income. (Check your budget.)
3. You have bounced a cheque in the last three months because you did not have sufficient funds in your bank account.
4. Your bank account has been closed, or you have been asked to return a credit or store card.
5. Most of your bills are two or more months in arrears.
6. You have problems juggling around whom you are going to pay each month.
7. You consider unused credit facilities as part of your wealth.
8. Someone has obtained a debt judgement against you.

There are two main areas where people fall into the debt trap. These are the misuse of credit and store cards and variable home loans.

Credit and store cards

Credit cards are fast becoming public enemy number one for people who tend to overload themselves with debt. You must see credit cards as cash that you have not earned.

There are a number of major problems with them:

- Credit and store cards make spending incredibly easy. The credit limits are often quite high, so you can keep on borrowing.
- They are also quite easy to obtain, and you can get a number of them. This means that the total amount you can borrow could be more than your annual income.
- Credit cards give you interest-free money, but only if you repay the full amount you owe before the repayment due date. If you are even one cent short after the repayment date you will pay interest at a very high rate on everything you have bought from the purchase date. Many people think that they will be charged interest only on the unpaid portion. This is not true. You will pay interest on every transaction. And remember that credit card interest rates tend to be very high.
- Credit card debt is so easy to fall into because it is what is known as unsecured debt. This means that because you do not have to provide any security, such as an assurance policy, you will pay higher interest rates. Secured debt is debt to pay off something like your home or a motor vehicle (where the motor vehicle or your home are the security). In other words, the bank will repossess your home or car if you do not pay up. Unsecured debt is given to you almost exclusively on what is called your credit worthiness. If you are considered a good credit risk because you always pay back debt on time, you will be able to borrow more money at a lower interest rate. If you are considered to be a bad credit risk, the amount of money you can borrow will be restricted and you will pay higher interest rates. If you do not repay unsecured debt you can be taken to court and any or all of your possessions can be taken away from you.
- Banks encourage you to use credit card debt by asking you to repay only a fraction of the debt every month – a minimum repayment. But remember

that high interest rates are charged on everything you bought during the previous month, plus the outstanding balance.

Golden rules for using credit cards

If you want or need to use a credit card you must follow ten golden rules.

1. Always repay the full amount due. Never make only the minimum repayment. The minimum repayment required by your bank is basically only the interest you must pay on the debt you have built up. So, if you repay only the minimum, you will never get rid of your debt.
2. Never use the 'budget' section of your credit card. This is definitely not a way of budgeting. It is a way of getting deeper into debt.
3. Do not see a credit card as a status symbol. See credit cards as a potential symbol of debt.
4. Never have more than one credit card. Every card has credit limits that you will be tempted to use.
5. Remember that credit card interest rates are punitively high.
6. Never impulse shop with a credit card. Credit cards encourage impulse shopping, but this will have a very negative effect on maintaining your budget.
7. Use your credit card to pay only for things for which you have budgeted.
8. Never use a credit card for a cash advance unless you keep your account in credit. You will pay interest from the moment you borrow money. Remember that this also applies to buying petrol on your credit card. This is counted as a cash withdrawal.
9. If you already have credit card debt consider paying it off with money you can borrow elsewhere at a lower rate, and then pay off that debt too.
10. Destroy your credit card now if you find that you cannot restrain your use of it. If you need a credit card for convenience or security you can ask your bank to reduce the credit part of your card to zero or a low amount, such as R1 000, forcing you to keep your card in a credit balance. In other words, it becomes a real credit card, not a debt card.

Variable home loans

These are home loans that you can use as a ready source of money. Increasingly, all of us are using variable home loans to fund any shortfall of money that we have. This means that there is less need for us to discipline our spending habits, falling back on any slack on our home loans.

The consequence of this is that when interest rates go sky high, as they tend to do in South Africa, many people lose their homes because they can no longer afford to pay the high interest bills. By maintaining a high level of home loan debt you are also spending a fortune in interest. As long as you are paying interest you will not be building wealth.

HOW TO GET OUT OF DEBT

There is no easy way to get out of debt. It will be tough going but it will be worth it in the end. Here are seven rules you must implement:

1. Cut back on unnecessary spending. This can be from little things, like taking sandwiches to work instead of eating out, to delaying the purchase of a big-ticket items, such as a new motor vehicle, particularly when your current car is in fine condition. A motor vehicle is a major expense, particularly when financed with a loan (you have to pay interest). Often the only reason to replace your perfectly good existing vehicle is to get one with fancy headlights.

2. Don't borrow any more money, particularly from loan sharks, whose interest rates are prohibitive and could lock you into years of misery.

3. Speak to the people to whom you owe money, particularly your bank. Your bank will do the best it can to show you the way out of your problems. If your creditors see you have a plan to get out of debt and are prepared to make sacrifices to get there, they will be more understanding.

4. Pay off high-interest, short-term debt first, particularly credit cards. If you can switch your debt from a high- to a low-interest loan, do so. This could be possible if you have a long-term, secured debt like a home loan. However, you must increase the repayments on the lower-interest loan.

5. Close accounts and tear up credit and store cards as you pay them off.

6. Don't gamble in the hope of scoring the big hit. The odds of it happening are very small. It is more likely that you will lose all your money, making your situation worse.

7. You should not be making investments while you have high debt. Always pay off debt before you start investing. There are two reasons for this:

- The interest you are paying is likely to be higher than the returns you will receive on an investment.
- If interest rates move to high levels you could be forced to sell your investments to reduce your level of debt. This may mean selling when the value of your investments is low. You should never be in a position where you are forced to sell your investments at the wrong time for the wrong price.

Once you have paid off your debt, start building up an emergency fund. Most financial advisers will suggest an emergency fund equal to at least three, but preferably six, months of your after-tax income. An emergency fund will help prevent your falling back into debt again if and when an unexpected event occurs.

Money in an emergency fund should preferably be held in an accessible interest-bearing investment, earning as much interest as possible. If you can build up a sizeable lump sum the best place to invest your money is in a money market bank account or unit trust fund – that is where you will receive the best interest rates.

Don't invest your emergency fund in shares or equity unit trust funds, as markets may be down when you need your money, and you will suffer a loss. Also avoid life assurance endowments, as your money is locked up for a minimum of five years. With all three of these investments, which are excellent vehicles for medium- to long-term savings, you need time for the costs to work out of the system.

A few more tips on debt

- Never use long-term loans, such as on your home loan, to pay for short-term borrowing, like buying furniture or food.
- Never borrow to pay for luxuries, such as a trip overseas.
- Always try to repay a loan early. You can save yourself many thousands of rands by doing so.

Build a reputation as a good borrower

Your credit worthiness is a very important asset. If you are considered a person who does not borrow too much and always repays debt on or before the due date, when you have to make a seriously large loan, such as borrowing to buy a home, you will be able to do so with ease. Plus you will be able to negotiate a lower interest rate. Do everything you can to protect your credit status. Once you have gone wrong, your name will appear on the lists of credit checking agencies. Your bank and any company from whom you want to borrow money has access to these agencies – and once they have you marked down as a bad payer you will have ongoing problems. If your name is already listed you are going to have to rebuild your credit reputation by paying off your debts and being able to prove that you will now act with financial responsibility.

Unless you get your debt under control you will not be able to have a successful investment programme, and you will not achieve your financial goals in life.

4

Saving

Saving and investing are similar, but they are not quite the same thing. Saving is about keeping some of the money you earn or receive to build up a lump sum for a particular purpose. Investing is using the money you save to earn more money. Chapter 18 will deal with investing and its risks.

A savings plan must be deliberate. There are two ways to go about saving: either time-based or amount-based.

Time-based saving

Time-based saving works on reaching a certain target in a defined period of time. So say you want to buy a car in four years' time, your plan will work like this:

Estimated cost of car	R100 000
Less expected return on savings	R 15 000
Required savings	R 85 000
Savings a month: R85 000 ÷ 48 months = R 1 771 a month	

Time-based saving is useful when you know you have a restricted period of time in which to meet your targets or goals, such as paying for the education of children and for retirement savings.

Amount-based saving

With amount-based saving, you target on reaching a certain amount, no matter how long it takes. Let's use the car example again:

Estimated cost of car	R100 000
Monthly saving	R 1 000
Period to reach target: R100 000 ÷ R1 000 = 100 months	

Investment growth has not been taken into account in this example, and it will obviously shorten the period of saving. Amount-based saving should be used for non-essential savings, such as buying a new car or taking an overseas trip.

COMPOUND INTEREST/GROWTH

This is the most important item that you will read in this book. Compound interest/growth is one of the most amazing things in your personal finances. In simple terms, it is reinvesting whatever interest or growth you get on your savings. You then get further interest/growth on your interest and/or your investment growth, and so it continues building up year after year. For example, R1 000 with a return at 10 percent gives you R1 100 (R1 000 plus R100 interest) at the end of the first year. The next year the value of your investment would reach R1 210 (R1 100 plus R110 interest), and so on.

To illustrate the power of compound interest more dramatically, let's do a comparison. Take two people: Jack and Jill. Jill starts investing R100 a month at the age of 21 until she reaches the age of 30. At age 30 she stops saving, but leaves her money invested. At the age of 30, Jack starts saving R100 a month. Even if Jack continues to save R100 a month for the next 30 years, he will not catch up with Jill. The reason is that by the time Jack starts saving, the interest Jill is earning on her savings is already more than R100 a month.

The sooner you start saving, the sooner you will have compound interest working for you.

The moral of this story is that the sooner you start saving, the sooner you will have that very strong investment friend, compound interest, working for you.

The Rule of 72

Here is a rough guide to work out the effects of compound interest. It is called the Rule of 72. With the rule you can work out how often your savings or investments can double in value, depending on the interest or growth rate.

The Rule of 72 gets its name from the calculation that at a compounded rate of interest of 10 percent your investment will double every 7.2 years. You can also use the rule to calculate how long it will take your money to double at any given interest rate. For example:

At 6% how long will it take to double your money?
(72 ÷ 6 = 12 years)

At 15% how long will it take to double your money?
(72 ÷ 15 = 4.8 years)

The Rule of 72 can also be used to calculate what compound growth or interest rate you need to double your money in a chosen number of years.

To double your money in 4 years:
72 ÷ 4 = required interest of 18%

To double your money in 8 years:
72 ÷ 8 = required interest of 9%

There are two types of interest rates. These are simple and compound interest. With simple interest you get quoted one rate for the period of your investment. With compound interest, you will be paid interest on interest. The interest could be added to your savings every month, every three months or every six months. Compound interest is obviously better than simple interest.

There are two ways of being told about interest: nominal and effective rates. Nominal rates are the rates that are quoted for one year. For example, 10 percent on R1 000 would give you a R100 a year in interest. Effective rates are more accurate. When you are quoted a nominal rate you will often find that you are actually being paid (if you have invested money) or are paying (if you have borrowed money) compound interest. This means that you are paying or receiving more than the nominal rate you have been quoted. If interest is paid to you more than once a year and the interest is added to your investment you will receive more interest. For example, say you invest R1 000 for a year at a nominal rate of 10 percent, but the interest is credited to you every six months:

Investment	R1 000
Six months' interest	R 50
Subtotal	R1 050
Next six months' interest	R 52.50
Total investment worth	R1 102.50

So by receiving interest every six months, you receive an extra R2.50. Your nominal rate is 10 percent, but your effective rate is 10.25 percent.

It is important to find out whether you are being quoted an effective or nominal rate. Many institutions quote you an effective rate when you invest money, but quote you the nominal rate when you borrow money from them. This can be very misleading. Always work with effective interest rates. They are more accurate.

WHEN TO START SAVING

The sooner you start saving, the quicker you will get into the habit. The difficult thing is to start. It is also always easier to start when you have a target or a savings goal. Unfortunately, nowadays it is quite easy to borrow money. This makes what is called instant gratification much easier, but there is a price to pay. If you borrow money to pay for something, in the end you pay much more than you would have paid if you had paid cash. These are the reasons:

- You pay the interest on your borrowings.
- When you pay cash for a purchase you can often get a discount. The result of borrowing is that in the end you actually own far less, and you have the worry of debt repayments.

Banks are about the best place to keep your savings until you start investing your money. However, you must shop around and compare bank savings accounts.

5

Banking

To manage your finances properly, banking is an essential service, but like any other service, you need to pay for it. Because of costs, you must be careful about the bank facilities you use. Banks encourage you to use high-cost services by having status-symbol accounts such as gold or platinum credit cards. They also want to lend you money on which they can charge you interest.

BANK ACCOUNTS

There is a wide range of bank accounts that you can use to save or borrow money, as well as to provide many other services to help you keep your personal and business finances in order. You must accept that the more services a bank offers you, the more you will have to pay. So don't step up the level of service you get just so you can look important by having a cheque account when a savings account will do.

When you operate a bank account you must do it in a responsible way. This is particularly the case with a cheque account. With a cheque account it is possible to issue a cheque without any money in your account. But doing this without the permission of your bank manager is illegal, and technically you could be sent to jail. Not only will the person to whom you gave the cheque be fed up, so will the bank. The bank will not pay up; it will charge you a hefty fee for sending the cheque back to the person who deposited it; and if you persist in issuing 'dud' cheques, your account will be closed and you will find it difficult to get banking facilities elsewhere. If you need to 'overdraw' your bank account, in effect borrow money from the bank, you must speak to the bank manager first. The bank manager will arrange to give you an overdraft through which you can borrow money if you are considered to be a responsible customer. Remember that you will be charged interest on the money you borrow.

The different types of bank accounts are savings accounts, transmission accounts, cheque/current accounts and credit card accounts:

Savings account

This is the most basic form of banking account. You can deposit and withdraw money, but have very few additional services. Most savings accounts provide you with access to automatic teller machines (ATMs) and can be used increasingly as debit cards in stores. A debit card allows you to pay for goods and services, as long as you have money in your account, but you can never borrow money.

Transmission account

Some banks offer what are called transmission accounts. These accounts are useful when you do at least 10 to 20 transactions every month. A transmission account is a type of savings account, but you are also able to make a limited number of cheque payments every month and have regular amounts deducted (stop or debit orders) to pay other people or businesses. The cheques can be obtained either through special bank ATMs or through call centres, where you give an instruction over the telephone for someone to be sent a cheque. As with a savings account you cannot use the account to borrow money.

Cheque account

A cheque account – also known as a current account – provides you with a wide range of facilities. You are issued with a chequebook to make payments to third parties. The most important service that you receive with a cheque account is that you can also be given loans (called overdrafts). Cheque accounts come in a number of different forms. You are given a number of cost choices. You can have accounts where you are paid interest on your money; others where there is a guarantee to anyone accepting your cheque that the bank will definitely pay up; and others where, if you keep a minimum balance, you don't pay bank charges. You need to compare the costs to see what is right for you.

Credit card account

These cards are exactly what they say they are. They are banking facilities that allow you to pay for just about anything without actually having the cash. Every month you are sent an account, which you must pay in full; otherwise you will be charged a very high rate of interest. Credit cards are definitely not for people who find it easy to spend money they do not have.

ELECTRONIC BANKING

Banks realise that they have to become more efficient to cut costs and to make it easier for us, their customers, to do our banking. A major expense for banks is all the branches they have around the country. They are also an irritation for us, as we have to stand in queues. So, banks now encourage us to do our banking from a distance. Electronic banking is also allowing new entrants into the market, offering far more competitive charges and interest rates (both for borrowing and lending). This is placing mainline banks under pressure to put a halt to ever-spiralling costs and to improve service.

The development of electronic banking has come in a number of steps. These are ATM machines, call centres and Internet banking

ATM machines

You will find ATMs in the strangest places, but effectively they give you 24-hour access to banking facilities, including depositing and withdrawing money and paying accounts.

Call centres

Telephone call centres are used by bank customers with transmission or current accounts. You dial a number and a bank official answers. You are then required to give certain codes so the bank official knows you are who you say are. Once you have been cleared you can give instructions for payments or other trans-actions to be made. With a call centre you do not have to use a chequebook, as the money is transferred electronically from your account to the account of the person or business you have to pay. All you need is the name, account number, bank and branch of the person you want to pay.

Internet banking

Internet banking allows you to access your bank account on your computer. You can give instructions for payments, check your balance and get statements. This is the banking of the future. Big bank halls and branches all over the place will soon become history as customers manage accounts from home. Computer banking allows for much easier management of your finances at a time that is convenient for you.

Here is a list you can use to make cost comparisons between the banks:

Service	Absa	FNB	Nedbank	Standard	NBS	Pick 'n Pay
Account name						
Interest rate						
Minimum balance						
Charge for using own ATM						
Charge for using other ATM						
Other transaction charge						
Monthly charge						
Deposit charge						
Cash deposit charge						
Any other charges						
Number of withdrawals allowed						

BANKING SECURITY

Banks are not 'safe as houses', as the saying goes. Many banks in South Africa have tried to escape their responsibility to look after your money properly. You have to accept a large degree of responsibility for the security of your money. Electronic banking has added a whole new spectrum of areas where you are vulnerable to fraud.

Banks are not 'safe as houses', as the saying goes.

There are a number of important areas where you must take special care.

Personal identification number (PIN) codes

PIN codes are issued to bank customers to access a variety of banking services. The most important of these are automatic teller machines, telephone call centres and Internet banking. A PIN code gives you access to your account, but if it is obtained by a criminal it also gives them access to your account. In most cases, you will find it extremely difficult to reclaim any losses from a bank if someone else uses your PIN code. Rules for PIN code security include:

- Do not keep your PIN code in the same place as an ATM card, and definitely do not write it on your card. It is best to memorise your code. Leave the record of your PIN in a safe place at home.
- Do not give your PIN code to anyone else – not even a family member.
- Do not use your PIN code as your log-on access number for your computer.
- If you suspect someone else may have your PIN, change it immediately. Banks make it easy for you to change your PIN.
- Do not use the same PIN for all your banking activities. If a criminal obtains a single PIN it provides access to all your banking.
- Treat your PIN as you would the cash from your account if it was in your pocket.

Automatic teller machines (ATMs)

You must be very careful when using an ATM. They have become prime targets of criminals. Here are some rules you should follow.

- Women drawing money from ATMs are often targeted by criminals. This includes the use of physical violence. Never use an ATM if you are suspicious of people in the area, if the ATM is in an isolated spot, if you are at all flustered or distracted and have your mind on other issues, or if it is dark.
- Place a limit on the amount of money that can be withdrawn from your account in any single day. You can do this yourself at the ATM. If there is an emergency and you need more money all you have to do is go to a bank branch with your ID book and ATM card. The bank officials will make an arrangement for you to withdraw extra money.
- If someone asks you for help at an ATM decline politely and refer them to the bank. Criminals often ask for help as a ruse to switch ATM cards and clean out your account.

- If your card appears to be jammed, phone your bank immediately and have the card cancelled. The banks all have emergency telephone numbers. Criminals often create a blockage in the ATM so that they can steal your card as soon as you leave.
- Do not let anyone see you entering your PIN code. If you are feeling crowded, ask the person or people to stand back, or leave and come back later. Also be aware that someone may be watching you through binoculars from a distance attempting to get your PIN code.
- If you are at all suspicious of anything, delay doing your transaction.
- Always remember to remove your cash, card and transaction record.
- Report a loss of your ATM card immediately to your bank so that it can be invalidated.
- Finally, if you are threatened at an ATM, rather let the people have the money. It is better than being injured. However, try to memorise what the people look like. Report any incident immediately to the police and to your bank.

Cheques

Chequebooks have over the years been a major source of fraud. Cheques are a form of money that can be abused in a number of ways. Take the following measures to protect yourself against cheque fraud:

- Keep your chequebook in a safe place. In the hands of a criminal, a cheque-book is like cash.
- Always check your cheque account statements (and all other bank statements) to ensure that they are accurate. Often, this is the first place you will detect a fraud. If you do notice something you do not understand, contact your bank immediately.
- Never sign a blank cheque. This means that you must never sign a cheque without completing the other details.
- Avoid issuing cash cheques. These cheques are like cash and can pass through many hands before being banked. This increases the chances of fraud.
- When making out a cheque you should follow these precautionary steps:
  - Clearly write out the name of the person to whom the cheque is to be issued. Always use the full name of the person to whom you are issuing a cheque. For example, if you are paying the taxman do not write SARS;

rather write 'South African Revenue Service'. The reason for this is that someone could make it payable to 'SARS Smith'.

- Write out the amount clearly, using all the space provided. If you have not used all the space provided draw a double parallel line through the remaining space.
- Endorse a cheque clearly and boldly across the top with the words 'Not Transferable'. This means it can only be deposited into a bank account of the name of the person or company to which you have issued the cheque. This is the only phrase that can be used. You cannot use wording such as 'account payee only' or 'not negotiable'. The bank will accept liability for the cheque being paid into the wrong account only if you have endorsed it 'Not Transferable'.
- Scratch out 'or bearer'. If you write merely the name of a person and do not scratch our 'or bearer' you are allowing the bank to pay out to anyone who has the cheque in their possession.
- Use a pen and not a pencil to complete a cheque.
- Do not make alterations. A bank will not accept any cheque with alterations.

• Avoid sending cheques through the mail. On no account should you ever send a cash cheque through the mail. If you do send a cheque through the mail ensure that it is endorsed 'Not Transferable' and that you scratch out 'or bearer'. Do not staple or use a paper clip to attach your cheque to an account. This is a giveaway for thieves working in post offices.

• Immediately report the loss of your chequebook or a cheque to your bank so that it can be invalidated (stopped).

Credit cards

Credit cards are becoming one of the major target areas of criminals. In combination with Internet shopping, a credit card account is very vulnerable to attack. All the fraudster needs is your credit card number. There is not much you can do to prevent the number of your card landing up in the wrong hands, as every time you use the card the number is printed on the slip. Here are some ways to protect yourself:

• Always read your credit card statements. This is the first place you are likely to detect a fraud. If there has been a fraudulent withdrawal on your card, contact your bank immediately. The bank will reverse the entry to the merchandise provider who accepted the fraudulent payment. The provider must give proof that you have signed the withdrawal.

- Retain your slips to check against your statement.
- Always keep your PIN secure to avoid cash withdrawals on your card.
- Always keep your credit card in sight. Do not allow it out of your sight for the processing at, say, a garage or restaurant. It could be run through twice.
- Always check that your card, and not that of someone else, has been returned to you.
- Do not leave your card, slips or statements lying around.
- Immediately report the loss of a card to your bank so that it can swiftly be invalidated.

Debit orders

Debit orders are increasingly becoming a source of massive fraud involving millions of rands. Here the banks do very little to protect you. A debit order is a deduction from your bank account by a third party. The third party should have your signed permission to make the deduction against your account.

Debit orders can be placed on your account, even without your knowledge. Where you have a debit order abused by a merchant or fraudster it can become very difficult to change it. To cancel a debit order you have to give the instruction to the merchant, not the bank. The bank will reverse an entry only after the third party's instruction has come through. If your account is subject to repeated unauthorised withdrawals insist that the bank closes your account and provides you with a new one. If it will not do this at no cost, take up the issue with the ombudsman for banking.

The most common types of fraud are:

- increasing an existing debit order amount slightly so you do not notice the deduction increase;
- making an additional deduction in any one month; and
- making small deductions from the accounts of many different people, using a merchant name that you may associate with a bank charge.

Here are some ways to avoid debit order fraud:

- Avoid signing debit orders. Rather use stop orders with which you autho-rise the bank to make a payment, or make the payments monthly yourself.
- Do not give the third party the right to alter the amount of the debit order.
- Read the fine print on a debit order very carefully and delete anything with which you are not happy.
- Fill in the maximum amount that may be debited.
- Make the debit order valid for fixed periods.
- Always check your bank and credit card statements carefully.

Protecting yourself against your bank

Banks must abide by a code of good practice. If you have any dispute with a bank you should take up the issue with the banking adjudicator (see p. 244 for contact details).

6

Spending Wisely

There is an old saying that a fool and his money are soon parted. Wise spending is essential if you want to achieve financial independence. People will try to con you into spending your money. It is up to you to know enough not to pay too much and not to buy inferior goods.

LEARN TO BE A SMART CONSUMER

If you plan your purchases you can find good deals and the best value for money. Say you are shopping for washing power, you will find umpteen brands in your local supermarket. So how do you make your choice? You need to make comparisons.

- Price: This is the first thing to compare. You must compare not only the total price but also the price per kilogram, which you should find recorded either on the shelf or on the box.
- Weight of the contents: Compare the weight of the contents. Often you will find a big box with what seems to be a lower price than a smaller box. With one brand you will frequently be offered a jumbo or economy pack. The implication is that the bigger pack is always cheaper. It is often not the case. You must compare the price per kilogram. That will give you the true story.
- Quality: You can sometimes pay less but get poorer quality. Ask around to establish the products with better quality. This is particularly important when you are buying high-price items such as a hi-fi set.
- Different stores: Different stores sell the same item for different prices. The more expensive the item you want, the more you should shop around.
- Advertising: Read any advertisements for special offers very carefully and look for any fine print.
- Guarantees (often called warranties): Different products have different

guarantees. This alone should tell you something about the quality. If one product has a guarantee of only six months while another has a guarantee of two years, it tells you how much confidence the producer has in the product. Guarantees come in two forms:

–   A full guarantee means that no matter what goes wrong your purchase will be repaired or replaced, or your money refunded.

–   A limited guarantee means that not everything in the product is guaranteed, or that the guarantee will be met only under certain conditions, or that the parts will be replaced at no cost but you will have to pay for the labour. Also check on the guarantee policy of the store. Some shops will handle a returned product for you without hassle. Others will expect you to deal with the manufacturer directly.

•   Always keep your receipts and any guarantee forms. Without them you will be unlikely to claim successfully if something goes wrong.

Here are 18 more ways to protect your money:

•   Don't keep up with the Joneses. It feels great to show off a smart new car to the neighbours, but think of it this way: would you like to boast about the debt that comes with it as well? Many people wearing the latest designer clothes and driving sporty little cars don't sleep at night because of the debt burden they carry.

•   Don't borrow to finance consumption. Borrowing to finance your daily living expenses will soon land you in debt, while also making each item cost you more.

•   Negotiate and compare prices. On any big-budget item you must shop around and compare prices. You will be amazed by how much you can reduce prices by negotiating.

•   Pay cash, as you can often negotiate a lower price. Never be embarrassed to ask for a cash discount. It is your money you are saving. Point out that if someone bought the product with a credit card the shop would have to give a discount to the credit card company, so you should get a discount as well.

•   Be wary of credit cards. They can be as easy to use for impulse buying as cash – and you can pay for large and expensive items with credit cards. If you have a tendency to spend easily, avoid getting one. More people get into financial trouble by using a credit card indiscriminately than in other ways. Never use the budget part of your credit card for anything. It is anything but a budget. However, if you find it easy to control your spending, a credit card does have advantages. You can get up to 50 days' credit before you must repay the debt. You can also get points in a loyalty reward programme, based on how much you spend on the card. The points can be used to buy almost anything from air tickets to hi-fi sets.

- Avoid store cards altogether. They are an even quicker way to buy things you do not need on credit. Again it is an easy way to build up debt and get into trouble.

- Avoid impulse shopping. One of the quickest ways to spend your money is impulse buying. Lots of shops bet on your spending money on impulse. That is why, for example, you will always find sweet racks at the check-out tills at supermarkets. You will save money by shopping with a shopping list – and sticking to it.

- Never pay for anything without knowing all the details. You will frequently see advertisements asking you to send something like R50 for a magic formula to make you rich. Don't send anything. The only person who will get rich is the person who put the advertisement in the newspaper.

- When setting up your own home for the first time don't buy furniture on hire purchase, as you will pay high interest rates. New furniture can lose 50 percent of its value on resale. Rather buy at flea markets, garage sales, through newspaper advertisements and at auctions. Whole households of furniture are often sold by people who are emigrating. At auctions, be careful that you do not bid beyond a price that you have already settled on in your own mind.

- Know the difference between a convenience store and a discount store. A convenience store usually opens early and closes late – and for this you will pay extra for that loaf of bread. Discount stores are major retail shops that offer competitive prices.

- Beware of shopping on the street. Street markets are becoming increasingly popular in South Africa. There are some great bargains, but there are also lots of scams. Among other things, stolen goods are being sold. When you buy off the street you usually have very little comeback if things go wrong.

- Cheap and counterfeit imitations of well-known brands are increasingly being smuggled into South Africa. Although you often pay extra for the name of a very upmarket brand, no imitation is worth much. About the only guarantee you will get is that it will not last.

- Beware of introductory offers. Introductory offers are frequently used for things such as music clubs. You pay a very low price for the introductory offer, but the follow-up prices are often as much or more than you would pay in a normal shop. You are also required to buy a fixed number of articles for at least a year, without being absolutely sure that you want what you will be offered.
- Be careful of best buys. When shopping for food, realise that offers at the end of the aisle are not necessarily cheaper. The product producer pays more for the special position. Store brands or no-name brands are often the best buy. Always compare prices.
- Clip and keep coupons wherever you see them. They can save you quite a bit of money over the long run. Coupons are also often available on supermarket shelves next to the product. But be careful: the price of the product less the discount on the coupon may still be more expensive than a similar product.
- Try to form lift clubs. You'll be amazed at how much money lift clubs will save you in petrol bills – and time, when you are transporting children. If you are forced to use your own transport, find people without transport who will be prepared to pay you weekly to help with your petrol bill.
- Don't carry large amounts of cash. Give yourself a cash budget every week and stick to it. Too much cash in your pocket leads to impulse buying. Most of us find that whatever cash we have in our wallets has an amazing way of disappearing.
- Beware of sales. The maxim 'the more you shop, the more you save' is misleading. People often go to sales looking for bargains – not for what they need.

> **The maxim 'the more you shop, the more you save' is misleading.**

CREDIT LIFE ASSURANCE

Credit life assurance is becoming an increasingly important part of spending, as almost every retail store has seen this as a way to multiply profits. You need to be very careful that you are not taking out expensive, unnecessary life assurance.

With credit life assurance you are taking out assurance on the possibility that you may die (or become disabled) before you are able to repay a significant debt. Whenever you buy something expensive on credit, like a motor car, you may be asked to take out life and disability assurance to cover the amount of your debt. Credit life assurance, although often necessary, is one of the areas of life assurance where you need to exercise care. In many cases, you do not need it, or you may already have sufficient assurance. It is increasingly being used as an easy source of profits by some life assurance companies, and an easy source of massive commissions by the motor vehicle industry, some banks and sales people.

If you do not have sufficient assurance to cover a major debt if you die or become disabled it is essential that you take out credit life assurance. You must take great care so that you get the right amount of cover, for the right period, and at the right price. There are five steps you need to take to achieve this.

STEP 1   DO YOU NEED IT?

There are two reasons why lenders, such as banks, require life assurance:

- It gives them the security of knowing that the debt will be paid to them directly.
- They will not have to go through the tedious process of claiming against your estate if you die.

You do need to take out life assurance against significant debts such as a home or motor vehicle loan. However, against this, many retail shops, such as clothing stores, have introduced various packages to pay off your account if you die, and then they add various other bits of fairly useless assurance to this, such as accidental death and funeral assurance. The premiums are normally higher and they do not have proper claims mechanisms in place. If a retail company insists on this type of assurance, rather close the account. You should not have a clothing account anyway.

The main reason why retail stores try to get you take out the assurance is the significant commissions and other fees they can generate.

STEP 2   KNOW YOUR RIGHTS

Although life assurance can be made conditional on giving you a loan, no one, by law, can insist on your taking out additional life assurance if you already have sufficient cover for any debts. Here are some issues you must take into account:

- Free choice: You must be given free choice as to what type of policy and which company will issue the policy. However, banks and motor vehicle financing companies have direct links with life assurance companies and you may be offered only the associated company's products.
- Contractual period: You cannot be forced to take out a policy for a period longer than the contractual repayment period of the loan.
- Assured amount: You cannot be forced to take out assurance for an amount greater than the debt.
- Add-ons: Many dubious operators, particularly in the motor vehicle and furniture field, will attempt to add on extras such as an investment portion. Again, the reason is that they are generating extra commissions. You cannot be forced to take any additional assurance other than pure-term life assurance equal to the amount and period of the loan.
- 'Negative-response' selling: Many retailers, such as clothing stores, have added to their unethical behaviour by using what is called 'negative-response' selling. What this means is that you are sent a letter by the retailer informing you that they have an assurance policy to cover you against various events, including death. They then tell you that if you do not want the assurance you must write and tell them. Most people do not read the bumpf they receive with accounts and before they know it premiums are being added to their account. Although this is not illegal yet, it is frowned upon by the government. If you find you have been subject to negative-response selling, you are entitled to cancel the policy and claim back all premiums plus interest.
- Written notice: If you are required to take out credit life assurance you must be given written notice stating the following:
  - You are free to choose an existing policy.
  - You are allowed to choose the life assurer and the intermediary if you buy a new policy.
  - When you are already assured against death and disability, you have a choice to take on extra assurance cover.
  - You may select to take out extra cover only to the extent that the debt exceeds the amount of your existing cover. You must confirm in writing that you have been given the written notice and you have not been coerced.

STEP 3 **GET THE CORRECT ASSURANCE**

In its correct form, credit life assurance should be what is called called 'decreasing term' assurance. This means that, as your debt decreases, so will the amount of assurance cover. For example, if you borrow R100 000 to buy a home, the assurance would pay out R100 000 initially if you died, but 20 years later, if you died as you made your last payment, your dependants would get nothing. However, in both cases your dependants would own the asset, your home, without owing a cent. If the policy is what is called 'level term', you will be covered for R100 000 from beginning to end, and will pay higher premiums for the extra cover.

If you have motor vehicle financing over five years, be aware that you do not need 20 years of life assurance to cover the debt. If you have calculated the debt into your existing life assurance, you don't need additional life assurance and cannot be forced to take out new assurance.

Assess your life assurance needs properly, preferably with a reputable, independent financial adviser. Do not confuse credit life assurance with your general assurance needs. Here are some other tips:

- Add-on investments: Do not be talked into adding on any investment assurance to credit life assurance that is not part of your financial plan. You should keep your investment goals totally separate from credit life assurance.
- Home-loan-linked endowments: Most banks have now withdrawn these products, with which you were encouraged not to repay the capital amount of your home. You were required to pay only the interest, with the balance going to pay the premium on a life assurance investment policy. The theory was that after 20 years you would have enough money, plus some, to pay off your home loan. These policies work only under rare circumstances – mainly when you are buying property as an investment, but even then you can be at risk when there are high interest rates.

STEP 4 **HOW TO BUY CREDIT LIFE ASSURANCE**

In most cases, credit life assurance will come looking for you, but remember that it is available from all life assurance companies. If you are required to get credit life assurance, ask for quotations in writing from at least five life assurance companies. (Remember: the higher the premium you pay and the longer the term, the greater the commission.)

As with all life assurance, credit life assurance against death or disability is a very competitive business. Premiums are easily comparable, particularly if you are not lured into anything more complex with a confusing array of bells and whistles. The premiums, like any other assurance on life and disability, will vary according to your age, state of health, job, hobbies and lifestyle.

STEP 5 CESSION OF POLICIES

When you take out credit life assurance, you will usually be asked to cede the policy to the bank. In effect, you are transferring the ownership of the policy to the bank. This can cause problems if you die during the term of the policy.

If you die, the policy may well be worth more than your debt. This is particularly the case if you have been lured into signing up for a policy with a value and term greater than the size and contract period of your debt. Depending on the policy of the bank and the life assurance company, the excess money may be paid into your estate and not directly to your dependants (as would normally be the case if you named beneficiaries to the policy). This will mean greater costs, and your dependants may have to wait months before getting access to the money.

There are a few ways around this problem:

- If it is likely that the policy will have more value than your debt, nominate a person as a beneficiary for any excess amount over the loan. You must notify the life assurance company of the name of the beneficiary. Then get written assurance that the excess money will be paid directly to your dependants who have been named as beneficiaries.
- Suggest to the bank that you would rather name the bank as a preferential beneficiary to the extent of the outstanding loan. This means that the loan will be paid off first, and then other beneficiaries, such as your dependants, will receive the rest of the money.

You will be required to sign an undertaking when you cede the policy or name a bank as a preferential beneficiary to keep the premium payments up to date. If you fail to do so, the bank may be able to recall the loan it has granted to you.

If you have ceded a policy to a bank you must ensure that the policy cession is cancelled and the policy documents are returned to you when the debt is repaid. Do not cancel the policy itself if you repay the debt early. First establish if it will fit in with your overall needs.

7

Women in the Workplace

For many years women have been discriminated against in the workplace. Areas of discrimination included the following:

- Temporary employment: Women were often made temporary employees, even though they were employed on an ongoing basis. This allowed employers to exclude them from employment benefits.
- Refusal of membership of a company-sponsored medical scheme, particularly when married to a member of another scheme.
- Refusal of membership of retirement funds: When accepted they were frequently discriminated against in the structure of their membership, receiving lower benefits than male counterparts.
- Limited promotion opportunities: Employers did not see female employees as having long-term career paths, because women were expected to get married and/or have children.

Although there have been significant legislative advances since 1994, many women still find that they are at a disadvantage in the workplace. Labour law is extensive and cannot be dealt with in detail in this book, but there are certain elements that are important to women. These issues include protection from discrimination, maternity leave, unemployment insurance and retirement.

Protection from discrimination

Discrimination against women and the protection in law against unfair labour practices have been enhanced by a raft of new labour legislation that followed the election of a new democratic government in 1994. The most important piece of legislation, from a discrimination point of view, is the Employment Equity Act. In terms of the Act, no employer or person may unfairly discriminate, directly or indirectly, against an employee in any employment policy or practice on any of the following grounds: race, gender, pregnancy, marital status, family responsibility, ethnic or social origin, colour, sexual orientation, age, disability, religion, HIV status, conscience, belief, political opinion, culture, language or birth.

The only exception is in the case where an employer is following an employment equity plan to bring previously disadvantaged groups, such as women, up to a level of proper representation within the company's structures.

If you are subject to discrimination or an unfair labour practice you can complain to the Commission for Conciliation, Mediation and Arbitration (CCMA) and/or take action through the Labour Court.

Among other things, in terms of the legislation, the following apply:

- You cannot be refused permission to apply for any job.
- If you do not succeed in a promotion or a new job application, an employer has to justify its decision to you.
- Your employment conditions must be the same as colleagues doing a similar job.
- You cannot be given reduced benefits or pay because you are a woman.
- You cannot be refused membership of an employer-sponsored retirement fund. However, if there is no fund you cannot demand that an employer provides one.
- You cannot be refused membership for yourself, or your dependants, of an employer-sponsored medical aid scheme if one is provided.
- You cannot be employed permanently on a contract without having access to benefits such as retirement and/or medical fund benefits.

Maternity leave

By law you are entitled to four months of unpaid maternity leave. It is left to the discretion of the employer whether or not you will be paid. Often, payment for maternity leave is determined by agreement with employee representative organisations, such as unions.

Unemployment Insurance

If you earn less than R7 774 a month, you must contribute 1 percent of your gross salary to the Unemployment Insurance Fund (UIF), and your employer must match that amount.

UIF pays jobless people who qualify for relief 45 percent of their last salary for a maximum of 26 weeks. Even if you are formally employed and have stopped contributing to UIF, you may still qualify for UIF benefits if you become unemployed. You will be able to claim 45 percent of the salary you were earning when you last contributed. The fund provides for loss of earnings because of unemployment under the following circumstances:

- You must have been contributing to UIF and have been employed for at least 13 weeks during the 52 weeks before the date when you lost your job.
- If you have contributed to UIF, are capable of and available for work and are actively seeking work, you may apply in writing for UIF benefits for a maximum period of 26 weeks.
- If you have the necessary UIF qualifications, you can claim illness benefits for a maximum of six months. To claim, you either have to be unemployed or you have to receive less than a third of your normal earnings from your employer during your illness.
- Maternity benefits are paid to women at a rate of 60 percent (as of 2001) of their salary for a maximum of 26 weeks from the date on which they become unemployed due to pregnancy; or if they are still working, but receive less than a third of their normal earnings from their employers during pregnancy.
- If you are female, unemployed and have applied to a children's court to adopt a child under the age of two years, you may claim UIF for a maximum of 26 weeks from the date on which you apply to the court. You have to apply for adoption benefits within 52 weeks of the date of the adoption, and you also have to provide certified copies of the birth certificate and the order of adoption.
- If you are a dependant of a deceased UIF contributor, you may apply for UIF benefits. Payment may be made to dependent children who are under 17 years of age at the time of death of the contributor. If there is no spouse or children, payment may be made to anyone else who was dependent on the deceased.

People excluded from UIF benefits include government employees, people who earn more than R97 188 a year, and domestic or contract workers. The new Unemployment Insurance Bill was gazetted in January 2002 and is expected to come into effect during 2002. The law will extend unemployment coverage to all employees irrespective of income and will include domestic workers for the first time.

Contribution levels will remain the same at 1 percent of your salary (paid by your employer), but people earning more than R97 188 a year will be deemed to be earning R97 188, and their contribution will be limited to this amount.

Retirement

Until the year 2000, on most retirement funds, women could retire five years earlier than men, with even the Receiver of Revenue structuring taxation of retirement funds around an earlier five-year retirement age. This anomaly has now been removed. No woman can be forced to retire earlier than a male colleague, and all women must have the same contribution levels and benefits as male employees. Many funds have had to make good the shortfall in benefits that were caused by the earlier retirement structures. The official level at which the Receiver of Revenue recognises retirement is 55 years of age, unless there are special circumstances to justify earlier retirement, such as ill health.

8

Tax

Women contribute less to the coffers of the state than men – not because they receive a favourable dispensation but because they are quite clearly discriminated against by the structure of society and employment practices.

Although women are often discriminated against in the workplace, there is no discrimination when it comes to tax.

The October 1997 Household Survey shows that 9 percent of men employed in the formal sector are in managerial positions, against only 5 percent of women. At the opposite end, 38 percent of the female workforce is employed in unskilled positions, against 21 percent of men.

Although women are often discriminated against in the workplace, there is no discrimination when it comes to tax. They are taxed as individuals in their own right, whether single or married.

BASIC PRINCIPLES OF TAXATION

There are some basic principles for the taxation of individuals that can help you to structure tax affairs to your best advantage. You are not entitled to evade tax, but you can structure your financial affairs to give yourself the best tax deal. The principles you can use include the following:

- Income-splitting: This is transferring income from a taxpayer with a high marginal tax rate to a taxpayer in a lower tax bracket, for example from yourself to your spouse. There are, however, regulations controlling this, and you must be sure you don't break the law, as the income will merely be deemed to be that of the donor spouse. It is a useful vehicle for investing, particularly when one spouse has no income or a lower marginal rate of taxation. It works like this: a spouse on a high marginal rate gives investment money to the other spouse to invest in their name. As a result, the returns on the investment will be subject to a lower rate of tax.

- Income-shifting: This is timing income to receive it in a year when your income will be lower than in another year so that you can take advantage of a lower marginal rate. It can also mean ensuring that deductions are taken in a high-income year.
- Investment choice: This is selecting investments in vehicles that have a lower taxable gain, such as an investment that shows capital gains (shares or unit trusts) with a lower rate of tax, rather than one that provides income (a bank deposit account) and is subject to a higher rate of tax.
- Tax deferral: This involves using tax incentives, such as those given for pension fund or retirement annuities, to postpone or defer tax to a later date. For example, you claim your contributions to a pension fund or retirement annuity against tax in the year that you make the contribution.

TYPES OF TAXATION

Taxes are collected in many different ways and at different levels of government, both local and central.

At the lowest level, people who own property must pay taxes to their local authority. These are called rates. Property rates are set on the value of the property and the value of the buildings on the property.

Most taxes are collected by the South African Revenue Service (SARS) on behalf of government, and are decided on each year when the minister of finance presents Parliament with a budget. There are two main ways to pay tax. These are 'direct taxation', which you normally have to pay directly to the SARS based on what you earn and own, and 'indirect taxation', which is normally collected by someone else (such as a shopkeeper) and is based on the money you spend. There are numerous types of tax within these two categories.

DIRECT TAXATION

There are a number of different forms of direct taxation. These include income tax, capital gains tax and transfer taxes, such as estate duty, property transfer and donations tax.

Income tax

Income tax is based on how much you earn, hence the name 'income tax'. If you are employed and are paid a salary every month you will find one, if not two, types of tax deducted from your pay. It does not matter how old you are; if you earn income from any source, both in South Africa or in foreign countries, you are liable to pay income tax.

There are a number of issues you must take into account with income tax:

ISSUE 1 **COLLECTION OF INCOME TAX**

Income tax is collected in three main ways. These are Standard Income Tax on Employees (SITE), Pay As You Earn (PAYE) and provisional tax.

SITE: If you earn below a certain level you will pay only SITE. In the 2002/3 tax year if you earned less than R60 000 you paid only SITE. The amount is adjusted annually. The tax is automatically deducted from what you are paid by your employer. Generally, you cannot get a refund for SITE unless your employer has not taken account of any contributions you may have made to a retirement fund or medical aid plan. The big advantage of being a SITE-only taxpayer is that you do not have to fill in tax forms every year, unless you earn additional money from another source, such as investments.

PAYE: If you earn above the cut-off level for SITE, you will also pay PAYE. The big difference between SITE and PAYE is that at the end of February and before the end of May every year you have to fill in a tax form telling the SARS how much you have earned and how much tax you have paid. The SARS then decides if you have paid too much or too little. If you have paid too much you are refunded, but sadly you have to pay in if you did not pay enough. Both SITE and PAYE are collected by your employer.

Provisional income tax: If you are self-employed, a director of a company, a member of a close corporation, or earn more than R10 000 a year from sources other than an employer (such as interest on investments) you may have to register with the SARS as a provisional taxpayer. If you are a provisional tax-payer you have to pay in tax a few times a year. You must make the following three payments:

- The first payment is due within the first six months of the tax year and must be equal to one-half of your estimated income tax for the year. The amount may not be lower than the previous year, unless you have permission from the SARS.
- The second payment is due on or before the last day of the tax year. The amount must be equal to the estimated tax that is due for the year, less what you have already paid. If you are more than 10 percent out in your estimation you will pay a penalty of 20 percent on any underpaid amount, plus interest.
- A third voluntary payment, payable within seven months of the end of the tax year allows you to make good any incorrect estimations.

ISSUE 2 REGISTERING AS A TAXPAYER

It is your responsibility to register as a taxpayer. Most employers will normally help you register if you are working for the first time. If not, look up the address of your local office of the South African Revenue Service (SARS) and send a letter asking them to register you as a taxpayer. When you are registered, you will be given a tax number, which will remain with you for the rest of your life. You can be prosecuted for not registering as a taxpayer.

ISSUE 3 INCOME TAX RATES

South Africa has what is called a progressive personal income tax system. To give you a very simple example of what this means, say you earned R1 000 for the year and the rate of tax on R1 000 was 10 percent. You would then pay R100 in tax, or R10 for every R100 you earn.

Now here comes the progressive step. Say you earned R2 000. The second step (or marginal rate) may be 15 percent. However, you still pay only 10 percent on the first R1 000 that you earned in the year. The 15 percent applies only to the second R1 000 that you earn. You can never pay a higher rate on that first R1 000.

Here is how you would do the calculation on this simplified example:

Income	Marginal tax rate	Tax payable
First R1 000	10%	R100
Second R1 000	15%	R150
TOTAL tax paid:		R250

You will often hear people claiming that they received less income in total when their salary increased because they went into a higher tax bracket. This is not possible: you always pay the same amount on the previous rand. It is the additional rands you earn in a particular bracket on which you pay more.

There are six marginal tax brackets through which the progressive rate of taxation is structured. The brackets for the 2002/3 tax year were:

Taxable income	Tax rate
R 0–R 40 000	18% of each R1
R 40 001–R 80 000	R 7 200 + 25% of the amount above R 40 000
R 80 001–R110 000	R17 200 + 30% of the amount above R 80 000
R110 001–R170 000	R26 200 + 35% of the amount above R110 000
R170 001–R240 000	R47 200 + 38% of the amount above R170 000
R240 001 and above	R73 800 + 40% of the amount above R245 000

ISSUE 4 AVERAGE RATE OF TAXATION

The average rate of taxation is used mainly to tax lump-sum retirement benefits. The average rate of taxation is the average amount of tax you pay on your income. For example, with an income of R240 000 you would be on the marginal rate of 40 percent, but your average rate of taxation would be 30.74 percent. In other words, after averaging out all the different marginal rate tax brackets, you would pay R73 800 in tax (before rebates) and not R96 000, which you would pay if you were paying 40 percent on every rand you earned.

You can calculate your average rate by using the following equation:

$$\frac{\text{Total tax paid}}{\text{Taxable income}} \times 100 = X\%$$

ISSUE 5 REBATES ON TAX

There are rebates, which are given against the tax that you must pay each year. There is a primary rebate for every taxpayer, and a secondary rebate for people over the age of 65. For the year 2002/3 the rebates were:

Primary: R4 860

Age 65 and over (additional to primary rebate): R3 000

ISSUE 6 DEDUCTIONS

There are a number of deductions you can make from your taxable income. These include:

- any expense involved in generating income;
- contributions to retirement funds, within defined limits; and
- medical expenses within limits.

ISSUE 7 NO INCOME TAX

There are levels below which you pay no tax. The tax thresholds (below which no tax is paid) for 2002/3 were:

Under age 65:	R27 000 a year
Age 65 and over:	R42 640 a year

Capital gains tax

Capital gains tax (CGT) was introduced on 1 October 2001 and is structured to be taxed as income. A capital gain is any profit you make on the sale of an asset. As an individual, 25 percent of the gain is subject to tax. There are a number of exemptions, and women are taxed separately on their assets, whether or not they have partners. There is one exception. The first R1 million in profit on a primary residence is exempt from capital gains tax. But a couple cannot have two primary residences. However, the R1 million can be divided in any proportion between the two.

In calculating the capital gains tax on any capital gain/loss you must follow these 11 steps.

STEP 1 KEEP GOOD RECORDS

Keep good records on any asset you acquire, whether you believe it is subject to CGT or not. For example, although your primary residence may be exempt from CGT while you live in it and use it exclusively for domestic purposes, this may not always be the case. In the future, you may move out and let it, or you may use part of it for business purposes. This would result in part of the gain, on disposal of the property, becoming taxable.

You need to have proper records of:

- the cost or value at acquisition of the asset (keep all of your receipts and invoices);
- the date of acquisition of the asset;
- the cost or value of any additions to the asset;
- the date of any additions to the asset;
- the cost or value at disposal of the asset;
- the date of disposal of the asset;
- portions of an asset used for business and private purposes; and
- periods of absence from a primary residence exceeding six months.

STEP 2 DID A CGT EVENT OCCUR DURING THE TAX YEAR?

You need not have bought or sold an asset to be liable for CGT. A CGT event occurs when what is called a disposal (not necessarily a sale) of an asset that you have acquired (not necessarily bought) takes place.

Events that are regarded as acquisitions of assets include:

- buying an asset;
- receiving an asset as a gift or donation; and
- inheriting an asset.

Events regarded as disposals of assets that may be subject to CGT include the following:

- A donation (except to public benefit organisations), expropriation (unless the proceeds are used to replace the assets within three years), conversion, cession (except where the asset has been ceded to a bank as security, or as part of a divorce settlement) or transfer of ownership (except from one spouse to another). A portion of donations tax is deductible from the capital gain.
- The change of ownership on emigration, whether the asset is sold or not, except immovable property, which is taxed when sold.
- The asset's forfeiture, termination, redemption, cancellation, surrender, scrapping, loss or destruction.
- The transfer of an asset to a trust, or the vesting of an asset in a beneficiary of a trust (i.e. the disposal of the asset to a beneficiary).

STEP 3 **IS THE ASSET EXEMPT?**

There are a number of assets that are excluded from CGT. These include:

- The first R1 million of gain or loss on the disposal of your primary residence.
- Personal-use assets, such as personal effects, jewellery, artworks, furniture, and vehicles not used for trade purposes. Items such as gold coins and boats exceeding 10 metres in length are not considered personal effects.
- Any retirement savings investments, both pre- and post-retirement. There is a moratorium on retirement assets for three years.
- Profits made on life assurance policies (the CGT will have been paid on your behalf by the life assurance company), with the exception of second-hand policies, on which any gain or loss in your hands will be liable for CGT.
- Any gains as a result of compensation for personal injury, illness or defamation. This applies only to natural persons and special trusts.
- Gains or losses made from any foreign currency that may be left over from your travel allowance.
- Gains or losses made from any legal South African gambling, including the Lotto.
- Donations to public benefit organisations, such as charities and educational institutions.
- The transfer of assets between spouses/partners.

STEP 4 **CONSIDER ROLLOVERS**

You can defer CGT if what is called a 'rollover' occurs. Rollovers include:

- Involuntary disposal: If the asset was lost as a result of expropriation, misplacement or destruction, and compensation, such as insurance, is paid on which a capital gain is made, the gain can be disregarded if the compensation is used to replace the asset. The replacement must be acquired within three years.
- The transfer of assets between spouses: An asset transferred between spouses is treated as being disposed of at the base cost. Tax will be payable on disposal to a third party on the difference between the disposal value and the base cost. The same applies when an asset passes from the estate of a deceased spouse to a surviving spouse and also with a transfer in terms of a divorce settlement.

STEP 5   ESTABLISH THE BASE VALUE

The base cost of any asset that is subject to CGT is the value of the asset on 1 October 2001 (the effective date of implementation of CGT), or its cost or value on the date after 1 October 2001 on which you acquired the asset. The capital gain or loss you make is the disposal value less the base value.

It is important that you calculate the base value correctly, as it will determine the amount on which you will be taxed, or on which you will be able to claim a deduction against other capital gains when you dispose of the asset. You will not pay CGT on capital gains made before 1 October 2001.

It is also important to know that the onus is on you to ensure that you can prove to the SARS the base value of any asset that is subject to CGT.

For assets acquired after 1 October, the base value is the acquisition cost or value plus the cost of improvements.

More problematic is the base value of an asset acquired before 1 October 2001 and still possessed on that date.

With some assets, the base value on 1 October will be set for you, but on others you will have to use one of a number of methods to establish the base value. Be warned that you cannot, of your own accord, set a high base value to avoid making a capital gain in the future. The SARS has the right to challenge any valuation, and it can impose severe penalties if it suspects that you have deliberately manipulated a value.

For the most part, you can divide assets into financial assets, on which the base value on 1 October will be calculated for you, and hard assets, such as property, where you will have to provide the base value.

Financial assets

For financial assets quoted on a local financial exchange (for example, the JSE Securities Exchange), such as shares, bonds and other securities, as well as collective investments, such as unit trust funds and wrap funds, you will be provided with the base value by the product provider.

The base value will be calculated from an average of the last price on each of the five trading days preceding 1 October.

If the financial assets are quoted on a foreign exchange, the last price quoted on the last trading day before 1 October will apply. For foreign collective investments, such as mutual funds (unit trusts), the value will be the last selling price published before 1 October.

Hard assets

These are mainly what are called hard assets, such as property, a boat or an aircraft. Three methods have been proposed, and you can choose whichever one suits you best, except in the case of the market valuation method. You do not have to commit to a method until such time as you dispose of an asset. You may use the market valuation method only if you have submitted proof of the valuation by 30 September 2003 (two years after the effective date) with your income tax return. In all cases, you must submit proof of your valuation with your tax return in the year in which you dispose of an asset.

These are the three methods:

Market valuation: The legislation does not prescribe how an asset must be valued – it is left up to you. However, there is less likely to be a problem if the valuation of a hard asset is made by a sworn appraiser; and the valuation of companies and close corporations and businesses is done by auditors with reference to quoted prices on the JSE. For individuals, the asset most likely to need valuing is property.

Time apportionment: You calculate the capital gain by apportioning the entire gain between the number of years the capital asset was held before and the number of years it was held after the implementation date of the tax. In other words, the valuation is calculated on the date that you dispose of the asset.

For example, if you acquired a second house in October 1991 and you sell it in October 2005, only four of the 14 years during which you owned the house will be relevant (October 2001 to October 2005). The total expenditure (the acquisition cost plus the cost of any improvements) is subtracted from the disposal proceeds. The capital gain is apportioned for the period before and after 1 October 2001. Where improvements to the asset have taken place before 1 October 2001, the maximum number of years you can take into account before 1 October 2001 is 20 years. This limit does not apply where the asset was not improved before 1 October 2001.

The 20 percent calculation: If you have no records at all of the acquisition of an asset acquired before 1 October 2001, or you have not used the market valuation method, you can use this method to calculate the base value. The base cost is calculated as 20 percent of the proceeds of the value of the disposal, less any expenditure on improvements after 1 October 2001. It does not matter on what date you dispose of the asset. As this method essentially creates an 80 percent capital gain, the market value method is likely to be preferable in most cases.

STEP 6 ADD TO THE BASE VALUE

You must ensure that you have added in any additional expenditure on an asset. This could reduce the gain or create a capital loss, and thus reduce the overall amount of CGT due. Additional expenditure includes the following:

- Anything related directly to the acquisition or disposal of the asset: This includes professional fees and commissions, such as legal or surveyor's fees, transfer costs, stamp or transfer duties, moving and installation costs.
- Any improvement of an asset or addition to an asset if it still exists when you dispose of it.
- Borrowing costs, including interest, on money borrowed to acquire a business, a listed share (but not an unlisted one) or a unit trust: These costs are not allowable for income tax purposes. In the case of borrowings to acquire a unit trust or listed share, a maximum of one-third of the interest is claimable for CGT purposes.

STEP 7 CALCULATE THE CAPITAL GAIN OR LOSS

Two calculations are required to ascertain the capital gain or loss of an asset at disposal: one for assets acquired before 1 October and another for assets acquired after that date.

STEP 8 CONSOLIDATE GAINS AND LOSSES

The total of your capital losses in any one tax year must be subtracted from the total of your capital gains. You cannot transfer capital losses between companies or trusts to reduce a gain made in a company or in your personal capacity. If you have made an overall loss, you may not deduct that loss from your taxable income for the year. The loss must be carried forward to a year when you make a capital gain. The loss can be deducted against a future gain.

STEP 9 REMEMBER THE EXEMPTION

Every year, individuals and special trusts (such as a trust established to care for an incapacitated child) are given a R10 000 exemption. This exemption does not apply to companies, close corporations or ordinary asset protection trusts. The reason for this exemption is to avoid unnecessary work, especially for people below the income tax threshold who do not have to complete tax returns.

If you have a net capital loss you cannot add the R10 000 exemption to the amount to make a greater loss; nor can you create a loss by deducting the R10 000 from a gain below R10 000. If you have a net gain, for example, of R8 000 before the deduction of R10 000 exemption, your gain will be reduced to zero, not to a loss of R2 000.

It is important to note that the annual exemption of R10 000 reduces both gains and losses. If the sum of your gains and losses for the year is a loss of R12 000, this will be reduced by R10 000, leaving a R2 000 loss to be carried forward to future tax years. If the net loss is R8 000, this would be reduced to zero.

If you know you are going to make a loss on the disposal of an asset, you should sell it either in the same year or in the year before you dispose of an asset on which there will be a capital gain. That way you will not see your assessed capital loss being eaten away by inflation. The exemption is increased to R50 000 in the year of assessment in which you die.

STEP 10 WORK OUT THE AMOUNT TO BE TAXED

If you have a net capital gain you pay tax only on a portion, not on the total amount. Individuals pay tax on 25 percent of the gain, and trusts pay tax on 50 percent of the gain. The taxable capital gain is added to your normal taxable income.

STEP 11 ESTABLISH THE CORRECT RATE

There is no standard rate of CGT. The tax rates are all based on the income tax rate of the person or body being taxed. The different tax rates clearly favour holding assets in your own name rather than in the name of a trust, company or close corporation, but you should consider the other non-tax reasons for holding an asset in a trust or a company before transferring it into your name.

So, if you as an individual have a taxable gain after all the exclusions and exemptions, you must declare 25 percent of the gain. The taxable gain will be added to your normal taxable income. You must then use the marginal rate that applies for your total income (normal taxable income plus the capital gain) to work out how much income tax you must pay on both your income and capital gain.

Transfer taxes

Transfer taxes are placed on assets that are transferred from one person to another. The main transfer taxes are estate duty, property transfer taxes and donations tax:

Estate duty: This is tax that is paid on all your assets when you die. It is payable only if your assets are worth more than R1.5 million. The only time this tax is not paid is when married, common law or traditional union couples leave their assets to the surviving partner. So, if you died and left everything to your spouse, no estate duty would be paid. But when you both die and leave your assets to an heir, then estate duty would have to be paid at a rate of 20 percent on any net assets (assets less liabilities) exceeding R1.5 million.

There is one way that spouses can, however, get the R1.5 million exemption twice. When the first dies, R1.5 million in assets (on which no estate duty is payable) should be bequeathed to the ultimate heirs and the rest of their estate to their partner. When the second dies, the R1.5 million exemption clicks in again. If the surviving partner still needs the assets, say a property, an agreement can be reached where the partner will have a usufruct (right of use) of the property until death.

Property transfer taxes: Every time a property or home is sold a transfer tax is placed on the selling price of the property.

Donations tax: You are allowed to give away your assets to someone else only at the rate of a value of R30 000 a year without any tax being paid on the gift. If the total value of the gifts you make exceeds R30 000 then you must pay donations tax at a rate of 20 percent. The only exception is to registered charities and educational institutions.

INDIRECT TAXATION

As with direct taxes, indirect taxes also come in different forms. Indirect tax is a tax that you do not pay directly from your income. Normally, an indirect tax is based on what you spend. You are not responsible for seeing that it is given to the SARS. Indirect taxes include VAT, fuel levy, import taxes and luxury taxes.

Value added tax (VAT)

VAT is the most common form of indirect tax. It is added to almost everything on which you spend money, whether they are goods or services. The rate of VAT is 14 percent. There are a few exceptions in the application of VAT, including some basic foods, mainly to help the very poor.

Fuel levy

For every litre of petrol you buy you are paying a levy to the government. Originally, this levy was intended to pay for better roads, but now it goes into the general government pot. You also pay VAT on this tax.

Import taxes

These are taxes that are paid on a wide range of goods that are imported from other countries.

Luxury or ad valorem taxes

These taxes are added to wide variety of goods. The most notorious are the taxes on booze and cigarettes, also called 'sin taxes'.

9

Buying a Car

You will probably spend more on motor vehicles in your lifetime than you will on property. Surprised by this statement? Well think of how often you are likely to buy a vehicle and how much you will be paying. Vehicles are a major expense, which will impact on your finances throughout your life. Depending on how often you replace your vehicle and the type of vehicle you buy, the effect on your overall finances can be significant.

FINANCING A CAR

The purchase of a motor vehicle is rarely an investment. To make matters worse, in most cases motor vehicles are 'depreciating assets'. In other words, from the day you buy a vehicle it starts to lose value.

From the day you buy a vehicle it starts to lose value.

As a general rule, you should not borrow money to finance anything that loses value, but clearly this would make a car unaffordable, particularly when you are young and have not accumulated savings.

These are the biggest mistakes people make in buying vehicles:

- They buy the biggest and the best, which are often out of their price range, saddling themselves with high debt.
- They buy new vehicles, when they could make a considerable saving buying a good, second-hand, recent model.
- They replace vehicles too quickly. Most will last you at least eight years, if not longer, depending on the mileage you do. If you keep replacing it every three years you are adding to your costs, as a new vehicle loses at least 20 percent of its value as you drive out of the garage.
- They choose an inappropriate form of borrowing, with high interest rates and other add-on costs.

- They buy vehicles that have high running and servicing costs, guzzling petrol and needing expensive spare parts.
- They forget that the more costly and sporty a vehicle, the more they will pay in insurance.
- They add on fancy parts, which are excessively expensive.

Over the years, motor vehicle companies have managed to change the ordinary motor vehicle from a functional tool that makes your life easier to a status symbol of power and wealth. The evidence is there to see: how many people driving expensive 4 × 4 vehicles actually need additional power and gears? Vehicle manufacturers also redesign their vehicles on a regular basis for exactly the same reason – so you can be seen driving the latest model. It is difficult to resist the urge to drive a fancy car, but do a rough calculation of how much you could save yourself in a lifetime if you bought only functional, comfortable and reliable vehicles.

There are three good indicators to judge whether you are buying out of your financial league:

- You have to borrow more than 70 percent of the cost of the vehicle.
- Your repayments are absorbing more than 20 percent of your after-tax income.
- The repayment period of the debt is longer than three years.

There are a number of financing options for buying a vehicle. These are discussed in order of merit starting with the best.

Cash

If you have the cash available you can always negotiate a better deal. Dealers are always keen to sell, so they will be prepared to give you a discount for cash. There is often more than one franchise holder in your area, so you should play off one dealer against another.

Using your home loan

If you have to borrow to buy a vehicle you should find the cheapest money available to you. For most people the money on which they pay the lowest rate of interest is their home loan. But be careful about how you borrow on a home loan. Most banks now offer variable (access) home loans, where you can borrow up to your limit at any time as well as make additional repayments. There are a number of issues you must take into account when using a home loan to finance a motor vehicle:

- By having arranged loan finance outside of the motor vehicle company you have put yourself in a position to pay cash and will be able to negotiate a healthy discount.
- Repay this section of the debt as rapidly as possible and don't stretch the repayment over the full period of the home loan. If you repay the motor vehicle over, say, the 20-year life of a home loan, you will still be paying off that debt long after your vehicle has passed on to the scrapyard, and you will be financing further vehicles along the way. This is not a good idea. You should repay the additional borrowing within four years or less.
- If you do not have sufficient leeway on your home loan, but your property has gone up in value, you can ask your bank to increase your limit. However, check the costs.

Consolidated debt loans

Increasingly, banks are offering single-debt facilities, which include your home loan and other financing deals, such as motor vehicles. Initially, these facilities were only for the wealthy. You had to earn more than R500 000 a year and own assets worth a few million. Banks are now starting to offer these facilities to ordinary customers in good standing. The interest rates are similar to those on home loans. Again, you have the same advantages as using a home loan facility, but you must repay the debt on the vehicle loan within a limited time.

Hire purchase agreements

These are loans that are made available mainly through banks but increasingly by divisions of motor vehicle manufacturers and larger motor vehicle retailers. The elements of these loans are as follows:

- You are leasing the vehicle until you have repaid the loan, then the vehicle becomes yours.
- If you default on the loan the financier of the deal is entitled to reclaim the vehicle and you can lose everything you have paid.
- You need a deposit of at least 20 percent of the cost of the vehicle.

- The repayment period is a maximum of 54 months.
- The interest rates tend to be higher than for a home loan; in some cases they are excessive. You need to negotiate the rate.
- There are likely to be additional administration charges.
- You will not find it easy to negotiate the price.
- The terms and conditions of a loan can be onerous. Check these carefully. One of the most important issues is repayment: some loans make it difficult to repay the loan quicker with penalties for early repayment.

Leases

Lease arrangements are different from hire purchase agreements in that you are in effect hiring the vehicle. These are the main elements of this type of financing:

- Lease arrangements are suitable for businesses and for people with car allowances, because you can claim the cost of the lease proportionally against business mileage.
- No deposit is required.
- The maximum lease period is five years.
- You effectively pay interest on the sale price of the vehicle at a higher-than-normal interest rate in most cases.
- You can take ownership of the vehicle when the lease period expires. The amount you pay will depend on the structure of the lease. Many of these deals have residual or balloon payments at the end. Residual value financing allows you to buy a vehicle that you would not normally be able to afford.

A residual payment is structured like this:

- You pay a monthly lease, which is lower than a hire purchase instalment.
- You leave an large unpaid sum, called a residual or balloon payment, until the end of the contract period. The average residual value over five years is anything between 20 and 35 percent of the new cost of the vehicle.
- In theory the residual payment should be equal to the resale value. So when the contract expires you should be able to sell the vehicle for its residual value and owe nothing.

There are two major disadvantages to taking out a residual value contract: higher costs and lower-than-expected value.

Higher costs

In the long run, a residual lease agreement will cost you a lot more than a straight instalment sale contract. For example, a R200 000 vehicle at an interest rate of 15.5 percent covering a period of 60 months would cost you almost R14 000 more with residual value financing than it would with conventional financing.

The interest on a standard instalment contract would be R84 958. The same vehicle on similar terms would cost you interest of R98 600 in terms of a residual value contract, with payment on 20 percent of the value of the vehicle deferred. But ultimately you would pay R138 600: R98 600 interest plus the R40 000 (which is the 20 percent residual) that was deferred.

Lower-than-expected value

There is a risk of the market value of the vehicle being less than the residual value at the end of the contract. In many cases, it is impossible to settle the contract early because there is very little capital redemption in the initial period of the agreement. You need to know from the outset how much the residual amount is going to be. Make sure that you are not relying on the sale of the vehicle to pay off the residual amount.

A residual makes ownership more affordable initially, and you might rationalise that your income will be much higher in four or five years when the residual payment is due. At that time, if you do not have the cash, you might be able to refinance the vehicle for the residual amount. Some banks will check the condition of your vehicle to make sure that its current value is more or less equivalent to the amount that you still owe.

As a general guide, any residual over 40 percent of the initial purchase price is too high and should be carefully checked out. Expect your vehicle to depreciate by 1 percent a month for the duration of your contract. So, if your contract term is 60 months, your vehicle will depreciate by 60 percent over the period. This means that you should not have a residual amount of more that 40 percent of its original value.

To avoid ending up owing the bank more than you could get by selling the vehicle, you could opt for a buy-back contract with a motor dealer who guarantees to buy back your vehicle for a certain value after a set time, provided you have not done more than a specified number of kilometres.

Other issues to take into account include the following:

- Abuses: There are some serious abuses of the residual system. Some franchise dealers who sell vehicles that don't retain their value well approach a bank and offer to place all their business with them in return for financing at least a 40 percent residual on every deal. These dealerships then advertise vehicles with super-low repayments such as 'only R999 a month'. It is a contravention of the Advertising Standards Authority's Code of Conduct not to disclose the residual value, so very often the information is buried in the fine print.
- Residual amount: The size of the residual the bank will allow you depends on the risk you pose to them. Ideally, it should be linked to the expected trade-in value of the vehicle, but banks may apply stricter credit criteria to residual value financing because of the buyer's responsibility to make good any shortfall between the actual value of the vehicle and the residual value of the vehicle.
- Final value of the vehicle: The actual residual value of the vehicle will to a large extent be determined by its condition and the distance that has been covered. Poor condition and a high reading on the odometer will result in a lower market value when you choose to sell it. As much as 20 percent can be deducted from the book value if the vehicle is in a poor condition with many kilometres on the clock. You could then find that your vehicle is worth only 25 percent of what you owe the bank or financier in order to settle the residual.
- If you are likely to run up a high mileage you should investigate the maintenance contracts offered by some motor dealers.
- Insurance: You must make sure that the insurance covers the entire value of your vehicle, including the residual payment. If your insurance policy does not cover the outstanding balance of your loan and you have an accident in which the vehicle is written off, you could find yourself carrying a very heavy financial burden.

OTHER ISSUES

Apart from financing, you need to take a number of other issues into account when buying a car:

Second-hand cars

The second-hand market can be dodgy and you need to take a number of steps to protect yourself. When you are purchasing a second-hand car, deal only with a reputable dealer. There are two reasons for this:

- There are many stolen vehicles in circulation. If you purchase a stolen vehicle it can be reclaimed from you without your receiving any compensation. You should check the registration and engine numbers with the police if you are at all suspicious. Also ask for guarantees from the dealer that it is not a stolen vehicle.
- There is a reputational risk for the dealer. Reputable dealers will not want to get a bad name by selling jalopies, so they are more likely to give meaningful guarantees.

Also make sure that you do the following:

- Use an expert: You should have any second-hand vehicle carefully checked. The best way to do this is to use the services of the Automobile Association (AA). You do not need to be a member to do this. The check is thorough, and you will be told about all the problems.
- Check the logbooks to see that the vehicle has been regularly serviced.
- Get proof that there is no outstanding debt on the vehicle. If there is, a bank may repossess it even though you have paid for it.
- Make sure that the vehicle is properly registered and have it registered in your name as soon as possible.

Guarantees

Carefully check what is guaranteed and what is not guaranteed. For example, is labour guaranteed? The terms of a guarantee are particularly important on used vehicles. On new cars they all tend to be fairly similar.

Maintenance contracts

These contracts are costly, but they ensure that you stick to the proper service intervals. Costs vary according to what the maintenance contract covers. Some include service costs, others include minor faults and others even include free tyre replacement after two years. The end result is that the vehicle could be in a more marketable condition when you trade it in or sell it.

Join the Automobile Association (AA)

The security of the AA is well worthwhile. Among other things, response is normally quick if your vehicle breaks down or you have an accident, tow-in costs are dramatically reduced and medical assistance is included.

Tax implications

There are no tax implications if you are buying your vehicle for private use. You cannot claim anything against tax. However, if you are using your vehicle for business purposes you need to weigh up a number of issues in deciding on the best way to finance it. There is no single best formula. Most of the banks with special motor vehicle financing divisions have computer programs that will help you out. The main issues you need to consider are:

- your business mileage;
- the cost of the vehicle;
- the interest rate on the financing arrangement; and
- your marginal tax rate.

You are usually best off paying cash if you are using your vehicle for both private and business purposes. Incidentally, many people are under the false impression that vehicle allowances are unfairly and punitively taxed. This is not true. The SARS considers any vehicle allowance to be normal income. However, because they expect you to use the vehicle for business purposes and to claim the usage against your taxable income only, 50 percent of the allowance is taxed under PAYE when you receive the allowance. If at the end of the tax year you have not done any or very little business travelling, it means that you will have to pay the tax on all or part of the other 50 percent you received as an allowance.

10

Your Own Home

After retirement savings the biggest asset most people acquire in their lifetime is a residential property. For most people, home ownership is a slow process with many hazards along the way. Many people start off by renting before buying property, and the first purchase is often a sectional title apartment, which holds its own particular problems.

Added to the normal hazards of property ownership, married women need to take particular care in case of divorce. With women living longer than men, they are often also left to make the decision about a retirement home. This chapter will take you through all the phases of renting and owning residential property.

RENTING A HOME

There are some good reasons for renting. You can live somewhere temporarily:

- if you are saving a deposit for your own home;
- if you are searching for a home; or
- if you are transient.

You should avoid buying property if you are not going to hold on to it for at least five years. In most cases, it will take this long to cover the costs of buying a property.

If you rent an apartment or house you will be expected to sign a lease agreement (the conditions under which you will rent the property). A lease agreement is in your interests as well as those of the owner, as it spells out the rights and obligations of both parties. Among other things, the lease agreement will state what you must pay in rent, when it must be paid, if and when the rent can be increased, how many people may stay on the property, and even whether you will be permitted to keep pets. The lease agreement protects mainly the owner of the property, as it ensures that rent is paid on time and that the tenant leaves the property in the same condition as they received it.

A lease agreement also protects you as a tenant. It will contain provisions for your privacy and your right to the use of the property. If you intend to share the accommodation, you must make sure that this is included in the agreement, including your right to collect rent from the other people sharing.

It is best to get someone who is knowledgeable about leases, like a lawyer, to look at it to ensure that you are properly protected.

Other issues you need to consider include the following:

- Utilities: Are there additional charges for water, lights or rates? These can all vary from paying nothing to paying a set amount or paying a share. If you are responsible for the utilities, you may also find that you have to get yourself connected. This will involve paying a deposit to the local municipality.
- The period of the lease: Many rental agreements are for one year. The minimum period of notice you are required to give is one month. A one-month notice requirement often applies if the lease is not formally renewed after the first year. You should have written into the lease agreement a clause saying that if, due to unforeseen circumstances, you have to move out, you should be allowed to find a suitable person to replace you.
- Furnishings: There are both advantages and disadvantages to furnished or partially furnished accommodation. Furnished accommodation tends to be more expensive but can be useful if you do not want the upfront cost of buying furniture. In apartments and houses the stove is normally installed.
- Security: How secure is the property? Are there burglar bars or alarms? If you have your own furniture the insurance company will charge you premiums according to the level of security on the property.
- Amenities: What amenities are offered? For example, is there parking? If there is a pool, can you use it? Are there laundry facilities, a TV and TV aerials?
- Other tenants: What are the other tenants like? If you are sharing accommodation take time to meet them to see if you can get on with them.
- Maintenance: Who is responsible for the proper maintenance of the property? This can differ from agreement to agreement, with your being responsible for some things and the lessor being responsible for others.
- Rent limits: Keep rent below 25 percent of your income. If you go above this level, it could seriously disrupt your budget, and your life could become a total drag, with no money to do anything.

BUYING YOUR HOME

There are many debates about whether you are financially better off buying or renting a home. The argument depends on underlying market conditions, such as property prices, interest rates and future rentals.

Still, there are very sound arguments for owning a home:

- You are the mistress of your domain, able to improve or alter your property to your needs and taste.
- You are effectively fixing your rent for as long as you own the house. Although interest rates on a home loan can vary, inflation works in your favour, lightening the repayment load year after year.
- You have security of tenure.
- You are building up a significant capital asset, particularly for retirement.

There are two main ways by which South Africans purchase residential property: freehold title and sectional title.

Freehold title

Freehold title gives you total and sole ownership of your property. You make all the decisions and are responsible for all upkeep. It is a form of ownership that applies mainly to free-standing houses on their own property. Where there is common ownership of the land, you can have sectional title ownership of a free-standing house.

Sectional title

Sectional title ownership applies mainly to blocks of apartments, where there is common property, such as walls and a garden. What this means is that you own and occupy your portion (or section) of the property and share common parts of the property with all your co-owners. You and your co-owners form a committee, called a body corporate, which decides how the property should be managed. You need to pay a levy for the maintenance of the common property and sometimes for things such as security services.

Sectional title holds many more potential pitfalls for owners than freehold title. Questions you must consider with sectional title include the following:

- What are the areas of common ownership?
- What common rules apply to the property? (Are animals allowed? What parking is available? What limitations are there in terms of noise at night?)
- Who are the property managers? What are their duties and how much are they paid?
- What is the monthly levy and what does it cover?
- Does the body corporate have any debts? If it has debts, you will be taking on a proportional share of the debt load.
- Does the body corporate have any assets? Likewise, you then own a share of the assets.
- Are any major renovations planned in the next year or so? This would involve extra costs.
- What is the general condition of the building and property?
- Who are the members of the body corporate? Meet them. They may not be very pleasant people, or they may have very different views from you about how the common property should be maintained?
- What conflict resolution mechanisms exist if there is a dispute?

WHAT TO CONSIDER WHEN BUYING PROPERTY

When buying property you are making one of the bigger investments of your life. You need to approach property ownership very carefully and must take a lot of issues into account. You should also look at a number of properties so you can get an idea of prices for areas, and the condition of different properties.

There are six steps before signing on the dotted line. These include assessing the property, deciding on how to own it, signing an offer to purchase, raising the finance, taking transfer and making it truly yours.

Assessing the property

You need to make a proper assessment of whether the property is suitable for you before you make an offer to purchase.

Position: The most important issue in buying property is position, position and position. The position of the property is absolutely important because it will determine how easily you will be able to resell. Issues you need to consider are crime levels, proximity to shops, schools and other amenities, noise levels (for example, is it next to a motorway), and the condition of nearby properties.

Accurate pricing: Ask the estate agent for a list of selling prices of other properties in the area to give you a guide. Do not agree to the asking price. Negotiate. Don't be pressured into buying. Agents commonly tell you that there are six other buyers waiting around the corner. If you miss a purchase, there will always be another.

Affordability: There are two main issues you need to take into account in deciding whether or not you can afford the purchase price. These are price and additional costs:

You cannot really afford the price if:

- you need more than 25 percent of your after-tax income to repay the loan; and/or
- you cannot put down 20 percent of the price as a deposit. (If you borrow more than 80 percent of the value of the property the banks are obliged by the Reserve Bank to charge you penalty interest rates on the additional 20 percent.)

You should also take account of what will happen if interest rates go up. In 1998 when interest rates skyrocketed to 25 percent many people lost their homes because they could no longer afford the repayments. This is something you must consider when interest rates are low.

Property transfer taxes can add considerably to the purchase price of a home. Companies, close corporations and trusts pay a flat rate of 10 percent. For individuals, the rates are as follows (effective from 2 March 2002):

Property value	Rate of tax
0–R100 000	0
R100 001–R300 000	5%
R300 001 and above	R10 000 plus 8% on the value above R300 000

Other initial costs include:

- bond registration agreements (R2 000);
- lawyers' fees (R500 or more);
- bank valuation fees (R1 000 or more);

- electricity and water connection deposits; and
- moving costs.

Also take account of annual costs. These include:

- Rates: These can be high if you are in an upmarket area. (Incidentally, ensure that rates and water and electricity bills are paid up to date or you may find yourself responsible for any backlog).
- Maintenance: It is estimated that these average about R500 or more a month for a three-bedroomed home.
- Water and electricity.

Condition: If the property is in a poor condition, you may be involved in significant additional expense. You must insist on receiving a list of all faults in writing. If a fault is hidden from you at sale you have the right to rescind the sale. If you are in any doubt about the condition of the property, get an expert in to inspect it.

Neighbourhood: There are two ways of assessing the neighbourhood:

- Get the feel of the area. Estate agents often drive you to the property on a route selected for its attractiveness, while a block away there may be a squatter settlement.
- Meet the people living next door to you. If the neighbours are crotchety you may have to live with endless complaints.

Building regulations: Check whether there are any special building restrictions that could limit renovations or alterations you may want to make in the future.

How to own the property

There are a number of ways in which you can own a property – from it being in your own name through to it being owned by a trust, close corporation or company. The issues you need to consider include the following:

- Your personal circumstances: For example, if you and/or a spouse are involved in a business partnership that leaves your personal assets vulnerable to creditors if something goes wrong in the business, you should consider placing the property in a trust.

- Capital gains tax: You will not get the R1 million exemption from CGT if the property is not owned by an individual.

Signing an offer to purchase

Most offers to purchase are fairly standard, but you don't have to accept all the clauses, and there is nothing to prevent you from adding other conditions.

Your offer to purchase must include all conditions, including:

- A description of the property.
- The offer price.
- The size of the deposit and how it will be paid. Insist that the deposit is held in a money market account with the interest accruing to you. If you do not ask you may not get the interest.
- How and when the full purchase price will be paid.
- The conditions of occupation. You must be particularly careful of occupational interest that you may have to pay before you take transfer. Negotiate a set figure that would be equivalent to rentals in the area. A normal monthly rate is 1 percent of the purchase price.
- When you want to take transfer into your name.
- What fittings will be included (you must list these).
- The financing of the purchase. If you are raising a home loan, the purchase is normally made dependent on your being able to raise the money from a bank.
- Other conditions of purchase, such as it being dependent on the successful sale of another property you may own.
- What repairs or maintenance need to done by the current owner.
- The provision by the seller of electrical and beetle certificates.
- Guarantees and undertakings on the condition of the property and the purchase agreement. Remember that most homes are bought 'voetstoots', which means 'in their existing condition'. You have a comeback only if the seller has deliberately hidden or misled you about a problem.
- Brokerage paid to the estate agent. Although this is paid by the seller, the amount can often determine the outcome of the purchase. Estate agents, despite the fact that inflation works in their favour, have managed to ratchet up commission levels to 7.5 percent of the purchase price, plus VAT. This totals 8.55 percent, which is ridiculous. If this commission is negotiated down to about 5 percent, which is still more than generous, it can affect the

price you will pay. Remember that commissions on lump-sum investments are normally about 3 percent, so it is very debatable that estate agents should receive so much more.

Any offer to purchase must be in the name of the entity in which you wish to own the property, for example your name or that of a trust or company.

Raising the finance

The financing of your property is extremely important. There are a number of factors you need to take into account.

Arrange your own home loan: Don't let the estate agent do it for you. You can often negotiate lower rates of interest with a bank by organising your own home loan (or mortgage bond). Estate agents get paid rewards from banks for bringing in home loans, and that fee will be included in what you pay in interest. People called mortgage originators can negotiate loans on your behalf, but remember that you are also paying them indirectly.

Negotiate: Establish the current prime interest rates; then approach all the banks and other home loan financiers, such as SA Home Loans, which recently introduced a new form of 'securitised' home loans. (SA Home Loans borrows money to lend money at cheap rates. Its entry into the market made home loans a lot more competitive.) Even half a percentage point difference in interest rates will make a substantial difference to your bond repayments. This is a significant area where a good credit rating will work in your favour.

Type of loan: Home loans are made available in a number of ways:

- Traditional home loans: Original home loans normally cover a period of 20 years, which you can pay off over the period. If you need more money, for say alterations, you have to apply for a re-advance. A re-advance takes time and will involve additional expenses such as valuation fees.
- Variable amount bonds: These bonds come under various names, but are mainly known as access bonds. They give you the discretion to increase or decrease the loan amount. While this is a useful facility, variable bonds are often misused, as people draw money for consumption expenditure, such as living expenses, and even worse for things such as holidays. You are

undermining your asset base if you constantly use a variable or access bond to fund your day-to-day expenses. It means that you are living beyond your means.

- Consolidated debt loans: Increasingly, banks are offering single-debt facilities, which include your home loan and other financing deals, such as motor vehicles. Initially, these facilities were only for people who earned more than R500 000 a year and owned assets worth a few million. But these facilities are now being offered to ordinary customers in good standing.

Interest rate structures: Home loan borrowers are being given increasing choices in interest rate structures. These include variable and fixed rates:

- Variable rates: This is the most common form of home loan. Your interest rate will move in parallel with the prime overdraft lending rate. So, if you have a rate one percentage point below prime, it will remain one percentage point below when the prime rate goes up or down.
- Fixed rates: Most banks will offer fixed rates for periods of up to 24 months. The rates tend to be higher than variable rates. However, you do have certainty on what rate you will be paying, particularly at times of interest rate volatility. In July 1998 when interest rates were around 14 percent, anyone who borrowed on a fixed rate was laughing when rates were nudging up to 25 percent by August. Fixed rates come with various bells and whistles, such as reductions if rates do fall.

Insurance: A bank will insist on numerous conditions, such as your having life assurance to cover repayment of the loan in case you die or are disabled and unable to earn an income, and short-term insurance to ensure that if there is significant damage to the property you can afford the repair costs.

Taking transfer

Once the seller has accepted your offer to purchase, and the bank has provided finance (if required), the lawyers take over. The lawyers register the property in your name; the mortgage bond is registered; you pay transfer costs; and the seller is paid out. A deed of sale, showing that you now own the property, is issued. If you have a mortgage bond, the bank retains the papers as part of its security.

Making it truly yours

Many people consider a house to be theirs no matter how large their debt. It is not. Your home effectively belongs to the bank until you have paid off your home loan. Most housing mortgage bonds cover 20 years. However, if you pay off the bond earlier you will save yourself a lot of money.

Let's take a mortgage bond for R200 000 as an example. If you are paying interest at a nominal rate of 14 percent a year, the minimum monthly repayment to repay the bond over 20 years is R2 487.04. This means that over the 20 years you will repay R596 889.60 – almost three times what you borrowed.

However, if you increase your repayments by only R100 a month, you will repay the bond in 16 years and 8 months and save yourself R78 964; if you increase your repayments by R500 a month you will repay the bond in 10 years and 10 months and save yourself a whopping R205 617.

The quicker you pay off the bond, the more you will save in interest charges and the sooner your home will be truly yours.

A HOME IN RETIREMENT

Many women, particularly if widowed, face the prospect of moving home at retirement. Retirement villages are becoming increasingly popular. They offer not only security but also companionship, and often provide special frail-care facilities. However, you need to be aware of the choices in retirement homes. There are four main choices: staying put, selling and renting, granny flats and retirement villages.

Staying put

There is nothing wrong with staying where you are if your current home meets your demands, particularly if your financial needs are not affected. Many people give up their current homes without properly considering the consequences. For example, they may move to the coast or the mountains thinking all will be great but leave behind family and friends. Often, the better choice is to take a regular holiday at the coast and stay right where you are.

There are a number of back-up services for senior citizens, such as meals on wheels, home nursing, and service and senior centres, which enable you to continue living in your own home even though you may require assistance.

If you would prefer to hold on to your home but cannot afford it, you can consider options such as taking in boarders, or joint ownership by selling half of your home to a friend who then moves in with you.

Selling and renting

If your home is valuable, you could consider selling and investing the money, which would provide the rental plus money for living expenses. You must, however, consider the risks of increasing rents and poor performance of investments.

Granny flats

The concept of an extended family with at least three generations living in a single home is nowadays generally limited to lower-income families, where choice is dictated by need. The need can be dictated by finances as well as by working parents, with the grandparents looking after children.

In recent years 'granny' flats have been gaining in popularity. Most 'granny' flats are small residences built on the same property as larger residences. There are many advantages, including greater security, maintaining a close-knit family, reducing overall costs, on-hand babysitters, an occupied property and closeness to grandchildren.

Retirement villages

Retirement villages are also becoming increasingly popular. They come in many shapes and forms and can vary considerably in cost depending on the location and services offered. They are also a form of communal living. If you find living in close proximity with others difficult, or like to be in total control of your destiny, a retirement village may not be right for you.

Don't see retirement homes as parking spots for people doddering around blindly. Many occupants are fit and healthy and lead active lives. Facilities often include things such as pools, tennis courts, and bowling greens, while golf-course-based retirement villages are on the cards for people who do not see retirement as a sedentary existence.

Don't see retirement homes as parking spots for people doddering around blindly.

If you are between 50 and 65 and are active and healthy, a village with sporting facilities may suit your needs better and could also be cheaper. If you are between 65 and 75 and require some help, but are not frail, you can consider moving to a complex that offers a communal centre, dining facilities, a clinic and a sick bay that caters for temporary stays. As a general rule, if you are nearing your 75th birthday or your health is failing, you should consider a retirement village that offers a full range of amenities, including health- and frail-care facilities.

There are a number of important issues you must take into account with a retirement village:

ISSUE 1 SECURITY OF TENURE

The retirement village industry has not had a very satisfactory history in South Africa. The biggest problem has been undercapitalised developers who took significant deposits from retired people and promptly went bankrupt. Even though the legal framework has been considerably improved, don't take chances. Before signing any agreement or deed of sale, have a lawyer check all the details – it will be worth the cost.

The Housing Development Schemes of Retired Persons Act, which was approved by Parliament in 1988, prohibits developers from using your money to develop a retirement complex. Any deposit you put down for a unit in a retirement village should remain in trust until you take transfer of the property.

ISSUE 2 RISKS

No matter how much protection you are given by the laws of the country, you will always find sharp operators who try to separate you from your money. Apart from scam operators, there are also a number of other risks:

- Scheme failure risk: A developer may be undercapitalised and may go bankrupt during operations. Although your capital is protected by law, in most cases other problems may occur – such as incomplete development or incompletion of promised facilities. Projects are often developed in phases, with revenue from the one phase financing the next. In effect, what happens is the financial risk stretches past the point where your unit is finished and occupied to when the last unit in the last phase is sold. The fact that a project is being financed by a large and well-known financial institution is not necessarily a guarantee to buyers. The bank will probably have a preferential right to any available assets.

- Resale risk: Buying in the right place at the right price. Compare facilities, locality and costs at different villages.
- Compare units: Don't inspect only the unit you are considering purchasing or occupying, also examine others in the same village and other villages. Make sure it meets your needs for now and for the future when you may become frail. If the accommodation is to be shared, meet the other residents to ensure that you will get along with them.

ISSUE 3 LEVIES

When comparing prices you must also compare levies. The cost of buying into one village may be far cheaper than another, but when you include the levies you could find yourself in a completely different league. You must also compare what you are getting for your levy, i.e. facilities and services. A developer may provide low initial levies to attract you, but will be forced to increase them substantially in the future. When visiting an established scheme ask about the levy history of the village.

There is a trend towards fixed levies, where a levy stabilisation fund is established to keep levies level. A stabilisation fund is normally funded by a percentage of the profits taken on the resale of units. See any village that has one as an advantage. It is an insurance policy against future financial problems.

ISSUE 4 MANAGEMENT

Poor management can make life in a retirement village unpleasant. You need to establish how the management is appointed, what experience the management has, who answers to who, how much say you have, and how often meetings are held with residents. You also need to know exactly what the management is responsible for, such as the maintenance of the communal buildings, electricity, plumbing in the units, maintenance of the exterior/interior of units, the gardens, security and the insurance of the building.

ISSUE 5 CONTRACTS

Not every contract is the same. Ask for a copy of the contract you will be asked to sign. Take it away with you and make comparisons. The contract should detail which services and facilities you can enjoy, especially on the issue of healthcare. Always have a lawyer go through the contract before you sign it.

ISSUE 6 VILLAGE LIFESTYLE

The general atmosphere in the village is important. Ask residents about relationships in the village (both between other residents and staff), security, restrictions on facilities, any past problems, the standard of meals (if provided), maintenance, and the quality of healthcare if you are taken ill.

ISSUE 7 HEALTHCARE FACILITIES

Frail- and semi-frail-care facilities are very important aspects of a retirement village. If you are moving into a retirement village because of its ability to provide frail care, make sure it is up to scratch. Also find out about doctors, dentist, nurses and other healthcare professionals. For example, are there regular visits by a panel of medical professionals? You need to take into account the cost of frail care, as well as worst-case scenarios, such as your spouse having to move to the frail-care centre while you continue living in your normal abode. You can expect to pay a fee of about R150 for every day you spend in frail care. Don't opt for frail-care centres that seem cheap. You should be ultra-cautious about anything that costs less than R100 a day. Some complexes will allow you a certain number of days a year in their facility at no cost.

ISSUE 8 GENERAL FACILITIES

Other features you should look for in a retirement village include parking for residents and visitors, social and recreation areas in the communal buildings (including dining facilities), covered walkways, a transport service, a laundry service, a library and social clubs.

ISSUE 9 CAPITAL AND FINANCIAL STRUCTURE (OWNERSHIP CHOICES)

There are five different types of capital structures on which ownership in retirement villages are based. These are full ownership or freehold title, part ownership or sectional title, share ownership or share block schemes, life right, and lease schemes. With the last two, you have no ownership rights.

The various options, which take account of how much capital you may or may not have, have different pros and cons. A retirement scheme involves several participants: the developer, the managers or administrators of the scheme and you, the buyer. If you obtain a loan from a bank to buy into the scheme, it will also be a party to the transaction.

Be aware that there are different termination or resale conditions, often with some type of penalty clause built in. For example, you may only be allowed to sell back to the project or through the project, and you may be given only a percentage of the profit made in the sale.

The five ownership choices are:

CHOICE 1 Full ownership or freehold/individual title

This is the simplest capital structure. As sole owner you hold the title deeds and the property is registered in your name. You enjoy protection under property laws and the Bill of Rights, which states that nobody except the state, and only under exceptional circumstances, can remove you from your property.

Buying into a scheme that gives you full ownership, or freehold/individual title, allows you to finance your house or apartment by raising a bond with a financial institution, without losing any rights. As the owner, you are fully responsible for maintaining the property and for paying for services, rates and taxes associated with the property.

Full ownership is probably the safest form of holding a stake in a retirement village. You will still, however, be required to contribute to any joint facilities or services, such as security, recreation and upkeep, the costs of which can be relatively high. You must take account of how common issues are governed and of the structure of the governing body.

CHOICE 2 Sectional title

Sectional title is similar to full ownership, but resources and responsibilities are pooled and shared, particularly as there is almost always commonly owned property. Your rights to your property are protected in law. A sectional title arrangement can make the burden of upkeep and facilities cheaper. The capital outlay is comparable with full ownership, but maintenance can cost less because of communal property and relatively smaller areas to maintain.

CHOICE 3 Share block schemes

In the past, share block schemes have been subject to criticism because of a greater risk. Unlike sectional title where you hold the title to a particular and identifiable piece of property in a common area, with a share block scheme you do not own an identifiable unit. Instead you are entitled to the use of a unit and your stake in the scheme comes from holding shares in the operating company of the facility. These schemes are often much larger and more complex with a greater risk than normal sectional title schemes, but because of their size and the resulting economies of scale, they generally offer more facilities at a lower cost per unit.

The difference between buying shares in a company listed on the Johannesburg Stock Exchange and a share block scheme is that, instead of receiving dividends, you receive the right to utilise the property within the rules of the company. These shares are usually transferable, so you can sell them again.

When buying into a share block scheme it is essential that you check the balance sheet. (Make sure it is audited by a reputable firm of accountants. If you have any worries about the financial affairs, ask the accountants, not the promoter.) The company could be carrying a large debt burden, a share of which also becomes yours when you invest. For example, you should establish what mortgage bonds are held on the property and under what conditions. If you buy into a financially fragile company, you could find yourself homeless if it goes bankrupt.

CHOICE 4 Life right

Life right was first set up in the 1970s by welfare groups and it is the most complex of capital structures. A number of people lost out because there was not adequate legal protection. Even though protection has been tightened up, again you do not have the level of security of someone who buys freehold or sectional title. These schemes are particularly attractive to people who are short on capital, as the costs to you are significantly lower than owning or having a share of a scheme.

Life right is exactly that: you have a legal right to occupy the house for the rest of you life. You do not actually buy any property or shares, so nothing in the village belongs to you. When you die you get nothing back.

A drawback is that you cannot sell the right, except back to the company that runs the village, and often only at the original purchase price. The principle is the same as a life assurance policy, with the scheme developers taking a bet on how long you will live. If you live for a long time, you win; if not, they win.

Some of the same risks attached to share block schemes apply to life right developments. Again, you should check the balance sheet very carefully to ensure it is a going concern.

If you are single and are considering moving into a life right scheme, check what effect a change in your marital status will have on your right of occupation.

CHOICE 5 Lease schemes

With lease schemes you don't put capital upfront. You simply lease a unit and have little security of tenure. Lease schemes are aimed primarily at people who have little capital to buy into a retirement village, but who are receiving an income stream, such as a pension. You are unlikely to be given any say in the running of the village. Your rent is subject to change, and you will not be able to make alterations within the unit to suit yourself. However, you can leave the village if you don't like it.

11

Timeshare

Many South Africans (more than 250 000) have invested in timeshare holiday schemes over the years. Most have done well, but there have also been some duds. Timeshare should be seen as a leisure purchase – both here and abroad – rather than a financial investment.

Although not an investment, once bought, timeshare is an asset. In most cases, it can be sold, donated or bequeathed. Timeshare can even feature in a divorce document with the facility being granted to one or other party, or being shared on, say, an alternative year basis. But it is very seldom that you will make a profit on the future resale of timeshare.

Timeshare covers only part of your holiday costs. If you cannot afford to go on holiday every year, you should be wary about investing in timeshare, particularly if it is at a resort that is far away and will involve significant travel costs. Make an accurate assessment of how much you can afford to spend on holidays before you think about buying timeshare.

Your choices of timeshare are almost limitless, both in resorts and ownership structures. The right choices will bring you back to work relaxed and happy; make the wrong ones and you could well condemn yourself to an expensive, decaying resort on the wrong side of the tracks.

What is timeshare?

Timeshare is based on the concept that you pay a lump sum for annual holidays today, and reap holidays well into the future. All schemes lock you into escalating annual fees, or levies, for as long as you are a member.

Most schemes are linked to exchange companies and clubs that enable you to swap your timeshare weeks, for a fee, at other resorts both within South Africa and abroad. Timeshare is based on the shared use of an asset, using one or other legal basis, including sectional title, shareblock or lease.

EIGHT STEPS TO BUYING TIMESHARE

STEP 1 UNDERSTAND THE DIFFERENT TIMESHARE STRUCTURES

Timeshare schemes vary – from conventional structures, where you have part ownership, through sectional title at a specific resort, to a points system, where you can claim holidays at a number of resorts. The choices are sectional title schemes, shareblock schemes, club schemes and point schemes:

Sectional title schemes: You own a part of a specific resort for a certain period. The resort is controlled by trustees elected by the timeshare owners. The scheme is likely to have managing agents who are often also the developers. You have security of tenure because of your part ownership. You have permanent ownership and are able to dispose of it by selling, donating or bequeathing it to someone else.

Shareblock schemes: A shareblock company owns or leases a resort. The developer sells shares in the resort to consumers, who elect a board of directors to an 'owners' association' to manage the scheme. You effectively become a shareholder in a company owning or leasing the resort. This ownership entitles you to use the resort for predetermined periods. You have permanent ownership of the shares (not the resort if it is leased) and are able to dispose of the ownership by selling, donating or bequeathing it to someone else.

Club schemes: Instead of having ownership in a scheme, you join a club. Your membership of the club gives you rights to use a resort for a fixed period. The club is managed by trustees, who are elected by the members. The club contracts to use the resort, which is normally owned by the developer. You have no permanent ownership rights. However, you are able to dispose of your club membership by selling, donating or bequeathing it to someone else, but your 'ownership' is limited to the period for which the club has leased the resort. The club, in other words, is self-terminating. You need to check on how long your membership will last.

Point schemes: These are the most hazardous of the timeshare schemes, so you must exercise extra care. You need to make very sure about the financial structures. These schemes may or may not lease and/or own resorts or parts of resorts. You buy points, in return for which the scheme managers promise to provide you with holiday accommodation for a predetermined period in the future at a range of resorts.

There are many problems with the points system:

- You have no ownership rights.
- Credible funding of future liabilities: You are putting money into a scheme that promises you holidays in the future. You need to ensure that the scheme managers are holding back sufficient money in trusts to meet the cost of your future holidays.
- The resorts into which the point schemes buy frequently constitute un-saleable timeshare.
- Prices are often way out of kilter with their counterparts in the more conventional timeshare schemes. For example, one club, which sells points for R1 200 each, requires you to have 26 points to spend a week at Sun City Vacation Club. That's R32 500 for a week. You could buy timeshare in 2000 at this resort for less than R15 000.
- The levies are structured in line with the number of points you own, which results in your paying higher levies than the more conventional schemes.
- Members often struggle to book peak weeks in upmarket resorts, because the schemes have access only during low-peak seasons. The scheme marketers will, however, not point this out when they sell you their plan. They will show you a glossy brochure of all the resorts to which you have access, but won't warn you that the scheme has access only to a few units and usually at the worst times of the year.

STEP 2 IS THE SCHEME RECOGNISED?

The Timeshare Institute of South Africa (TISA) is a self-regulatory body, which attempts to keep the industry in order. Before contemplating the purchase of any particular timeshare scheme, make sure that both the marketers and the scheme are registered members of TISA. Don't deal with a scheme or marketers who claim they are planning to become members of TISA. Be particularly careful to check whether a 'points scheme' is a TISA member.

TISA has a strict, but not always enforceable, code of conduct governing the industry. Sometimes TISA blacklists and suspends operators, including sales agents. It works closely with the Department of Trade and Industry's Business Practices Committee to help root out questionable practices.

Glossy brochures may make the resort look like paradise on earth, but you could find something totally different when you visit.

All schemes that are members of TISA must have their timeshare agreements with members checked by TISA lawyers to see that they comply with the law and the code of conduct. The agreements must have minimum levels of disclosure about the scheme details.

TISA, which in the past has come to the aid of members in failing schemes, also requires schemes to provide details of finances every six months.

STEP 3 ASSESS THE RESORT

Don't buy into a resort you have not visited. Glossy brochures may make the resort look like paradise on earth, but you could find something totally different when you visit. As a buyer, you are essentially buying an interest in a going concern. If the business is mismanaged or goes bankrupt, you will lose your money. Assess the following factors:

- Ensure that the resort is well managed and in good order.
- Check the financial health of the development. Make sure that the developer's levies are up to date on unsold units. You can request to see an audit certificate. Also make sure that your agreement provides the registered addresses of the developers and spells out whether a mortgage bond is registered over the property and how the bond will be repaid.
- Find out whether the development is complete. If the first five units have been built, it is not impossible that the other 45 will never appear on site, leaving you and the other owners with bigger bills for rates and taxes. Ask to see an architect's certificate.
- Find out whether any major renovation plans are under way at the resort. You could find yourself loaded with additional costs if the majority of owners have decided to refurbish the resort.
- If you buy a fixed week at a specific time of year, for example Easter, make sure that the scheme has taken into account that these dates fluctuate from year to year. If you don't, you could land up paying more than you should for a week you can't use.

- If a developer sells you timeshare in a resort that has not yet been built, make sure that your money goes into an attorney's trust account. Ask to see a feasibility study conducted by professionals in the tourism industry.

STEP 4 ASSESS THE RCI RATING

Resort Condominiums International (RCI) is an international timeshare exchange company. It rates all affiliated timeshare resorts and awards points to each resort, so that if you exchange resorts you will get equivalent value for money. The points are based on unit size, season, quality, and supply and demand for the resort. You should not consider buying timeshare unless you are armed with RCI's trading points manual – even if you do not want to use your timeshare for international exchange. The RCI grading of a resort will give you an idea of the value of the resort as a desired holiday destination.

The booklet can be difficult to obtain, but you should ask the salesperson for a recent copy. There can be significant differences between the price being charged and the RCI value. There can also sometimes be numerous reasons for this, including the underlying ownership structure of the resort. For example, if you bought into a club scheme it is likely to be cheaper than a separate title scheme, but the two chosen resorts on a week-for-week RCI swap basis could have the same RCI points value.

RCI also has an additional classification for top resorts, which is reviewed annually. Gold Crown status is awarded to the cream of timeshare resorts, and the Resort of International Distinction (RID) designation is given to the next 20 percent. All other resorts are seen as standard. RCI also honours a handful of resorts, which may not have the facilities of a top resort, with hospitality awards.

STEP 5 ESTABLISH THE COSTS

The initial lump-sum payment can cost you anything from R999 for 15 years' worth of annual holiday to more than R1 million. The costs depend on:

- the ownership structure;
- the standard of the facilities – from the accommodation to extras such as swimming pools and tennis courts;
- the popularity of the resort; and
- the time of the year in which you want to use the resort. Timeshare calendars are broken up into seasons, with the most expensive peak times generally

falling into government school holidays. Calendars can differ markedly between resorts and holiday regions. Many resorts offer you flexible options in which you can book any week in a specific season.

You should weigh up the price in relation to the length of time you will be given access to a resort; it is sometimes cheaper to buy into a scheme that lasts indefinitely than one that expires after a fixed number of years.

An increasing number of people are buying local timeshare with a view to swapping it, thereby cutting costs for decent accommodation for foreign holidays.

Costs include initial costs and annual levies, so check both of these.

STEP 6 BEWARE OF AGGRESSIVE MARKETING

Many of the timeshare marketers use hard-sell tactics to get you to sign on the dotted line. Up to 60 percent of the initial lump sum will be paid to a marketing company and agent for selling you timeshare. Agents selling directly for developers are not compelled by law to disclose their commissions. Commissions can be as high as 20 percent.

These hard-sell tactics include:

- Supermarket canvassing: Be particularly careful of marketers who approach you outside supermarkets with offers of prizes, including motor vehicles, to attend a presentation. The prizes are often a ruse, with no motor vehicle ever being won by anyone. You may see a brochure that claims a motor vehicle has been won, but it seldom happens.
- 'Sign now' tactics: Be warned that some scheme marketers do not allow you to take the documentation away until you have signed up for their scheme. If this happens you should rather not sign up.
- Not providing proper information: You will be promised the moon but nothing will be in writing. Ensure that you get all details in writing.
- 'There are almost none left': This is one of the oldest tactics in the book. Don't fall for it.

STEP 7 SIGNING THE AGREEMENT

Before signing an agreement get your own lawyer to read over the documentation and explain the legal ramifications before signing up: it could save you money and help you keep your holidays.

STEP 8 **COOLING-OFF PERIOD**

Because of the high-pressure sales tactics, you have a five-day cooling-off period after you have signed the contract to reconsider the deal. Use the period to read the documentation carefully and reconsider all the reasons why you made the purchase.

Again, you must consider whether you can afford the timeshare. Remember that most timeshare is a 'use it or lose it' facility. If you don't use the facility you are writing off both a portion of your initial capital and the levy you have paid for that year. In most cases, however, you do have an option (but you must check this) to sell or give the timeshare to someone else to use for that year; or you can bank it through organisations such as RCI, to be used at a later date. Still, there are usually expiry periods, normally two or three years.

12

Love
and Marriage

Any relationship needs to have ground rules. These ground rules will differ, depending on the legal nature of the relationship, the contribution being made by each party, and the duration of the relationship.

Love is not merely a state of mind. It also requires a legal basis, mainly to take account of what happens if the relationship sours.

You will need different plans for the various stages of your life.

SINGLEHOOD

If you are single and employed you should be developing good financial habits and laying the platform for your future financial health. One of the most important things you can do is start savings and investment plans. If you get into the habit of saving and investing you will have two significant advantages:

- The longer you leave off starting a savings plan, the more difficult it is to start one, particularly as you move into a permanent relationship; there will be more demands on what you earn.
- Compound investment growth takes time. The earlier you start, the more you will score.

Remember the Chinese saying: 'The longest journey starts with the first step.'

If you follow the financial planning steps in this book you will be well on your way. Remember the Chinese saying: 'The longest journey starts with the first step.'

LONG-TERM, LIVE-IN RELATIONSHIPS

Over the years the legal rights of people living out of wedlock, whether the relationships are heterosexual or same-gender, have increased considerably. For example, if your partner dies you are entitled to a share of his retirement savings if you can prove that you were a dependant. The law, however, still favours conventional husband–wife relationships. Unmarried couples operate without the safety net of tax and property laws that favour married couples. If you have lived together in a relationship for many years and even if you have had children together, this is still the case.

Without special planning you may find that you will not be able to inherit each other's property without significant tax consequences or even speak or take action on behalf of each other in a life crisis, such as serious illness.

The best protection you can give yourself is to make sure that your financial relationship is based on rules. The important issue is that you agree with your partner on how you structure your live-in relationship.

In some cases, these relationships are quite simple, but in others, particularly when it comes to joint ownership of property, they can become complex.

You need to structure three agreements:

- How will you structure your finances in the relationship?
- What will happen if the relationship falls apart?
- What will happen in a life crisis such as death or disability?

Put these agreements in writing. You can give legal status to any agreement by having a lawyer draw up what is called a 'cohabitation agreement'. If there are children or substantial assets involved, such as joint ownership of property, you should draw up legal agreements with the assistance of a lawyer.

MARRIAGE

Marriage is love built on a business contract, and you should not let your heart rule your head. It can be a thrilling time, but make an effort to ensure that it is based on a solid foundation that will take care of what may happen in the future.

Before you get married, both you and your, hopefully, partner for life need to understand that marriage is not only a union of love but also a contract.

Marriage contracts come in many different shapes and forms, some of which will suit you, and others that will not. You need to take into account a wide range of issues, including current wealth, earning power, lifestyle, dependants (now and in the future), past relationships and, most important of all, what will happen if your partnership collapses.

To find your way through the choices, you must get legal assistance from a lawyer who specialises in family law. A call to your local law society will give you a list of family lawyers.

It is not crass or a lack of good faith to insist that any relationship, whether marriage or live-in, is legally structured. It is in both your interests.

There are many types of marriage contract – both formal and informal. There are laws to protect the parties in customary marriages, but it is best to choose from a pick of three. They are 'in community of property', 'out of community of property' and 'out of community of property with accrual'.

In community of property

This is the original marriage contract brought to South Africa from Europe. Until quite recently, this form of marriage virtually reduced a woman's financial status to that of a child. Although it is not quite so bad today, you will still need your husband's permission to undertake a number of financial transactions.

Being married in community of property means that you are equal owners of everything in the relationship – both the assets and the debts. So, if your partner runs up a debt, you are equally responsible for it. Any assets that you or your spouse bring into the relationship are also pooled.

One of the flaws of this marriage arrangement is that if one spouse runs into financial problems the assets held by the other spouse are vulnerable to seizure by creditors.

In divorce, your assets are divided, but obviously this is not compulsory. Divorce settlements are now the norm where things such as the division of assets and future income are settled with agreements confirmed by the divorce court.

Out of community of property

You marry 'out of community of property' by signing an antenuptial contract, commonly called an ANC.

In simple terms, marriage out of community of property means that what is yours is yours, and what is his is his. As a woman, you can enter any financial contracts without consulting your spouse.

If your marriage breaks up you are entitled only to the assets that are in your name, but again obviously the courts will expect a proper settlement, particularly if there are dependants involved.

The major problem with this choice is over the division of assets if one spouse does not work and all assets are placed in the name of the partner earning the money. The system is a major advantage for people entering marriage with substantial assets, as these assets will be protected, remaining in their name. If the less well-off spouse has large debts, creditors cannot claim repayment from the wealthier partner.

Also, the system does not prevent one partner giving assets to another. Although you are taxed separately, spouses can give and receive gifts from each other without any tax consequences. So, if you are staying home to care for your children you should insist that a fair share of assets is registered in your name. This is particularly the case if your husband runs his own business. For example, ensure that at least your home and furnishings are in your name so that if the business gets into trouble you will not lose everything.

Out of community of property with accrual

In many ways, this option is a combination of marriage 'in' as well as 'out' of community of property (ANC). In brief, the assets you take into wedded bliss remain yours; you share the assets you build up together during your marriage; and you have the freedom to conduct your own financial affairs

Although creditors cannot claim against one partner for the other partner's debt, there could be debt consequences if the marriage dissolves. If the marriage dissolves, both what you owe and what you own are divided. So, if you or your partner run up high debts you will both have to shoulder the load when you get divorced.

No marriage contract

If you do not draw up a marriage contract to be married out of community of property (with or without accrual) or married in a customary marriage, you will be considered to be married in community of property. You can contract after marriage. This contract is called a postnuptial contract. But be warned that the process is a lot more expensive and complicated than having an antenuptial contract signed before you are married.

ON BEING DIVORCED

Divorce, as well as marriage, can be a relationship until death do you part. Divorce as a legal procedure can be fairly straightforward. Parting couples need merely claim an 'irretrievable breakdown of the marriage' as sufficient reason.

But after this, there can be a nightmare of negotiations and consequences. These can lead to a different type of dependency and friction – sometimes far worse than any previous destructive relationship. This is particularly the case if there are children involved.

Financially, the whole is normally better than the half. Very few people come out of a divorce situation financially stronger than they were when they were married. Obviously there are exceptions to this, but generally you are dividing what was there before. You are setting up two separate households with all the financial implications that holds.

The better you have prepared in the past, the easier the future will be. The two main factors in this are:

- Your original marriage contract: If you initially had a poor marriage contract you could find yourself significantly worse off.
- Your level of dependency: If you allowed yourself to become totally dependent on your partner, both emotionally and financially, then your problems multiply. However, if you retained your individuality and control over your own finances you will be far better prepared for what lies ahead. It is in divorce that you pick up the dividend for letting your head rule your heart.

Use the law, but don't become a law junkie. The more friendly your divorce settlement, the more likely you are to have a better settlement. A long, drawn-out divorce war is hardly likely to benefit anyone but a bevy of well-fed divorce lawyers. The first offer is often the best offer. One of the worst mistakes anyone can make is to try to structure a divorce settlement in an attempt to exact revenge on a partner. Again, lawyers are the most likely to benefit.

Getting the best deal in divorce

Although divorce is always a painful experience, you should try to negotiate the basis of a settlement between yourselves. If you cannot do it verbally try to do so in writing. You need to follow a number of rules, including the following:

- Avoid a do-it-yourself job. Unless you have no dependants, your financial affairs are quite simple and you are not expecting to be paid any alimony, avoid a do-it-yourself divorce. However, if a full financial settlement can be reached between both partners, consider the clean-break principle. There are guides available at your local bookshop, which will tell you how to do it yourself. This can substantially reduce costs and can be the best option if you are really parting ways never to see or have anything further to do with each other again.
- Draw up a draft settlement. Try to get a draft agreement of your preferred financial settlement before visiting a lawyer. This on its own will reduce the legal costs of a divorce.
- Use legal advice. You must involve a lawyer who will give you individual advice to ensure that the settlement is fair and legally sound.
- Remember that a divorce settlement is not one-way traffic. What's good for the goose is good for the gander. Many women are the breadwinner of the family, and claims can be made equally against them as against a male breadwinner.

There are a number of issues that must be taken into account in a divorce settlement. These include alimony, maintenance and custody of children, division of assets, medical insurance, life assurance, group life assurance and retirement savings.

Alimony

This is any amount that your ex-husband will pay you after divorce, or vice versa. The amount, if any, depends on a wide range of factors. These include your potential to earn money, including whether you have worked before and whether you are working at the time of divorce, and the ability of your former husband to pay.

Although maintenance of children is a separate issue in a divorce settlement, account will be taken of whether you are able to contribute. It will also include factors such as whether you are unable to work because you have to care for minor children. Alimony is often granted for a limited period to allow a partner (usually the woman) to find a job and rebuild an income.

Maintenance and custody of children

If you have minor children this makes divorce more complicated. The court will need to know that the divorce is structured in the best interests of the children. Children give love but they also add to the load of women.

In most cases, women get the custody of their children. This brings with it a lot of responsibility and potential financial stress. The odd thing, though, is that the father normally remains the guardian of the children and has control over any assets owned by minor children, unless the courts rule otherwise.

Children require special consideration in any divorce action, not only for their sake, but also for the sake of the mother. The financial problems of a mother can grow enormously if she is left with the entire responsibility of children. This responsibility can have enormous consequences, particularly later in life when most other people are looking forward to a secure retirement. It is important for your own sake that you take particular care in any divorce settlement that you get the best deal.

There are two main issues involving children, which will have to be settled when you get divorced:

- Guardianship: If you have minor and dependent children, the court of its own accord can take action to ensure their well-being. You will not get a divorce until the court receives a report from the family advocate stating that the settlement is in the best interests of the children. This does not mean that children will now live in heaven; it simply means that the best possible settlement has been reached.
- Access to children: Custody does not mean the other partner no longer plays any further part in the upbringing of your children, apart from footing the bill for food, clothing and education. Arrangements must be made for the father to have access to your children, unless this places them in danger. The arrangements must be of particular convenience to the children themselves.

Division of assets

The division of assets is one of the more problematic areas. A lot will depend on your marriage contract. However, a marriage contract is not the final word. If the contract was intrinsically unfair a court can decide on a more equitable division. However, you should remember that courts have tended to stick to a game plan of awarding no more than one-third of net assets (assets less liabilities) to a dependent spouse. So, in any dispute over assets you must take account of the marriage contract, any current ownership rights and also what the court is likely to consider a fair division of assets. If you have structured your asset ownership properly during your relationship, the issue is easier to resolve.

Often overlooked is the cost of the transfer of an asset from the name of one partner to another, particularly of a house. Even the right to use a property can cost money, including tax (e.g. registration of a usufruct on property), depending on how the deal is structured legally.

Medical insurance

This is a key issue. If you have children they will in most cases continue to be covered by the same medical aid, as long as they remain dependants of the scheme member. However, you will probably find that you will lose benefits. Make sure that if you lose membership of your partner's medical aid you have a replacement plan.

Life assurance

You need to take account of any existing life assurance, particularly if you are receiving alimony and/or maintenance for children. Ask yourself what happens if your ex-spouse dies or becomes disabled. It is best to have any policy ceded to you, as a beneficiary named in a policy can be changed by the policy owner. Once it is ceded to you, it is yours. However, you need to have a method of checking that the premiums are paid when they are due; otherwise the policy will lapse. The life assurance company should be informed of the details of the divorce settlement and the cession. Ask them to let you know immediately if a premium is unpaid. You will have to keep a reserve to pay the premium yourself if the premiums go unpaid by your ex-partner. A life assurance policy should also be unencumbered. In other words, you must make sure that it is not being used as collateral for a loan or has a loan made against it.

Group life assurance

If your husband is a member of an employer-sponsored retirement scheme, there will be group life and disability assurance attached to the scheme. Although a member of a retirement fund can advise the trustees of the fund of the preferred beneficiaries, the trustees must take account of all dependants. In terms of the law, all dependants are entitled to a share of any group life or disability benefits. You cannot be excluded merely because your partner does not want you to benefit. It is important that you advise the fund of your new legal status. The division of group life assurance can be included in a divorce agreement. The principal officer of the fund must be provided with a copy of your divorce agreement.

Retirement savings

You may be entitled to part of the retirement benefits of your former husband, and these must be written into any divorce settlement, and a copy given to the fund.

Factors that must be taken into account include the following:

FACTOR 1 ENTITLEMENT TO RETIREMENT SAVINGS

Spouses have the legal right to share in their partner's retirement nest eggs when they divorce, but they can lose out severely if the divorce takes place many years away from the date of payment. The spouses of retirement fund members face a double jeopardy, because other legislation gives their partners the right to recover tax from them if tax was not taken into account at the time of the divorce.

Retirement savings in pension funds, provident funds and retirement annuities often form a major part of a couple's assets, and it is only fair that both should share in retirement assets built up during the course of the marriage. This right – enshrined in the Divorce Act – evens out the situation where one spouse, who may have left a job to take care of the family, has little or no retirement savings and is left with practically nothing, while the breadwinner accumulates a comfortable nest egg.

Legislation allows pension sharing between spouses in all marriages other than marriages concluded out of community of property after 1984, in terms of which the antenuptial contract excludes community of property, profit and loss and the accrual system.

In practice, the divorce order will set out how much of the retirement assets should go to the non-member spouse, but she will get the money only when her partner leaves his retirement fund – this would be when he retires, resigns, is retrenched or dies.

The legislation falls short in that it does not allow for interest to accumulate on the portion allocated to the non-member spouse between the date of divorce and the date of payment.

For example, she may be entitled to half of her husband's pension fund, which, at the time of divorce, is worth R400 000. So, she would be allocated R200 000, which would remain in the fund until he leaves it. The longer she has to wait before he retires, the more she will lose out. If he retires 20 years later, her share would still be R200 000, because the legislation does not allow for any investment growth on her share. The fund member, on the other hand, gets to enjoy investment growth over the 20 years on the full amount.

However, remember that what is written in law is a minimum benefit to which you have a legal claim. In your divorce settlement you can agree to exclude yourself from any claim against a retirement fund altogether, or you can agree to better the benefits.

When you get divorced it is better to include the value of your spouse's pension to which you are entitled in the total value of the assets being redistributed. An equivalent value can then be paid out in a lump sum, or in instalments. This option, of course, works only if your spouse has the capital to pay you your share, as the retirement fund cannot, in most instances, simply be cashed in, and even if it could there would be tax consequences.

If your spouse is not in a position to pay you – even over a period of time – then you will have to rely on the legislation.

FACTOR 2 TAX

The proceeds paid out from an employment retirement fund or a retirement annuity fund are taxed at retirement date or if there is an early withdrawal. Until November 1999, retirement funds were obliged to deduct tax from the member when paying out an amount to the spouse, and there was nothing the member could do about it. While this is still the case, i.e. that tax is deducted, the South African Revenue Service amended the tax legislation, so that a spouse now has the right to recover the tax he or she paid on the ex-partner's share of the pension, provident or retirement annuity fund.

But the right to recover tax is not always fair to both partners. For example, assume the spouses divorce close to the date of retirement when the value of the member's provident fund is R2 million. In terms of the divorce settlement, the non-member spouse is entitled to 50 percent of the pension.

On retirement, let's say two years later, the fund value is R2.5 million. If the fund member pays tax at, say, 40 percent on the full value less the R120 000 (the tax-free lump sum allowed), the after-tax value of his fund would be R1 428 000. Of this amount, R1 million would be paid to the ex-wife, and he would be left with a far smaller amount of R428 000. In this situation, it would be unfair if he were to bear the R400 000 tax on his wife's portion. By being able to recover the tax from her, he would be left with R828 000, and she would have R600 000.

A different situation arises if a couple divorces 20 years prior to the member's retirement. In this instance, assume the value of the fund is R500 000 at the date of divorce and the spouse is once again entitled to 50 percent – R250 000. In 20 years' time, when the member retires, the fund has grown to, say, R4 million. Assume this member's average rate of tax is 40 percent. His ex-wife would be paid R250 000 without any growth – plus, he is entitled to recover R100 000 in tax from her.

You need to assess the tax implications at the time of dividing up the assets, and only then divide the after-tax amount between them. It should be clearly stated in the divorce agreement that tax has been accounted for, and that the right of the member to recover any tax afterwards is waived.

FACTOR 3 RETIREMENT ANNUITIES

In terms of the Pension Funds Act, a retirement annuity policy cannot be ceded to an ex-spouse, but a spouse does have rights to the benefits.

FACTOR 4 LAWS UNDER REVIEW

The legislation on retirement fund benefits at divorce is dynamic and you need to be sure you keep abreast of legislation. At the time of publication of this book, draft legislation – the Division of Pension Interests on Divorce Bill – had been out for comment for two years. The legislation intends to spell out in more detail a fair distribution of retirement assets.

FACTOR 5 INFORM THE FUND

Any retirement savings divorce settlement must be given to the retirement fund. The fund will require copies of the divorce settlement. Also keep the fund informed of any change of address. Use actual figures and assumptions when dividing up the pension assets, rather than percentages, so that it is clear to the trustees of the retirement fund how much should be paid out.

ON BEING WIDOWED

As a widow you do receive a tax benefit on the death of a spouse, so no estate duty or capital gains tax is payable on any assets you inherit. You need to know how any death benefits will be paid out from life assurance policies and retirement funds. If you have minor children, with a defined benefit retirement fund you will lose the benefits when the children stop studying or reach a certain age.

You may have to negotiate with a retirement fund on how benefits are distributed. You do not have automatically to accept the decisions of the trustees in the distribution of retirement saving benefits.

ON REMARRYING

Many people remarry after being widowed or divorced. This can create new issues that impact on your finances.

On remarrying after divorce

Issues you must consider are the status of any benefits you may lose because of remarriage. This could include medical aid benefits, life assurance, alimony and use of an asset. In some cases, you may be better off living with a new partner rather than remarrying.

On remarrying as a widow

You need to check the rules of the funds of which you are a beneficiary to ensure that you are not excluded from any benefits by remarriage. This can be the case particularly with a defined benefit retirement fund, which may have rules that exclude you from a pension if you remarry.

The blended family

One of the major problems on remarriage is merging two families, particularly if both you and your new partner have minor children. You will have to consider all the implications of the demands on the family finances, especially if there is a major imbalance in earning power and assets. It is very important to structure life assurance and wills correctly.

13

The Cost
of Children

Few of life's events focus the mind more quickly than having children. Though they bring great pleasure, children also bring great responsibility. Having a child is a major financial commitment, so you need to restructure your finances. You can ease the financial sacrifices you will have to make if you plan properly in advance. It is difficult to give a ballpark figure as to how much a child will cost you from birth to empty nest. There are certain costs that can be estimated, such as the future education of children, but other costs, such as feeding and clothing, can differ dramatically.

There are a number of steps you must take as soon as you know you are about to be a parent. These steps must be repeated with the arrival of every child.

STEP 1 CHECK EMPLOYMENT CONDITIONS

If you are employed find out what rights you have to maternity and other leave. The rules differ from employer to employer. You may be able to combine maternity leave, accumulated annual leave and unpaid leave to stretch out the period between the birth of your child and your return to work. Remember that your employer, by law, cannot discriminate against you because you are having a child. If you take unpaid leave you may be required to make additional contributions to an employer-sponsored retirement fund. Your employer is entitled to ask you to contribute its share for the period you are on unpaid leave but not during annual or maternity leave. Depending on what you are earning and your employment status, you may also be entitled to the government-sponsored Unemployment Insurance Fund (UIF) maternity benefits. (See p. 50 in Chapter 7 for more information.)

STEP 2 CHECK YOUR MEDICAL AID COVER

Check that you are properly covered by your medical aid. Remember that the birth of a child is not covered by a medical aid fund if you join up after you have fallen pregnant. Find out what proportion of birth costs will be paid by your medical aid and start saving for the balance. After the birth of the child, make sure that your child is recorded as a beneficiary by your medical fund.

STEP 3 RESTRUCTURE YOUR BUDGET

Your spending habits will change – with a definite increase in spending – while your level of income could be affected if you stop working. As a young parent, you may find this restructuring quite painful. The additional costs, apart from the responsibility, will have an effect on your lifestyle. It will probably take a few months to get the restructure right as you discover the full extent of additional costs. Even the initial costs of buying a cot, pram and clothing will set you back.

STEP 4 REVISIT YOUR FINANCIAL NEEDS ANALYSIS

In revisiting your financial needs analysis you will have to restructure your financial plan to include the following:

- Increase your emergency cash fund: There are now more things that may make extraordinary demands on your finances.
- Review your life assurance against death and disability: You need to know that you have sufficient assurance to cover your family if either you or your spouse should be disabled or die. If you decide to be a full-time mother you should also ask yourself what financial stress would be placed on your family if you are no longer able to fulfil the role as a result of death or disability. If you take out a life assurance policy you must name the child as the beneficiary, with instructions on how that money is to be held if the child is still a minor.
- Review your savings goals: You will probably have to restructure your savings goals for a number of reasons. These include:
  - Providing for future education costs: These costs are likely to be high, and you will need to start saving immediately. (As a suggestion you should encourage friends and relatives to donate to your education fund rather than provide soon-to-be-forgotten presents.) In 2001, an average

university degree or technikon course cost about R14 000 a year. To this you must add the cost of books (about another R3 000 a year) and ordinary living costs. The costs do not start at university level; they start at school level. The better schools have significant school fees, which can be as expensive as university fees.

- If you stop working, your joint income will be reduced for a limited or extended period.
- Your retirement plans could be affected if you are no longer working. If you are paying into a retirement annuity you need to check that there will be no penalties in reducing or temporarily halting contributions.

You need to structure your affairs so that your dependants are protected in the way you would like to see them protected. This includes issues such as guardians for children.

STEP 5 ADJUST YOUR RETIREMENT FUNDS

Ensure that both your and your partner's retirement funds are aware of your child as a dependant. This will ease the position if you die or are disabled.

STEP 6 REVISE YOUR ESTATE PLANNING

You will need to revise your estate planning. In other words, consider what will happen if you or your partner dies. This involves a number of different issues:

- Draw up a will. If you already have a will, update it to take account of your child. Your will should take account of how your assets will be distributed as well as what will happen if both you and your partner die simultaneously or soon after each other.
- Appoint a guardian who will care for your child if you and your partner die simultaneously. You will need to discuss this with the person you want to appoint as a guardian. Establish what you expect the person to do and what they can expect from you, particularly in terms of financial assistance.
- Appoint an executor who will look after the finances. (It is best to appoint different people as guardians and executors.) There are various ways to protect the assets you set aside for the upbringing of a child. This includes holding the assets in a trust until the child is no longer dependent. The trust can then be dissolved and any remaining capital given to your child or children. As further children are born you can alter the structure of the trust

so that there is no distribution of the assets until the last child is no longer a dependant. In setting up a trust, you will have to decide on the trustees. The trustees should preferably include someone, such as a relative, who will act in the best interests of your children, and an independent trustee, such as a lawyer, who will make carefully considered and unemotional decisions.

If you have a mentally or physically disabled child who is unable to earn a living, you will have to take special steps to ensure their long-term well-being. The government makes allowance for you to establish what is called a special trust (see p. 240 in Chapter 22 for more information), with tax dispensations, to help you ensure the well-being of the child.

14

Life Assurance

Insurance is often dismissed as an unwanted product that an over-aggressive, foot-in-the-door salesperson attempts to foist on you. This may be the selling approach, but many people have had reason to thank hard-sell sales people when the unexpected has happened.

There are two types of insurance:

- short-term insurance, which is mainly protection against the loss or damage of your possessions; and
- long-term assurance, which is mainly protection against your dying or being disabled earlier in life than you would normally expect.

This chapter is about the importance of long-term assurance against dying or being disabled. It is not about short-term assurance, which is dealt with in Chapter 16, or investment through assurance policies, which is dealt with in Chapter 19.

As a general warning, investment assurance should not be directly linked to assurance against death or disability. In most cases, your investment needs are different from your life assurance needs. You often need to cover your investment goals, such as the education of children, with life assurance, in case you die or are disabled before your children can survive on their own.

Life assurance is essential for most people. It helps you balance the risks of life. Without assurance companies many people would be left destitute in the event of an unexpected disaster. However, you must be on your guard against becoming another statistic by buying a poor product. Deal only with companies that have a sound reputation and track record.

Life assurance is not a 'one size fits all' product. You have to take care that you don't get too little or too much assurance.

Women must take special care in taking out life assurance and in ensuring that their partners are properly insured, particularly if you have other dependants, such as children or elderly parents. Your particular circumstances, i.e. whether you are single, married and working, married and not working, or divorced, will all alter the approach you need to take to assurance on your life.

If you are not properly insured, you or your dependants could face extreme financial difficulty at a time when you least need it.

Nothing is constant in life. You are born; you grow up; you are educated; you are single and need to earn a living; you may get married; you may get divorced; you will probably have dependants (either children or elderly parents); you will get ill; you may not be able to earn a living. As life changes, you need to ask yourself two questions continually:

What will happen if I am no longer able to earn a living? The answer to this question is not 'My partner will look after me'. You can never be sure of anything in life, because circumstances can alter very rapidly in extraordinary and unexpected directions. It cannot be repeated enough that you must look to yourself to be self-supporting. To be self-supporting you need to know what will happen if you are unable to work because you become seriously ill or disabled.

You cannot get much assurance against unemployment or the loss of your job, but you do need assurance against being disabled or too ill to work.

There are limits on how much disability an individual can take out. This is done to prevent fraud. The limit is normally worked out as a percentage of your earnings and takes account of disability assurance from all sources.

Married women who stop working for a certain period may find the limits seriously reduced because they are no longer earning an income. When you take out disability assurance check whether it carries through if you stop working for any reason. You also need to establish which company will give you the most favourable treatment. Disability assurance is extremely complex because of the different ways in which benefits may be paid. For this reason, it is discussed in more detail at the end of the chapter.

What will happen to my dependants if I am no longer able to earn a living? When you have dependants, you must also take account of assurance against dying. Many couples, for example, do not realise that the woman in the family makes an enormous contribution not only by earning a salary but sometimes also as a homemaker and caregiver. Children still have to be cared for after the death of a mother, and this may necessitate the employment of someone who could not be afforded if it were not for life assurance.

In deciding how much life assurance you require, follow these 10 steps.

STEP 1 · UNDERSTAND THE REASONS FOR LIFE ASSURANCE

The main reasons for assurance against dying or disability include the following:

- Protection against loss of income: You need to be sure that your dependants (and you, if you become disabled) can continue living at the same level as they could reasonably have expected when you were alive.
- Protection of savings plans: You may have savings plans for specific items (eg. education of children.) that will be at risk if you die or become disabled.
- Protection against debt: People to whom you owe money have first claim on your assets when you die. For this reason, you should make sure that there is sufficient money in your estate to pay off all debts.
- Protection against taxation at death: Estate duty of 20 percent is applied to any amount above R1.5 million in net assets (your assets less your debts) in your estate. Death is a capital gains event and all your assets are liable for capital gains tax. There is, however, no estate duty or CGT payable on any bequest by one spouse to another. You can get life assurance that will pay out on the death of the surviving partner to cover estate duty that will become payable on the inheritance.
- Protection of business interests: If you own your own business, and particularly if it is a one-person business, it will probably need money for it to continue operating as a going concern after your death. You may be a vital partner in a partnership with all the partners being essential to the success of the business, and your family may need to employ an outside manager.

Disability assurance can be attached to life assurance. Although you can assure against death without attaching disability, it is very seldom available as a stand-alone product (unlike disability assurance).

STEP 2 · TAKE ACCOUNT OF LIFE'S STAGES

As you advance through life's stages you may need to take out assurance for your particular circumstances. As different demands face you, you assure for that period. For example, if you have children, you can take out fixed-level term assurance from the day they are born until they reach, say, 21.

STEP 3 CALCULATE HOW MUCH YOU NEED

You can have too little and too much life assurance. Very few people have too much. The worst thing you can do is make a final decision on a rough guess of how much you need. Financial advisers, as a guide, recommend that you should have anything between 15 to 30 times your annual income available as capital if you die or become disabled. But the only way to be sure is to have your financial adviser take you through a financial needs analysis, which will identify and prioritise your financial needs and those of your dependants. It will also help you come up with an affordable plan. Everyone's financial situation is different.

This is a rough guide to help you assess whether you have sufficient life assurance:

Annual income required

Total family income	R
Reduced by 20% ($\times$ 0.8)	
= Income required	R
Subtract income of surviving spouse	R
Subtotal	R
Subtract income from retirement fund	
= TOTAL income required	R

Capital needed to generate required income

Divide income required by real return percentage of 3% ($\div$ 0.03)	
= Capital amount required	R
Subtract:	
Savings and investments	R
Retirement fund lump sums	R
Other life assurance benefits	R
Subtotal	R
Add:	
Debts	R
Special goals	R
Subtotal	R
= TOTAL capital amount required for life assurance	R

STEP 4 REMEMBER GROUP LIFE ASSURANCE

In calculating how much life assurance you need, also take account of any group life and disability assurance you may have. If you are employed and belong to a retirement scheme you will have what is called group life and disability assurance. Most group life and disability assurance is provided as a multiple of what you earn as a pensionable salary. (Your pensionable salary does not normally include allowances such as car or cellphone allowances.)

Issues to remember with a group life and disability scheme include the following:

- You do not normally need to have a medical check-up to qualify.
- It is only in force while you are employed by the company sponsoring the scheme (unless it is a union or industry fund), and will fall away at retirement.
- The premiums for the group life and disability assurance attached to a defined contribution scheme normally come from the total contribution from your employer. If the costs of group life and disability assurance increase because of, say, AIDS, the amount being paid into your retirement savings could be reduced.
- You cannot decide how the funds will be distributed when you retire. The decision is left to the trustees, who must apply the rules of the fund in seeking out all your dependants and deciding in what proportion each dependant will benefit.

STEP 5 MAKE THE RIGHT CHOICES

With life assurance against dying or disability you have many choices, which are structured to meet different needs. Here are some of the different options:

Fixed-level term assurance: This is the simplest form of risk assurance. You buy assurance for a fixed period, which pays out on death. The amount assured remains the same (it is level, hence the name). The premium, however, is not necessarily level. It may change if it is not guaranteed for the period.

Increasing term assurance: The amount by which you are assured will go up by a predetermined amount each year. Your premiums will also increase. The main reason for increasing term is to keep pace with inflation. Normally, the percentage increase in premiums is greater proportionally than the percentage increase in the amount assured. The reason for this is that as you get older the likelihood of your dying increases, so you need to pay higher premiums relative to the amount assured. Normally, you do not need to have any further medical check-ups.

Decreasing term assurance: The amount by which you are assured decreases by a set amount each year. In most cases the premium is level. This is useful if you are covering a reducing debt or are building up savings for, say, the education of children. This assurance is normally linked into a universal policy, which has an increasing investment portion with risk cover decreasing.

Convertible term assurance: This gives you the option to renew a policy at the end of a pre-selected term. The advantage of this is that at the end of the initial term you do not usually need another medical check-up. So, even if you are in worse health this will not be taken into account when you renew the policy. Your premiums will go up because they will be re-assessed, based on your age at the date of the conversion or renewal of the policy. However, some renewable term policies require you to pass an HIV/AIDS test.

Joint life assurance: This assurance is aimed at couples who are married or live together. Joint life comes with three options:

- It will pay out when the first of the two die. When the second dies there is no further payout.
- It will pay out on the last partner dying.
- It will pay out fully on each of the partners.

Disability assurance: This assurance will pay out either an income or a lump sum if you are disabled and unable to earn a living. This assurance choice is very complex and causes much dispute, so it is dealt with in more detail at the end of this chapter.

Chronic or dread disease assurance: If you suffer from a serious disease, all or part of your benefit will be paid out. Dread diseases include heart attacks, cancer and strokes. The list of what is included varies between life assurance companies.

Terminal illness assurance: If you develop a disease from which you are almost certain to die, all or part of the benefit will be paid out when the disease is confirmed by a medical doctor.

Premium waiver assurance: This assurance covers payment of premiums, under particular circumstances, such as disability or death, if it is a savings plan or joint life assurance.

Accident indemnity insurance: This is an additional benefit you can add or have as a stand-alone policy, which will result in a bigger benefit being paid out if you die or are disabled in an accident during the term of your policy. The benefit is normally doubled.

All these options are not necessarily stand-alone. They can be mixed and matched to meet your requirements.

STEP 6   CONSIDER YOUR CIRCUMSTANCES

Consider your current lifestyle and circumstances in deciding how much life assurance you require. Here are some examples:

Single without children: Unless you are supporting, or are likely to support, your parents you do not need any life assurance. You should not be taken in by the argument that life assurance is cheaper when you are younger. The only problem is that you may not be able to get sufficient disability assurance without life assurance. However, disability assurance is likely to be attached to your retirement savings plan.

You may also be required to take out credit life assurance for a loan, for example a home or motor vehicle loan. But, on the whole, don't worry about credit life assurance and don't take it out for any period longer than the actual debt. Also, avoid being talked into adding investment or any other bells and whistles on to credit life assurance.

Single with children: You definitely need both life and disability assurance. You must do a proper financial needs analysis to ensure that you are properly covered for both death and disability. (See Chapter 22 on trusts to see how to ensure that your children are financially protected in the event of your death.)

You do not need to assure your children, although some life assurance sales people will try to argue that you need such things as funeral assurance. Unless you are very vulnerable financially this is not really a financial need.

Married without children: Assuming you are working, both you and your spouse are in much the same position as if you are single. This means that you do not really need life assurance unless the standard of living of the surviving spouse is likely to fall after the death of the one partner. Often, however, credit life assurance on loans on major assets, such as property and motor vehicles, is sufficient. Again, always remember any life cover you have on a retirement savings plan.

Married with children: Both you and your spouse need life and disability assurance. You need to take different factors, such as your savings, into account in assessing how much assurance you need if you are married with children.

Divorced and receiving alimony and/or child support: If you are divorced you fall into the category of a single-parent family with a few additions. You definitely need life and disability assurance. If you are divorced and are receiving alimony and/or child support you need to ensure that you will continue to receive this money in the event of the death of your former spouse.

Your divorce settlement must deal with the issue of life assurance. Your former spouse must carry sufficient life assurance to cover the alimony and child support in the event of death. It is definitely not sufficient for your former spouse to notify the life assurance company that you are a beneficiary of the policy. The beneficiary can be cancelled.

You must ensure two things in a divorce agreement:

- Cession: You must ensure that any policy is ceded to you. A cession is different from merely being a beneficiary. Cession means you take ownership of the policy. Make sure you get and keep the policy documents.
- Premium payments: You must ensure that the divorce settlement contains a clause compelling your former spouse to keep paying the premiums. If the premiums are not paid the policy will lapse and be worthless. You should make it a condition that the premiums are paid directly to you, so you will know if the payments stop. If your former spouse does stop paying the premiums then you should do your best to prevent the policy from lapsing by making the payments yourself.

STEP 7 **PAY THE RIGHT PRICE**

The premiums you pay will depend on a number of factors:

- Your age: The younger you are, the cheaper your assurance will be, because you are not expected to die young.
- Your state of health: If you are sickly you could well die earlier.
- Your personal habits: If you smoke your health will be undermined.
- Your job and hobbies: If you are employed as an armed-response security guard during the week and skydive at weekends you can expect to pay more.
- Your lifestyle: If you are in what is called a high-risk category (i.e. there is a high risk of your dying) you are likely to pay more. An example is someone who is a drug addict, not only because of the addiction but also because of the higher risk of contracting HIV/AIDS.

Once you know how much assurance you need, shop around. Get quotations from three or four assurance companies on the level of premiums. Life assurance is a competitive business, and you will find that premiums differ between companies. However, you must not only compare premiums, you must also ensure that you are comparing apples with apples. Remember to take account of premium guarantees. Always check whether the premiums you pay on your life assurance are guaranteed or not. (If the premiums are not guaranteed you should establish the conditions on premium adjustments. Premiums are adjusted – mostly upwards – for a number of reasons, including more people than expected dying from, say, AIDS.) Find out under what conditions premiums may be guaranteed and for what period. For example, if you exclude any claim as a result of dying from AIDS you may get a guaranteed premium for the life of the contract; or you may agree to pay a little extra for the guarantee; or the premium may be guaranteed for say 10 years.

Beware of buying life assurance directly. Avoid buying any assurance in reaction to television advertising. There are two reasons for this:

- This type of assurance is normally expensive. You will nearly always find cheaper life assurance elsewhere. You should in any case always compare premiums. The amount you pay can build up enormously over a long period.
- The assurance you get is likely to be inappropriate. You need to make sure that the life assurance you take out meets your needs, which can be properly assessed only with a financial needs analysis. By buying directly

from a television advertisement or cutting out a coupon, you are unlikely to get the balance right.

STEP 8 — WATCH THE EXCLUSIONS

Many assurance policies will have exclusions, such as death as a result of AIDS and suicide. The most contentious area is with disability policies where there can be substantial exclusions. You need to be aware of the exclusions.

And remember: never lie or keep quiet about facts that could affect the level of the premium you pay. If you give false or incorrect information knowingly and the life assurance company finds out, it will repudiate your claim. In other words, you and/or your dependants will not be paid out. It is better to pay a higher premium.

STEP 9 — NAME BENEFICIARIES

Generally, you should name a beneficiary for any type of life assurance policy. There are various reasons for this:

- If you name a beneficiary the money will be paid to them within days of your death. If you do not name a beneficiary the money will be paid into your estate. It could take months before your dependants, who may not have an alternative income, see any cash.
- There will be no executor fees payable on the policy amount to the executors of your estate. This is a saving of about 3.5 percent plus VAT. The amount will, however, be subject to estate duty.

However, make sure you leave enough money directly to your estate to ensure payment of tax or debt claims against it. If you do not leave sufficient cash in your estate, other assets may have to be sold at an inopportune time.

Incidentally, if you have a policy that includes assurance against dying, disability or on your health, a creditor (someone to whom you owe money) may not claim the first R50 000 of your benefits. This is to protect your dependants from being left destitute if you die.

STEP 10 — READ THE POLICY

When you receive your policy document, read it. If it is not what you wanted, you have 30 days in which to cancel it and get the premiums you have paid returned to you.

DISABILITY ASSURANCE

Disability assurance takes over where health assurance leaves off. Health assurance covers your costs while you are ill; disability assurance provides you with an income when you are too ill or disabled to earn a living.

Also known as income protection assurance, sickness assurance and dread disease assurance, disability assurance is one of the most complex types of assurance and leads to many disputes.

Disability assurance is important, because you need it to cover yourself as well as your dependants. You may not need life assurance against dying until you have dependants, but anyone who is working needs disability assurance from the day they start work. If you are disabled on your first day at work, you will still need an income for the rest of your life.

Until recently, mothers who stayed home to look after children could not take out disability assurance. This could be problematic for single-parent families in particular, as well as for providing the back-up that would be required if a mother became disabled. Now, however, it is available for stay-at-home spouses. The amount is limited and is paid only on total disability. The maximum claim varies from company to company.

How to buy disability assurance

Many of us who have regular jobs make the fundamental mistake of believing that the disability assurance attached to our group life assurance is sufficient for all our needs. Unfortunately, it is highly unlikely that it will meet more than the most basic necessities.

As with life assurance, you need a basic level of disability assurance to carry you through your working life. The amount of disability assurance should be variable, altering to meet your changing circumstances. You need to follow a number of steps to establish how much you need.

STEP 1 **KNOW THE DIFFERENT TYPES**

Disability assurance and income protection plans come in many different forms. Most people are covered for disability through schemes set up by employers as part of retirement funds, or through disability assurance added on to a life assurance policy. Recently, a stand-alone disability or dread disease product was introduced for the first time.

The choices, limits and exclusions with disability assurance and income protection plans create a legal and technical minefield. Every year, the office of the life assurance ombudsman resolves many problems relating to the interpretation of what is and what is not disability.

With many policies you may find that there will be no commitment to pay out for the rest of your life. Because of the extensive fraud that occurs, most life assurance companies employ experts to ensure that the claimed disability actually exists. The companies are also developing rehabilitation programmes aimed at getting disabled people back to work.

Definition of disability

The contentious issue is what is meant by 'unable to work' because of a disability. Policies differ on the definitions. The main benefit categories are:

- Own occupation: This is disability assurance that is paid if you can no longer continue in the same type of job you are currently doing. Policies in this category are normally restricted to professionals.
- Own or similar occupation: This is disability assurance that covers you if you cannot do your current job or a similar one. If you have this type of disability cover, you may have to take on a similar job that pays less or provides fewer promotional chances and hence a lower earning potential. This category is based on experience, training, employment and personal history.
- Any occupation: This disability assurance is paid only if you can do no job at all. If you have this cover and are disabled but not incapable of working you will be forced to take up any job, even a menial one that pays virtually nothing.

The premiums you pay will be higher for the 'own occupation' than for the 'similar occupation' category.

A newer type of disability assurance, which doesn't take account of whether you can work or not, has recently become available. Instead, the assurance is against particular medical conditions, such as heart disease, that will affect your ability to work. Each condition is precisely defined in medical tems.

Reputable financial advisers say that it is advisable to have both types, as this is likely to provide you with better cover.

EXCLUSIONS

This is the area that causes the most dispute. Most policies have exclusions of one type or another. For example, back disorders and/or depression may be excluded. The exclusion clauses differ between different types of policies and between different companies.

You must read the policy to establish the exclusions before you sign up. A condition from which you already suffer, such as arthritis or AIDS, is likely to be excluded from being covered.

STEP 3 **LOOK AT THE BENEFIT DIFFERENCES**

Just as there are differences in the structures of disability assurance, so there are differences in how benefits are paid after a successful claim. Disability assurance benefits pay out in two main ways:

- Income disability: This is disability assurance or income protection that will provide you with a monthly income if you become disabled. If your disability or income protection scheme is attached to a retirement fund, the amount will be paid until you become entitled to a pension.
- Capital disability: This is disability assurance or income protection that pays out a lump sum if you become disabled. You are given a capital amount, which you must invest to provide an income.

There are many differences in how and when the benefits are paid out. These differences include:

- Delay before initial payment: In most cases, there is a delay before you are paid a benefit. This could vary from a week to up to a few months. For this reason, as an employee you need to investigate how much sick leave your employer will give you before reducing your pay.
- Temporary payment: Payments may be temporary in nature and the life assurance company may require you to undergo rehabilitation to get back to work.
- Scaled payment: With many policies you are paid 100 percent of your income for the first two or three years. The amount is then reduced to 75 percent of your income for all subsequent years. This is to make the temptation to make a fraudulent claim less attractive.
- Inflation-related payment: Your payments are increased at a pre-selected rate.

It is particularly important for working women who have disability assurance to check what happens if they stop working for a short while to, say, have children. The benefit may be reduced.

STEP 4 EXAMINE THE ADD-ONS

There are bells and whistles you can add on to a policy to provide you with more than basic disability assurance. These include:

- Hospital and/or medical expenses cover: With this assurance you will have your medical expenses paid out. Often, this assurance is paid only on specified illnesses.
- Accelerated payment: You could be paid out early if you suffer from a chronic or terminal disease, such as cancer. These diseases will be specified in the policy.
- Loss of limb or faculty: With this add-on you are paid out extra in the event of your losing a limb or the sight in an eye.

STEP 5 BE AWARE OF THE LIMITATIONS

There are limits on the maximum amount of disability assurance you may have. You must be very aware of these limits. Some people assure themselves for millions and then find they are way over the limits and don't get paid out.

The life assurance companies have agreed on maximum amounts because the temptation for fraud is great. Very few people would kill themselves to get a payout on life assurance, but quite a few more may consider chopping off a hand. It has been done!

The life assurance companies agreed that anyone claiming disability benefits should not receive more money from disability assurance than they would normally earn.

The guidelines used by assurance companies to determine disability benefit limits are:

- the equivalent of 100 percent of your monthly earnings on the day you were disabled for the first two years and 75 percent for each year after that, if you are being paid out the assurance on a monthly basis (the amounts can be increased to keep pace with inflation); and
- if you get a lump sum, 120 times the monthly benefit.

Note: These limitations are a total from all sources, including your group disability assurance provided by your employer or retirement fund. However, claims against motor vehicle assurance and against assurance for loss of the use of something like an arm or an eye are excluded.

Age is also normally a limiting factor, with benefits usually paid only until normal retirement age or until the age of 70. Compare the conditions of different assurance companies.

STEP 6   WORK OUT HOW MUCH YOU NEED

For most people, disability assurance is just an add-on to life assurance, either on to individual life assurance or on to a group life scheme. You should conduct a proper financial needs analysis to assess how much you actually need – and you need to review the position on a regular basis, particularly when there is a significant change in your lifestyle, such as when you get married or have children.

You can get disability assurance in two ways. Firstly, if you are employed or belong to a retirement scheme you probably automatically have disability cover. However, this is unlikely to be sufficient. You will need a separate disability policy, which you can get from a life assurance company.

You can buy a stand-alone disability assurance policy but it is more usual to add disability to a life assurance policy or even a retirement annuity, either when you take it out or later on. If disability is added to your retirement annuity, you can then access your retirement funds earlier than the normal minimum age of 55, if you are disabled.

As with assurance against dying there are a number of factors you need to take into account when calculating the amount of disability assurance you require.

STEP 7   CALCULATE HOW MUCH TO PAY

The cost of the monthly premiums will be set, depending on your risk profile, i.e. the probability of your becoming disabled, and the level of disability assurance you require. The most important issue is your health, and you will probably be required to undergo a full medical examination. The premiums will also depend on a number of other factors, such as:

- your age;
- your personal habits (e.g. whether you smoke or drink heavily); and

- your job and hobbies.(If you have a high-risk job, such as working down a mine, or you find hang-gliding relaxing, you may pay more).

The fewer exclusions you have from your policy, the more you will pay. So, if you have a heart condition and you want to be covered against dying because of a heart attack, your premiums will be higher than they would be if you excluded death from a heart attack from the policy. You must take account of the level of assurance you need, particularly in the definition of job type.

STEP 8 DON'T DISQUALIFY YOURSELF

When applying for disability assurance you must disclose everything about your health, lifestyle and the health of your close relatives. If you do not tell the truth, even on small details, the life assurance company is legally entitled to refuse to pay out if you claim.

If you change jobs you must inform your assurance company. Your cover may fall away if you change your job or occupation without informing the company, even if you continue to pay the premiums.

15

Health
Assurance

Everyone should have health assurance to cover all or part of their costs if they become ill. Medical aid schemes (medical plans) are like any other assurance: you never think that they are important until you need them. If you had a very bad motor vehicle accident and landed up in hospital for six months, or if you caught a bad case of malaria while visiting a game reserve, would you be able to pay the bills?

If you are employed you are likely to be on a group medical aid scheme. However, if you are self-employed you will need either health assurance or membership of an open medical aid scheme. There are increasing choices in health cover under both medical schemes and individual health assurance. In selecting a healthcare solution, you need to take a number of issues into account.

ASSURANCE OR MEDICAL AID?

You need to know the difference between a medical aid scheme and medical assurance so that you can choose the option that suits you best.

A medical aid scheme

A medical aid scheme is a non-profit organisation governed by the Medical Schemes Act. No one may be refused entry to a medical scheme on any grounds, for example state of health or age. There are both open and closed (restricted membership) schemes. Open schemes are open to anyone, while closed schemes are normally sponsored by an employer.

Medical assurance

Medical assurance is not governed by the Medical Schemes Act. It falls under either the long- or short-term insurance legislation.

If you choose to buy a health insurance plan rather than join a medical scheme, you can be risk rated, which means that you are assessed as an individual on the probability that you will make a claim. So, if you have some type of illness, certain exclusions could be placed on your policy, or you may have to pay higher-than-average premiums, or you can be refused cover altogether. The risk to you is that if you fall ill at some future date, when the renewal terms comes up, the assurer may refuse to extend the assurance cover, leaving you with no healthcare cover.

YOUR LEGAL RIGHTS

In terms of the Medical Schemes Act, you cannot be refused membership of an open medical scheme. However, if you do not work for an employer you can be refused membership of a closed scheme.

You cannot be kicked off your medical aid scheme willy-nilly. If you are a member of a medical scheme of any type you cannot be dumped if you become ill or old. If you are married, your spouse and dependants can continue membership after your death. Once you have joined a fund, the benefits continue until death.

Other important legal issues include the following:

- Waiting periods can be applied, at the discretion of the scheme, when you join, particularly for pre-existing conditions. These periods are:
  - a general maximum waiting period of three months during which time you will not be able to make any claims;
  - nine months for pregnancy (you cannot be pregnant when you are accepted for membership); and
  - up to 12 months for any specific illness or medical condition.
- Late-joiner penalties: If you have not been a member of a scheme before the age of 35, penalty fees can be applied. The penalties are backdated to the age of 30. The longer you wait before joining a scheme, the higher these penalties will be. If you were previously a member of another scheme, any years of membership will be subtracted from your current age and the

resulting age band and penalty rate will be determined on that basis (in other words, age at application minus years of creditable coverage). You have to provide proof of previous membership. This proof can be provided at any stage. When provided, your new scheme must recalculate the penalty.

- Community rating: This means that all members must be charged the same. The only factors that can alter how much you pay are your level of income and the number of dependants you have.
- Contributions/benefits: The contribution (what you pay for membership) and benefit (what is paid out to you) levels of schemes can be altered. There is no law or regulation that prescribes maximum contributions, but there are regulations that set down minimum benefits. These benefits include treatment for HIV/AIDS at public hospitals.

You also need to be aware that with an employer-sponsored closed scheme your employer can alter its contributions, depending on the rules of the scheme and employment contracts with employees.

THE CHOICES

There are increasing choices being made available in medical schemes. The choices break down into three main areas: traditional schemes, managed schemes and new-generation schemes. There are fundamental differences between the three choices.

Traditional medical schemes

Until recently, all medical aids worked in much the same way. The basics are:

- Contributions: Both you and your employer contribute if it is an employer-sponsored scheme, or you alone if you are self-employed. The amount you pay each month is based on your level of pay and the number of dependants you have. (The number of claims you have and your state of health are not taken into consideration for contribution purposes.)
- Claims: Claiming procedures are complex and vary from scheme to scheme. They include the following:
  - RAMS: Most schemes pay between 80 and 100 percent of what are called the Rates of Medical Societies (RAMS). These are rates set down by the Association of Medical Aids. However, not many doctors stick to these

rates (and they are not obliged to). If your doctor is not a member of RAMS then you have to pay the difference between what you would have paid under a normal RAMS rate and the rate charged by your doctor. For example, say you consulted your doctor, and you were charged R200. The RAMS rate is R140, and you can claim 80 percent of your doctor's bill on this rate. So, you would pay the R60 difference between the two rates plus the 20 percent of R140 (R28). Your share would be R88. Your medical aid would pay only R112.

- Caps on claims: Every year you are given limits on how much you may claim, known as 'caps'. If you are allowed to claim R15 000 a year, once you pass that point you would have to pay everything. With most schemes there are limits on dentist bills, for glasses, for ordinary doctors' fees, for hospital bills, etc.
- Exclusions: Many schemes will not pay out on certain medical bills. For example, if you want plastic surgery to reduce the size or shape of your nose, it is highly unlikely that a medical scheme will pay. Many schemes also refuse to pay for some things for which you would expect them to pay, like birth control pills. The same scheme will, however, be prepared to pay out thousands of rands on the birth of a child!

Always check all the conditions, particularly what you may or may not claim, of any medical scheme. You may find that you will need to buy additional medical assurance or switch options within a scheme.

The problems with traditional medical schemes

The structures of traditional schemes result in a number of problems, which in the end raise costs. These problems include the following:

- Use it or lose it: There is no incentive on members to keep costs down. They know how much they can claim and will go off to a doctor for the smallest ache or pain. If no claims are made, you have been paying contributions for nothing, as you get no credit for not claiming.
- Doctors' bills: As someone else (the medical aid) is paying the bill, you do not negotiate with your doctor to keep the bills down.
- Unrealistic costs to individual members: Premiums are based on things such as family size and members' income, rather than on the possibility of claims.

- Younger, healthier people are staying out of schemes: This reduces benefits and cross-subsidies, and pushes up costs for older and unhealthier members.
- Medical scheme administrators: Many of the scheme managers are paid a percentage of claims or contributions, so, the higher the bills, the better it is for them. There is no incentive for them to keep costs down.
- No pre-funding: Traditional medical aid schemes work on a year-to-year basis. In simple terms, contributions are made and claims are deducted. If there are more claims than contributions, the costs to members and employers go up. No account is taken of how each member's claims could increase as they get older. In other words, no money is put aside for what is likely to happen in the future. This type of structure is called 'pay as you go'. In terms of regulations, however, schemes are now required to build up reserves equal to 25 percent of annual contributions. This requirement will, in the short term, place further strain on all medical schemes.

Managed healthcare

Managed healthcare comes in many shapes and forms. Agreements are reached with healthcare providers, such as doctors, pharmacies and hospitals, about costs and levels of health service provided. In the past, a major criticism of managed care schemes was that members were given little freedom in their choice of healthcare service provider, and as a result could receive sub-standard care. Although there is now greater freedom of choice and patient control, you are, in most cases, still restricted to choosing from the panels provided by the managed care system. The upside is cost containment.

Managed schemes are often attached to other new-generation funding vehicles, so always compare schemes. The issues you should compare include:

- Contribution levels.
- Benefits: Don't examine only the amounts paid out; also look at the various quirks. For example, if you are hospitalised, does the scheme pay out for each day in hospital, or do you have to be admitted for, say, three days before you can claim?
- The network structure: For example, what is your choice of hospitals and where are they? If you are ill, you don't want to be admitted to a hospital many kilometres away.
- Choice of healthcare service providers, such as doctors and dentists.

New-generation schemes

Most of the new-generation medical schemes are based on the principle of reducing cross-subsidisation and getting you to save now for the likelihood of poor health when you are older. The structures are also being changed to get rid of many of the problems of traditional schemes, like overclaiming.

The new-generation schemes are designed to be tax efficient, to put the onus on you to control your own medical costs, and to reward you for keeping down claims and costs.

The fundamentals of new-generation schemes

There are four legs to the new-generation schemes, which among other things dramatically reduce cross-subsidies between the young and healthy and the old and unhealthy, hopefully keeping down costs. These are:

- Savings schemes: You put a certain amount aside every month in what is effectively an interest-earning savings account on which you draw to pay for day-to-day medical needs, such as influenza injections. If you do not use all the money in one year, your contributions are reduced for the next year.
- High-cost cover: You virtually buy assurance for high-cost critical medical needs and major calamities, such as hospitalisation.
- Investing for the future: Funds similar to retirement provident funds are established, so you can save for higher medical costs that you will more than likely face when you retire.
- Options: Most new-generation schemes offer various options – from very simple schemes with comparatively lower contributions, which cover you for high-cost health events, through to comprehensive options with high levels of contributions, which provide cover for everything from chronic medicines through to hospitalisation. If you join a low-cost option, be aware that when you need a higher level of cover, the option will not be exorbitantly expensive.

You need to compare the schemes that you are offered. For example, what is covered by your savings account for day-to-day expenses and what is considered to be a major cost? Some schemes, for example, will pay for your hospitalisation after a motor vehicle accident, but expect you to pay for physiotherapy while you are recovering.

LIMITATIONS

Limitations can be placed on scheme members in a number of different ways. Before joining a group or individual scheme you need to check these limitations so you can take counter-measures, or get what is called top-up assurance to cover any deficiencies. These limitations include the following:

- Contributions: If you are a member of an employer-sponsored scheme, you need to establish the level of your and your employer's contributions both for the period you are working and after retirement and whether these can be altered at the discretion of your employer.
- Waiting periods: When you join a scheme, there may be waiting periods before you can claim, particularly if you were suffering from some ailment when you joined the scheme.
- Freedom of choice: This applies particularly to managed schemes. You may be limited in the choice of service providers, such as your doctor or dentist.
- Exclusions: All schemes have exclusions. Some do not pay for birth control pills; many do not pay for cosmetic surgery; while most cover you for hospitalisation. One of the most important exclusions to check on is pregnancy and childbirth.
- Claim ceilings: Claim ceilings are applied in a number of ways, including.
  - a total amount you may claim in any one year; and
  - a total amount you may claim on different aspects, such as an amount for dentistry and another for hospitalisation.
- Proportional claims: You will often find that your scheme will pay out different percentages of your claim. For example, it may pay out 100 percent of hospital bills but only 80 percent of all dental bills. Most claims are also based on the Rates of Medical Societies (RAMS).

TAX AND MEDICAL AID

Medical contributions and other medical costs are deductible against taxable income, but the exemption is aimed mainly at people with low incomes or those people suffering from ill health with extremely high medical bills.

If you are 65 or older, you can subtract all health costs that you have not been able to claim against a medical aid or medical assurance from your taxable income. This includes your contributions to a medical aid scheme.

If you are under the age of 65 you may claim some of your medical expenses against your taxable income, but the deductions are limited to 5 percent of your taxable income.

Included in the amounts that can be claimed against tax are:

- your contributions to any medical care fund;
- any costs that arise from a medical disability; and
- medical expenses that cannot be claimed from your scheme. The medical expenses must be paid to a registered medical practitioner, like your doctor, or organisation, like a hospital.

For example, Mr X has a child suffering from a debilitating disease. His taxable income is R100 000 a year.

Medical contributions a year	R 4 000
Plus costs not covered by medical scheme	R10 000
Total medical costs to Mr X	R14 000
Less 5% of salary	R 5 000
Amount claimable against taxable income	R 9 000

MAKE COMPARISONS

When joining a scheme you need to check a number of factors:

- Administration: This has become a significant factor, as a number of high-profile schemes recently got into trouble because of poor administration. This means that your bills do not get paid in time and your doctor gets irate. Other consequences are that you will have to pay cash for medical care and then claim. The best way to check on administration is to ask your doctor and pharmacist about their past experience with a scheme.
- Administration costs: Some schemes charge far too much for administration. The Medical Schemes Council recommends that administration costs be in the region of 10 percent of contributions. Often, these costs are tucked away, so you should ask for details of all 'non-healthcare funding costs'.
- Commissions: These are supposed to be limited to 3 percent of your first year's contributions. However, many schemes are paying up to 6 percent of your contributions in annual fees. You need to establish what your health scheme broker is being paid and what he or she does for that fee. Remember that you are paying the money.

- Contributions and benefits: You should not choose merely the cheapest contribution rate. Compare contributions and benefits.
- Reserves and risk rating: Schemes have to build up reserves to 25 percent of annual contributions. A scheme with low reserves may be in trouble. If you suspect a scheme may be in trouble, check its risk rating. If it does not have a risk rating you should be even more suspicious.

KEEP DOWN YOUR COSTS

It is in your interests to keep down your own medical costs, particularly if you are not fully covered or have tight limits on your benefits. Here are some ways to keep down costs:

- Negotiate: When you visit a doctor or any other medical practitioner for the first time, ask about the charging structure. For example, is the structure within medical aid limits or not? Don't be afraid to negotiate with your doctor or other healthcare provider.
- Don't be a hypochondriac: Keep your visits to your doctor to a minimum. Don't go to your doctor for every imagined illness merely to be fashionable. However, have regular check-ups to catch any problem early.
- Choice of fund: Preferably opt for a new-generation fund, particularly if you are healthy. If this choice is not available, suggest a change of scheme to your employer, or ask if you may go outside the company.
- Levels of benefits: With new-generation funds you are often given choices on levels of benefits (what you can claim). Decide what you can afford to pay out of pocket and where you will need assistance. You will also probably be given choices on what you want covered for major trauma, like hospitalisation.
- Medicines: Always try to use generic (or no-name brand) medicines rather than brand names. Ask both your doctor and your chemist for generic medicines.
- Paying cash: Doctors and chemists will normally give you a cash discount. These discounts can be as high as 25 percent. Don't be afraid to negotiate.
- Compare prices: Check to see whether products at your local supermarket are not cheaper than at your chemist, and vice versa.
- Chronic illness drugs: Drugs that are needed for a chronic illness like heart disease can be bought on a contractual basis from a bulk supplier by mail

at considerably lower prices. Your medical scheme should be able to provide you with details.

- Hospitals: If you are being hospitalised, check how the charging structure works. Depending on what time you check in and out, you can be charged for one day less or more.
- Eye problems: Spectacles, particularly frames, are far cheaper at some of the discount opticians than at traditional opticians.
- Stay healthy: This is the best way to keep down medical costs. Live well, get enough sleep, exercise often, eat healthily, feel good and take time to smell the roses.

RETIREMENT

Plan for healthcare in retirement. Accept that your medical costs are likely to be significantly higher after you retire. More than 60 percent of medical costs of an individual occur after retirement. The other problem is that employers are reducing the amount they are prepared to pay in contributions for their retired employees. You need to build this into your retirement plan.

More than 60 percent of medical costs of an individual occur after retirement.

CONCLUSION

Health assurance is very complex and is changing all the time. You should take time in reaching a decision about what scheme suits you best, but remember that it is not a choice of whether you should or should not have medical assurance; it is matter of getting the most affordable scheme to meet your needs.

16

Protecting
What You Own

South Africa, unfortunately, has a high crime rate, which means that you have a fairly strong chance of losing a valuable possession. There are many ways to reduce risks, such as installing efficient alarm systems, but you can never achieve 100 percent protection. On top of this, everyone is subject to everyday risks, such as motor vehicle accidents or storm damage to their homes.

This is where short-term insurance comes in. It is protection mainly against losing what you own or against serious damage. It is one of those costly but necessary extras. As with life assurance, it is a balancing of risks. Look at it this way: you can probably afford to lose R1 000 without having a life crisis, but could you afford to lose R100 000?

The principle of short-term insurance is that you share the risks with others. By paying a percentage of the value of what you own, if you lose or damage possessions under predetermined conditions you can claim back the value.

Short-term insurance is an area of great dispute. You are very much in a 'buyer beware' situation because of the many pitfalls involved. When you buy insurance you are signing a contract with an insurance company: the company agrees to pay for a claim under certain conditions. It is these conditions that often cause problems.

There are three main areas where most people need short-term insurance. These are on motor vehicles, your home and the contents of your home. Each area has its particular peculiarities, but there are five important factors that apply to short-term assurance generally: period, conditions, exclusions, premiums and excess.

FACTOR 1 PERIOD

Short-term assurance normally applies for a maximum of a year and is then renewable. If you make many claims, the insurance company can increase your premiums at the end of the term or even decline to insure you again.

FACTOR 2 CONDITIONS

All policies lay down conditions under which companies will pay for a claim.

FACTOR 3 EXCLUSIONS

Most policies have exclusions under which certain items or events may not be covered. Always read the exclusions. You need to take account of how you will cover them if they occur.

FACTOR 4 PREMIUMS

The amount you pay will be affected by many different factors, including:

- Where you live: If you live in a high crime area, you will pay more.
- Your age: Motor vehicle drivers under the age of 25 pay considerably more because they have more accidents than older drivers.
- Your previous claims record: If you have made many claims you are likely to pay higher premiums, but if you have few or no claims you will pay less.
- Any measures you have taken to protect what you own (e.g. burglar bars and alarm systems): These will reduce your premiums.

FACTOR 5 EXCESS

This is either a voluntary or compulsory amount that you must pay before a claim is paid. Compulsory excess is put in place to stop small claims, which are expensive to administer, and to reduce risk to the insurance company in areas where it knows there could be many claims. Voluntary excess can reduce premiums.

ADEQUATE COVER

When buying short-term insurance you must follow a number of steps to ensure that you are adequately covered:

STEP 1 MAKE THE RIGHT CHOICES

You have three choices with insurance: self-insurance, partial self-insurance and comprehensive insurance.

Self-insurance: Self-insurance is becoming an increasingly popular choice because of the ever-climbing costs of short-term insurance, and the hassles with making legitimate claims. This choice involves the following:

* Setting up a separate savings account and paying into the account what you would normally pay in insurance premiums.
* Self-discipline: You need the discipline to build up a cash reserve to provide for any loss, and not to draw on the money for other purposes.
* Assuming risk in the early years before you have built up sufficient savings: One way to deal with this is to continue to insure, say, your motor car, but not the contents of your home.
* Setting the correct savings targets for covering any loss.
* Getting a better deal when you claim. It is common knowledge that as soon as any supplier, such as motor vehicle repair company, knows that you are making an insurance claim the costs goes up. Against this, if no insurance is involved you normally get a better deal.

Partial self-insurance: There are a number of ways that you can set up partial self-insurance using this system on a permanent basis or on the way to becoming self-insured. This choice involves:

* Deciding what risks you can afford yourself and what you need to share with others: For example, you could insure your motor vehicle but not your household effects. Or you could exclude, say, all your books when you insure for household insurance.
* Using voluntary excess: By using voluntary excess you can reduce your premiums. So instead of, say, R2 000 compulsory excess, you increase the amount to R5 000. This will reduce your premiums. In effect, you are self-insuring for the first R5 000.

Comprehensive insurance: Comprehensive insurance means insuring for full value. In most cases, you will still, however, be required to pay compulsory excesses.

STEP 2   VALUATION

It is important that you insure the value of your goods correctly. You can usually choose to insure either on replacement value or actual value. Obviously, to ensure on replacement value will be more expensive.

If you have not provided correct values, you could be subject to what is called 'averaging' by the insurance company. For example, if you have insured items with an actual value of R100 000 but the declared value is R80 000, when you make a claim it could be reduced by 20 percent because you are 20 percent undervalued.

With a motor vehicle you do not have much of a problem because values are freely available. Most difficulties in this area occur with household items. Insurance companies supply valuation charts for you to fill in and make value assessments.

STEP 3   KEEP GOOD RECORDS

Keep receipts and other documentary evidence of all purchases, so that you can prove your claims if the insurer requires you to.

STEP 4   TRY TO REDUCE PREMIUMS

There are numerous ways of reducing premiums:

- Secure your possessions properly. If you can prove to the insurance company that you have taken special measures to improve security, you will pay less insurance. For example, the fitting of a home burglar alarm system with active response will bring down premiums.
- Increase your voluntary excess.
- Make sure that you are not over-insured. An ongoing racket over the years by both brokers and insurance companies has been to keep your premiums in line with the insured value of a motor vehicle at the purchase price. Against this, the value of your motor vehicle has been dropping and you are paid out only the lower actual value. You need to reassess values constantly to make sure that you are not over- or under-insured.
- Never allow an insurance premium to be added to a debt when you are required to take out insurance on an item against which you have a loan, such as a motor vehicle or home. Interest will be charged on the premium, pushing up the cost of the insurance.

STEP 5   GET APPROPRIATE INSURANCE

You need to make sure your insurance is appropriate. Here are a few examples of types of motor vehicle insurance:

- Third-party insurance through the Road Accident Fund insures third parties injured or killed in an accident. This insurance is compulsory with the premiums collected through petrol sales.
- Third-party, fire and theft insurance covers your vehicle against fire and theft and the vehicle of another driver if you are at fault in an accident. This is useful if you are driving a low-value, older jalopy.
- Comprehensive insurance covers you for loss or damage in most eventualities.

Note: You can cover your car radio in two ways – either through your car insurance or your household all-risks policy. You need to calculate which is better for you – taking account of any excess on both policies, maximum amounts that will be paid and any loss to a no-claim bonus.

STEP 6   USING A BROKER OR GOING DIRECT

There is an increasing number of direct-sale, short-term insurance operations through which you can insure directly. There is not necessarily a cost saving in this. A broker can help you to make comparisons and get the best deal, but remember that they are paid a commission based on a percentage of the premiums you pay. This can be a perverse incentive to make sure that you pay the highest premiums. This does not mean that all insurance brokers will exploit you, but you need to be wary.

In choosing a broker you must ensure that they belong to a voluntary broker association and that they are in fact licensed to represent different companies. Avoid dealing with brokers who are licensed to sell the products of only one or two companies, as you need maximum choice. Always ask a broker to justify the advice being given in writing.

STEP 7   MAKE COMPARISONS

Not all policies are the same. You must compare the following:

- Premiums and other costs: There is an increasing tendency for costs to be loaded with various add-on charges and administration fees. Compare total costs, which, by law, must be declared to you in writing.

- Compulsory excesses that you must pay on any claim.
- Which items are covered by the policy.
- What is expressly excluded: By excluding significant events from claims, you may be offered a lower premium, but you are not saving anything if the event occurs.

STEP 8 **CHECK YOUR PROTECTION**

You are protected by the policyholder protection rules for the short-term insurance industry. In terms of these rules, you have to be properly advised of the conditions of your policy so that you can make an informed choice. These rules place disclosure obligations on both insurers and brokers. If you feel you are not being provided with sufficient information, you can complain to the Financial Services Board, which regulates the industry.

STEP 9 **PROVIDE ACCURATE INFORMATION**

Answer all questions on a proposal (application) form fully and correctly. If you try to mislead the insurance company with incorrect statements or by omitting information, you give them the right to repudiate a future claim. Don't take the chance of having a claim rejected; rather pay a higher premium. Insurance companies have various ways of checking up on your statements. Here are some important areas in which misinformation is often provided:

- Information on previous claims: You will nearly always be asked to state your previous claims so that the company can assess how much you will be charged in premiums. The insurance industry maintains a claims register in which they compare claims, so it will easily discover if you have lied.
- Usage: If you are using your motor car or home for business purposes, your premiums are likely to be higher. If you do not disclose this fact your claim can be repudiated.

STEP 10 **REMEMBER YOUR NO-CLAIM BONUS**

Most insurers, in different ways, credit you for not making claims. If you change insurance companies, you are allowed, in most cases, to carry your no-claim bonus from one company to another. You will probably have to get a letter from the previous company confirming your no-claim record. A five-year no-claim bonus can reduce your premiums by as much as 60 percent.

STEP 11 MAKE SURE THAT YOU ARE FULLY COVERED

Don't make assumptions when a third party is involved in arranging your insurance, such as when you have a loan on a motor vehicle or your home. Watch out for these two examples in particular:

- With homeowners' insurance, the bank that has provided you with a mortgage loan will often only be concerned that the extent of your loan is covered. You need to watch the value, particularly when you do renovations. When a bank does its initial valuation of the property, it will charge you for the service and will do so again if you apply for an increase in your bond. However, if you are asking for a valuation merely for insurance purposes, you must strongly resist paying for it, as the bank is already getting some commission from the insurance company.

- When you have a loan on your car, the outstanding capital amount you owe is often more than the value of the car. The reason for this is that your debt reduces slowly, with the biggest reductions coming at the end of the payment period, while your vehicle initially depreciates in value rapidly after the purchase. You can buy top-up cover through your bank or you can include it with your car insurance premium. Make sure you know what you have. You are most vulnerable for about a year after you have bought the vehicle.

STEP 12 GET FULL DOCUMENTATION

You are entitled to full documentation, detailing all aspects of the policy. Don't accept abridged documentation or verbal assurances from a broker. Most important of all: you must receive the policy. There has been a long history in South Africa of insurance brokers taking premiums without any policy being issued.

You must not only ensure that you get the documentation, you must also read it carefully so that you understand what is covered and what is not covered.

Note: You do not have to accept standard policies. If you want extras added or excluded, you can negotiate this with the insurance company.

STEP 13 REMEMBER YOUR RIGHTS

One of the rackets in the short-term insurance industry is conditional selling. This occurs mainly on items against which you have a loan. For example, if you have borrowed money to buy a motor vehicle or a home, the financier will insist that you take out insurance to cover loss or damage to the item. They are entitled to do this, but only a financier of a home loan may insist on a particular insurer to provide the cover.

This privilege to banks creates its own problems. By remarkable coincidence, most of them have their own associated insurance companies, which provide the cover. All these insurance companies charge virtually the same premiums, which are higher than what you can obtain elsewhere. This situation also creates opportunities for unfair exclusions.

Apart from financiers of home loans, no other institution or lender can insist on a particular company. In fact, you have to be told of your options. Many unscrupulous people will try to mislead you, or slip in documents in a big pile for you to sign so that you will end up paying higher premiums than necessary.

STEP 14 PAYMENT

Preferably make all payments directly to the insurance company. Some brokers are licensed to collect money on behalf of the insurance company, but you must get proof of this from the company. You can make payments either annually or monthly. An annual payment should be cheaper, as you will be paying in advance, so check that you are getting a discount. If you are paying monthly and you miss a payment, your policy is likely to lapse.

STEP 15 UPDATE INFORMATION

You must keep your insurance company informed of any changes in your circumstances that may affect your insurability. These include:

- any change of addresses;
- a change of motor vehicle;
- improvement in security to your home;
- alterations improving the value of your home; and
- any major acquisition that will be included in your existing policy, such as a Persian carpet.

STEP 16 PROTECT YOUR ASSETS

There is an onus on you to protect whatever you have insured. This includes:

- keeping your motor vehicle roadworthy;
- keeping your home in good repair; and
- ensuring that any security systems work properly.

MAKING A CLAIM

When it comes to making a claim you must also exercise great care to prevent the insurance company from using a technicality to repudiate it. There are a number of issues you must take into account:

ISSUE 1 KEEP IT HONEST

There is a great deal of fraud in the short-term insurance industry. The industry is quick to track down false claims and will repudiate your entire claim if it finds provable fraud. Insurance companies are also laying more and more criminal charges. Fraud includes allowing a service provider to inflate the cost of rectifying the damage or loss so that you do not, in effect, have to pay the excess.

ISSUE 2 ALL CLAIMS ARE VALID AS LONG AS YOUR POLICY IS IN FORCE

There is no limitation on the number of times you can claim on an in-force policy, as long as your premiums are up to date, and you have not made any fraudulent claims. No extra fee or premium may be charged when you make a claim or numerous claims on the same policy. But bear in mind that on when the policy is renewed on its annual renewal date you may be charged a lot more.

ISSUE 3 THE PREMIUMS MUST BE PAID FOR THE WHOLE YEAR

An insurer may reduce the amount of a claim by an amount equal to the premiums due for the remaining period of insurance. In other words, you will continue to pay insurance on a car that's been stolen or written off in an accident.

ISSUE 4 NO-CLAIM BONUSES

Even if an accident or a loss is not your fault you will lose your no-claim bonus if you make a claim. A no-claim bonus is not a no-blame bonus. Your first motor vehicle accident can take two years off your no-claim bonus, which means that you will need two accident-free years before you are entitled to the full discount once more.

> **A no-claim bonus is not a no-blame bonus.**

ISSUE 5 WEIGHING UP THE ADVISABILITY OF A CLAIM

It is not always advisable to claim, particularly for a lower amount where you may lose your no-claim bonus. In deciding whether to claim, you must take account of a number of factors, including:

• the amount of the claim less your excess;
• a comparison of the actual amount you can claim against the loss of your no-claim bonus and the additional premiums you will pay in future years; and
• whether you can have the damage repaired at a lower cost than what the insurer will be paying. (Remember that the cost is often inflated in an insurance claim.)

ISSUE 6 CONSIDER THE SMALL CLAIMS COURT

If you have been involved in an incident in which another party is responsible for the damage, consider using the small claims court as an alternative. However, you must inform your insurance company that you are using this option and that if you are not successful with your claim you may still lodge it with the company. You must ask for confirmation that the claim time limitations will be extended.

Don't consider making claims against the other party's insurance company. The company will merely reject your claim, often with unjustified threats. Your claim is against the offending party.

The small claims court is a useful and cheap alternative to making claims. If you have a claim against another person and you want to make a claim in the small claims court you must follow a number of steps:

- Send a letter demanding payment and giving the person 14 days to reply. State clearly that if they fail to reply, you will issue a summons through the small claims court. The letter must be delivered by hand or sent by registered mail.
- Visit the small claims court where you will be assisted in issuing the summons, and a court date will set. The summons will be delivered by the office of the sheriff at nominal cost – about R50 – which is the only cost you will incur.
- At the court appearance, no one is allowed to have legal representation: the court will resolve the issue as informally as possible.

ISSUE 7 WHEN YOU CLAIM

When you lodge an insurance claim you must follow specific steps. These include the following:

- When an accident or incident occurs, as a result of which you are likely to make a claim, never make any admissions of fault. Record all details of the incident as well as the names of all other parties involved and/or witnesses who can substantiate your statements. If you are involved in a motor accident, draw a sketch of what happened and record things such as time, weather conditions and place.
- Report any accident or theft to the police within 48 hours, making a full statement on what happened. Get a case number from the police. (Note that damage such as storm damage to your home does not have to be reported to the police).
- Report a claim to your insurance company as soon as possible, as most of them have time limitations on lodging a claim.
- If you have a broker, get assistance with the claims process.
- Don't be intimidated by an insurance claims assessor. They have no right to subject you to undue pressure or bully you. If this happens refuse to have any further dealings with the assessor, and report the behaviour to the insurance company.
- You cannot be forced to take a lie detector test if you have not agreed to do so in your policy.

ISSUE 8 REPUDIATION OF CLAIMS

An insurance company may repudiate or reduce a claim on a number of grounds. These include:

- fraudulent claims;
- not meeting conditions of policy (such as making sure your car has a working and approved alarm system or not making the claim within the required period);
- exclusions in the policy;
- lack of proof;
- under-insurance; and
- failure to take due care. For example, you may not have kept your motor vehicle roadworthy or had the roof of your home serviced to stop leaks.

ISSUE 9 WHAT TO DO IF YOUR CLAIM IS NOT MET

If your claim is reduced or not met, you must follow a number of steps:

- Ascertain the reasons for the rejection of your claim. Ask for confirmation of the repudiation or reduction of your claim in writing.
- Compare the reasons for repudiation or reduction of claim with your policy to see if they are valid.
- Consider whether you have sound arguments for challenging the view of the insurance company. If you feel you have been unjustly treated, write a letter to the insurance company challenging its view. For example, if an insurance company attempts to repudiate a claim against theft of a vehicle because you had smooth tyres, you would have reason to be aggrieved.
- Consider taking legal action, including use of the small claims court, against the insurance company or appealing for assistance from the ombudsman for short-term insurance. You cannot use the offices of the ombudsman if you have already instituted legal action. You can, however, still take legal action if your appeal to the ombudsman is unsuccessful. There are no costs for using the ombudsman.

17

Choosing an Adviser

Choosing a financial advisor has been one of the more difficult problems for individual investors. Until recently, there has been very little regulation of financial advisers. This has effectively left the door open to:

- honest advisers who are not properly qualified to give advice on the vast array of financial products, including the tax and estate-planning implications;
- knowledgeable but greedy advisers who give advice based on commissions rather than in your interests;
- advisers who are swimming pool salesmen one day and financial advisers the next, without the skills to do either job; and
- charlatans who see the financial services industry as an opportunity to rip off innocent investors. Prime targets are the elderly and women who have been recently divorced or widowed and previously had little or no say in the family finances.

For most people, the problem is identifying an adviser who fits the bill, i.e. someone who is qualified, experienced, honest, and who will give advice in the client's best interest. An underlying problem has been the financial services industry, which, in the past, has often designed financial products around the maximum commission and other incentives to advisers, rather than in the interests of consumers. There has also been a lack of proper regulation of advisers.

NEW LEGISLATION TO PROTECT YOU

Since 2000 the position in the financial services industry has changed substantially. Four major steps have been taken:

- The Medical Schemes Act now requires financial advisers selling medical scheme products to be registered and to have minimum qualifications.
- The policyholder protection regulations under the Long- and Short-Term Insurance Acts now set down rules about who may sell lifelong and short-term insurance products and how they may be sold.
- The Financial Advisory and Intermediary Services Act will regulate and register all people giving advice on financial products (due to be promulgated in late 2002).
- There is new legislation establishing an ombudsman (who now covers all areas not covered by the voluntary ombudsmen for life assurance, short-term assurance and banking) as well as the pension fund adjudicator. The new super-ombudsman will, among other things, deal with complaints about advisers who are not subject to the controls of the voluntary ombudsman.

The role of ombudsmen

The new super-ombudsman and the pension fund adjudicator are appointed by a panel selected by the minister of finance; while the ombudsmen for long- and short-term insurance and banking are selected by panels appointed by the various sectors of the industries they govern. The duty of an ombudsman is to resolve disputes between consumers and the financial services industry by finding fair solutions rather than resorting to the letter of the law. Ombudsmen level the playing field between large companies and consumers, because there is no cost to a consumer to appeal to an ombudsman.

In essence, all this legislation and attached regulation aims at providing investors with the following:

- proper disclosure of information about the financial product being sold, your advisor and the financial product provider;
- measures to improve the quality of advisers; and
- remedial steps that can be taken if things go wrong.

However, no legislation can protect you against every eventuality. You still have to be on your guard, and arm yourself with knowledge about your financial needs. The legislation does not establish a force of exceptional advisers; it sets minimum requirements. Your skill needs for a financial adviser will depend on the level of complexity of your financial affairs. The best-qualified financial advisers in South Africa are advisers who are Certified Financial Planners (CFPs), accredited through the Financial Planning Institute of South Africa. There are also a number of voluntary financial intermediary organisations with codes of conduct, which work at improving the status of intermediaries.

TYPES OF ADVISERS

Financial advisers come in different shapes and sizes. You have a choice between dealing with an agent, a general agent or an independent adviser.

The company agent

A company agent is appointed as a staff member of a particular financial services company, normally a life assurance company, to sell its products. The main issues to consider with a company agent include the following:

Limited number of products: A company agent is normally authorised to sell the products of only one company. They cannot sell you the products of any other company. An agent will be able to sell you the full range of products of the company, including assurance against dying or disability, life assurance investment products such as endowment policies, life assurance retirement products such as retirement annuities and annuities (pensions), healthcare products and unit trusts. Top agents are increasingly being authorised to sell the company's own linked investment products, such as living annuities.

Peace of mind: The company can be forced to stand good for any bad advice you receive. A company agent has to tell you that he or she is an agent and which company they represent. Companies keep a close check on the activities of an agent and can take quick action when it sees something going wrong.

Payment: Company agents can be paid in a number of different ways. They may receive a salary, or a commission, or both a reduced commission and salary.

Skills: Different agents have different levels of skills and experience, and they should inform you of their particular qualifications to be your adviser. Most life assurance companies nowadays insist that their agents do courses and write examinations to ensure they are knowledgeable about the company's products.

Back-up: An agent has a readily available research base to provide answers for difficult questions or needs of clients. Most life assurance companies have significant back-up facilities and research teams providing advice on a wide range of issues, including estate planning, tax and general financial issues. An agent is as good or bad as the company: if the company provides poor service and investment performance the agent cannot do anything to rectify the position.

The general agent

A general agent is a relatively new category. They are much the same as a company agent, but they are also permitted to sell the financial services products of other companies. These products must, however, be approved by the company employing the general agent. You have the peace of mind of knowing that if something goes wrong the company will be responsible and is subject to the authority of the ombudsman's office.

The independent financial adviser

An independent financial adviser is, in most cases, not employed by any one financial services company that supplies financial products. These are the main issues to consider with an independent financial adviser:

Not necessarily independent: Not all independent financial advisers are fully independent. For example, many work for banks as bank brokers, selling the products the banks have decided should be on the list of sales. Other independents may be licensed to sell the products of a limited number of companies only. Others have franchises and are permitted to sell the products of that one company only. The intermediary is obliged to tell you which companies he or she can represent.

Wide range of products: An independent financial adviser can sell you the products of any financial services company. This can result in your getting a better deal, as costs of assurance differ between different companies, and investment returns can also be dramatically different. A properly skilled individual investment adviser has far greater choice in putting together the right package for you.

Peace of mind: If you receive bad advice from an independent financial adviser you are unlikely to be able to call on the company supplying the product to stand good for any loss you may suffer. Many advisers are members of professional organisations that have codes of conduct, which will take action on a complaint. If you want to recover your money because of bad advice you will have to take the adviser to court.

Skills, training and experience: An independent financial adviser need not be skilled either by qualification or experience. Much of the bad advice given by independent financial advisers is as a result of poor knowledge rather than malicious intent. However, there are many highly skilled financial advisers who provide their clients with superb and knowledgeable service.

Back-up: A financial adviser operating as a one-person show is unlikely to provide the full range of services you require. Nowadays, no individual can have the full range of skills required to cover all the fields of financial planning, such as tax and investment. Any adviser requires significant back-up. Increasingly, brokers are joining forces, and there are now some substantial broker companies with the ability to provide the information and skills required.

Payment: Independent brokers get paid in different ways. Brokers are working increasingly on a fee-only basis. Others take a fee and commissions; others take only commissions. Using a broker can be more expensive than using an agent, but the broker will argue that they provide a far more comprehensive service.

So the question about whether you should use an agent, a general agent or a broker does not have an easy answer. There are upsides and downsides to both. Just as you get good, highly skilled agents, so you get bad, poorly skilled independent financial advisers. You will find the highly skilled Certified Financial Planners working as both agents and independents.

The answer often lies in the complexity of the advice and products you require. The more complex and the wider the range of the solutions you need, the more likely you are to need the services of an independent adviser. This is particularly the case with investment advice.

GUIDELINES FOR SELECTING AN ADVISER

Here are some further guidelines, not only for deciding between the three, but also for selecting any financial adviser, whether they are agents or independents:

- Ensure registration in terms of the Financial Advisory and Intermediary Services Act. Don't deal with anyone who is not registered as a financial adviser, as you will have little or no comeback if something goes wrong.
- Get advice from more than one person if you are in any doubt about the advice you are being given. Two should normally be good enough. Perhaps pick an agent and a broker.
- Always ask for references of clients with whom the intermediary has had long-term relationships.
- Always check on the credentials of the person giving you advice. Establish (in writing) which company or companies they are authorised to represent, their qualifications and their experience.
- Ask how much of your investment is going towards costs and how much of that is commission. In the past there have often been problems with products paying high commissions being sold by brokers. With an agent being paid a salary, or an independent working on a fee-only basis, the chances of commission-driven selling decreases. Be prepared to pay for financial advice, particularly when it is complex. Many people think they should get it for free. Advisers also need to earn a living. You should discuss how your adviser is to be paid upfront.
- Ensure that an adviser or agent has the skills, including computer skills, to provide you with a proper service. If the adviser does not have the skills, they may be able to access them from other people. The skills you should be checking on include:
  - qualifications that show an understanding of life assurance, investment, tax and estate planning; and
  - computer skills to do a proper financial needs analysis that can provide a breakdown of your needs and the steps you have to take to achieve them.

In the end you should select an adviser with whom you can establish a long-term relationship based on trust and good service, and who will provide you with ongoing advice.

18

Rules of
Investment

Men generally die at a younger age than women. The result of this is that many women are faced later in life with the investment of large lump sums of money coming from a number of sources, such as retirement funds and life assurance. A large proportion of women receiving these lump sums has never handled large amounts before, and many have not been involved in investment at all.

Widows are often the targets of unethical financial advisers who are driven more by commission than their clients' interests. You don't need to be an investment expert to make sure that things don't go sour, but you must understand the basics of investment, and the different investment products and their uses. If you have an understanding of the basics and follow a number of simple rules, you should be able to protect your money.

For a widow who has recently come into a large sum of money, the rules of investment are no different from the guidelines for someone who has received her first pay cheque and wants to start building real wealth. If you know your financial self, have a financial plan and (it is hoped) have no or little debt, you can start preserving and building wealth.

Don't see investment as a way of generating vast amounts of wealth. The first objective is to preserve your wealth. Wealth essentially comes from doing what you are best at doing, namely what you do to earn money, and then saving a portion of your money. You will not become wealthy if you do not earn and save money. With your financial needs analysis (see p. 16 in Chapter 2) you will have identified your economic requirements and how much you can afford to pay yourself by way of saving to meet your needs.

Saving, however, is not investing. Saving is accumulating money without placing it at risk – e.g. placing it in an interest-earning bank account – where you know you will get a certain interest rate paid to you at a regular period, and you will always get your capital back.

Investment is about making your money work for you. If you simply invest your money in a bank account, over the long term it is very unlikely that you will protect its value. The reason is that you have two significant enemies. They are inflation and tax. If you are on a marginal income tax rate of 40 percent and the inflation rate

Investment is about making your money work for you.

is 6 percent, you need a return of more than 10.3 percent a year to get a positive return – something you will not often get from an ordinary bank deposit. The higher your marginal tax rate and the higher inflation, the higher the return you must get on your investment.

Defining inflation

Inflation means a general and sustained increase in prices of products and services over fixed periods. It can be caused by a number of things. There are two main types:

- Push inflation: For example, if the price of petrol goes up it affects a wide range of product-producers, forcing them to push up the prices of their goods. Increases in salaries and wages can have the same effect.
- Pull inflation: This happens when there is too much money and too few products. This means that producers can charge more for their products. The situation is often caused by people borrowing too much money to spend on consumer goods, particularly luxuries.

As a general rule, when you save money you should work on your money growing by what is called a 'real' rate of growth. This takes account of inflation. A real rate of return is calculated by subtracting the inflation rate from the interest rate you are earning. For example, if the interest rate your bank gives you is 15 percent, and the inflation rate is 10 percent, then you are actually receiving 5 percent a year.

To make your money work for you, you need to take considered risks. Investment is about making capital gains. In other words, you invest in something because it will improve in value. For example, if you buy a bottle of wine for R10 and then sell it six months later for R50, you have made a capital gain of R40. However, you have to take the risk that you will be able to sell the bottle of wine for R50. You will make a capital loss if you are forced to sell it for R5.

Balancing risk and reward

There is risk in investing, but you can reduce the odds against yourself substantially, mainly by applying common sense and improving your level of knowledge. The more risky an investment, the greater the need for you to apply your mind. By building up a bit of knowledge about the basics of investment you will soon tell the difference between chancers and genuine financial advisers who know what they are doing and who will act in your best interests.

INVESTMENT RULES

Here are 14 basic rules, which, if followed, should protect you from being ripped off:

RULE 1 DON'T BE RUSHED

Never at any stage be rushed into making an investment decision. There are many opportunities available and missing one will not undermine your wealth. This rule applies particularly when you are at your most vulnerable (e.g. after a death or divorce) and may need to invest a large sum of money. It is best to put the money into a bank money market or fixed deposit account for a few months while you adjust to your new circumstances.

RULE 2 DON'T SWITCH INVESTMENTS

Many irresponsible financial advisers will attempt to get you to switch your investments between different products. The main reason for this is to generate additional commissions. You must accept that markets will go up and down. Investment is for the long term.

RULE 3 NEVER BELIEVE THE EXTRAORDINARY

If someone offers you an investment with a, say, 30 percent or higher return a year, the chances are that you are being had. It is not that there are no safe investments that do at times make very high returns; the issue is whether someone can safely predict that such high returns can be made on a consistent basis. No one can, and if they could they are hardly likely to share this wisdom with you. You should compare any promised returns with the current interest rate you pay on a home loan. If the returns promised are higher than this amount, then you should exercise caution.

RULE 4 DON'T BE CONFUSED

If you cannot quite understand the investment you are being offered or it seems extraordinarily complex, then avoid it. You should invest only in products that you understand thoroughly. So keep it simple.

RULE 5 ALWAYS GET IT IN WRITING

At all stages you should get everything in writing. This includes the initial proposal as well as all documentation that updates your investment performance. If a verbal promise is made to you ensure that you also have it in writing.

RULE 6 GET A GOOD ADVISER

Investment can be fairly straightforward, particularly if you have simple savings targets. However, if you are unsure of yourself or have a large sum of money to invest it is best to get sound advice. There are, however, a number of rules you must follow:

- Check the qualifications and experience of the person providing advice. A good place to start is with someone who has a qualification from the Financial Planning Institute of South Africa. Someone who is qualified and is a member of the Institute is allowed to be called a Certified Financial Planner (CFP).
- Ask for proof that the person is registered to sell the investment products. Check with the company.
- Preferably deal with someone who has the backing of a large group of brokers. This is particularly important if you need advice over the wider field of financial planning, including investment, estate planning and tax.
- Be prepared to pay for advice and assistance, but be aware of what and how you are paying. There are many ways for financial advisers to be paid – from the direct payment of a fee by yourself to commissions and/or fees paid indirectly on your behalf by the company providing the financial product. These commissions and/or fees may be paid once or annually.

- Always ask for references.
- If you are unsure of the advice that you are receiving then try to get a second opinion.
- Any payment you make should be made to the company providing the investment product. Never make out a cheque in favour of, or give cash to, a financial adviser.

RULE 7 BEWARE OF EXTRAORDINARY GUARANTEES

If someone offers you a guarantee that 'you will make a high return and you can be sure you will get your capital back', take care. Very few institutions offer guarantees on returns or capital, and they employ specialists to ensure that they can meet the guarantees.

You need to establish:

- whether the guarantee is genuine or merely sales talk;
- whether the guarantee is on being repaid your capital in full;
- whether the guarantee is only on a specific portion of your capital (say 80 percent);
- whether the guarantee is on your return;
- whether the guarantee is on an income stream generated by the capital;
- whether there is a guarantee on a combination of capital and return and what it is on each;
- who or what is providing the guarantee (if it is not a major financial services company, life assurance company or banking institution, then take extra care); and
- what the cost is: Remember that when you are given a guarantee it will come at a cost, normally in lower potential returns. Be particularly careful if words like 'costs are embedded in the product' are used.

RULE 8 AVOID BORROWING TO INVEST

If someone encourages you to take out a loan, particularly against your home, to invest, have no further dealings with the person. Borrowing to invest is highly dangerous, and should be avoided. It is a high-risk strategy that requires sound investment knowledge.

RULE 9   NOT INVESTING IS ALSO A RISK

Not investing can be as risky, if not riskier, than investing. Putting your money under the mattress or leaving it in a bank will not protect it. You need to invest it to beat inflation and because it is virtually impossible to time markets consistently. You need to be out of the equity market only for a few days every year to miss the biggest rises. If you are investing for the long term, you will increase the value of your investment over time.

> **Putting your money under the mattress or leaving it in a bank will not protect it.**

Historically, equity markets have provided the best long-term performance.

RULE 10   ASK DUMB QUESTIONS

First of all, your questions will not be dumb. It is your money, and you should ask as many questions as you want about all the aspects of an investment. Here are some questions you should ask:

- What are the costs, both initial and annual?
- What commissions are paid, both initial and annual?
- What is the investment period?
- What are the underlying investments, for example are they shares, or bonds or something else?
- How often will you receive reports on your investment?
- Are there any guarantees on capital and/or on growth?
- What has been the investment return on the investment for the past five years?
- What are the tax consequences?
- What is the name of the company marketing the investment?

Remember to get replies in writing. If you cannot get satisfactory replies or if the salesperson patronises you, walk away.

RULE 11   DON'T PANIC

Investment markets go up and down in value all the time. The biggest mistake you can make when markets lose value is to panic and sell your investments. This means you could make an actual loss. If you leave your investments where they are you have made only what is called a paper loss. When the investment markets recover, as they will, you have made no loss if you have not sold. Also, don't panic if someone else tells you they are making money on another investment. Stick to your investment strategy.

RULE 12 MAKE SURE IT'S LEGAL

There are many people out there, of whom you will never have heard, who want to separate you from your savings. Their names are often pretentious, such as the Royal and International Investment Bank. Here are a few ways to spot them:

- Neither the company nor their investment products will be registered with the Financial Services Board (FSB), which regulates investment in South Africa. As a general rule, you should never invest through a company or a product that is not registered with the FSB. This applies to both local and foreign products. (Contact details are at the back of the book on p. 244.)
- Scam companies are normally what are called unlisted companies. In other words, they are not listed on a stock exchange and are not subject to much, if any, regulation.
- They seldom have proper offices and operate out of hired office suites.
- They will often entertain your sumptuously.
- The initial contact will normally come out of the blue by way of a telephone call. These people trawl through things like share registers to find out who has money to invest.
- They often operate out of foreign bases.

Rather stick to companies and the products of companies that are registered with the FSB. There are many good, registered products available. There is no need to take a chance with something that is not properly registered. You are unlikely to receive better returns and are placing yourself at greater risk by dealing with an unregistered company or product.

RULE 13 DON'T START WITH THE PRODUCT

You should never start your investments by choosing a product first, particularly because you have heard that Aunt Sophia has been making a fortune from it. Companies that provide investment products are much like motor vehicle manufacturers. They keep altering the shape and style to make it seem bigger and better. You must start from the point of knowing why you are investing, and then constructing an investment strategy around your needs. Many people selling dud products will ignore any overall investment plan and attempt to steer as much of your money as possible into the product.

RULE 14 DON'T PUT ALL YOUR EGGS IN ONE BASKET

Scam operators often make their wares sound so good that you are tempted to put in as much money as possible. The more money they can convince you to invest, the more goes into their back pockets. Many pensioners, for example, put their life savings in the infamous Masterbond property scam in the late 1980s, thinking they would double their wealth overnight. They lost everything. The reason for the hard sell was that the eventually jailed crooks behind the scheme were paying financial advisers a commission of 20 percent of the investment value. The more money the financial advisers could generate, the more money they earned and the more the master-crooks could pocket. If you want to take a chance on a risky investment, use only a small proportion of your capital – preferably less than 5 percent.

19

Investment
Made Simple

Investing can be fairly simple if you understand the basic building blocks and know what you want out of a particular product. There are thousands, if not millions, of investment opportunities around the world, and you need to narrow down your options by building an investment strategy based on the correct choice of building blocks to meet your particular needs. In building your investment strategy you need to accept that there is no off-the-shelf solution that will suit everyone.

Here are 18 rules to getting your investment strategy right:

It's a marathon

Understand that investment is akin to a marathon; it is not a 100-metre sprint. If you want to succeed, you must plan carefully for the full distance, understand your destination and get there in good condition. There is no such thing as a get-rich-quick investment scheme. Investments do not include:

- pyramid or multilevel marketing schemes; or
- gambling, including casinos, the Lotto and horse racing. Gambling differs from investment in that you are placing your entire 'investment' at risk of loss, and the odds of making a return are extremely low.

Get good advice

There is no reason why you should not handle your own investments, but if you have any doubts seek advice. There are various people and companies available with expertise in investing, but there are also those who profess to have expertise who are not properly qualified. You must find the right person for the job. Many financial advisers tend to be product sales people rather than investment advisers. You must know the difference. Proper investment managers who have the discretion to make investments on your behalf must be registered either as stockbrokers or as investment advisers with the Financial Services Board.

Owning your own portfolio

If you have your own portfolio or want to invest directly in shares and other financial instruments, you have several options:

- Do it yourself over the Internet. There are a number of companies that offer direct Internet investment services. Most of the services will also provide back-up services on how various investments, including market sectors, companies and unit trusts are performing. But you must know what you are doing to use this option.
- Consult a stockbroker. You can get different levels of service from a stockbroker – from simply carrying out your investment orders through to providing you with ongoing advice and even having full discretion over your portfolio. You must be careful when giving full discretion, as some stockbrokers have a reputation for unnecessarily turning over your portfolio to generate more fees. Buying and selling any investment pushes up your costs and creates potential tax hazards.
- Consult a qualified investment adviser. If you can get someone who is a Certified Financial Analyst (CFA) then you will know that they at least have relevant qualifications.
- Consult a specialist investment portfolio company, such as a private bank. These companies/banks provide much the same service as stockbrokers. In recent years, a number of new market entrants have been involved in dubious activity, including taking good investments and switching them into investments in shares of their own company (often unlisted shares). These companies operate mainly by cold-calling you on the telephone. It is simply safest to have nothing to do with any company that cold-calls you.

Pooled investments

If you are investing in pooled investments such as unit trusts and/or life assurance policies you can in most instances use all the same people or institutions you use to own an investment portfolio, but in this case financial advisers are also available to you. Preferably use someone who is a Certified Financial Planner (CFP).

Income or capital growth or both?

There are three basic ways that you can earn money on your investments:

- Interest: This is money that is paid to you for money that you have invested. In other words, someone or an institution pays you 'rent' to use your money.
- Dividends: This is the share of profit that is paid to owners of a company of which they own a share.
- Capital growth: This is profit you can make by buying something cheaply and then selling it at a higher price.

These three ways of earning money come from two distinct investment groups:

- Lending investments: These are investments where you lend money to your bank (an interest-earning savings account), or a bond (where you lend money, for example, to the government).
- Ownership investments: These include investments in property or shares in companies.

The trick is to get the correct combination of the two. Most investments are structured to give you either income (mainly lending investments) or capital growth (mainly ownership investments). If you are saving for a long-term target, the investment product will be aimed primarily at providing you with capital growth, using ownership investments. If you need a regular income, your investment product should be focused primarily on lending investments.

An example is retirement. You would invest mainly in ownership investments until you retire and then you would invest mainly in lending investments that will give you an income. You would not, however, invest all your money to give you income. You will still need capital growth to ensure that you have enough money until you die.

Income investments are normally those that pay interest. They can include bank and money market deposits. Capital growth investments include options such as bonds and shares in companies.

Decide between asset classes

All lending and ownership investments are based on what are called asset classes. A first division between asset classes is what are called financial assets and hard assets.

Hard assets

Hard assets are investments in items such as artworks, stamps, carpets, diamonds, gold coins and tank containers. Hard asset investments can be highly speculative and are not normally advised by good financial advisers. If you want to invest in hard assets you must understand everything about the type of investment you have selected – from purchase and resale prices to the quality of the goods and the difficulty in reselling the asset.

Financial assets

There are three main 'financial' asset classes. These are cash, bonds and shares. Property can be both a hard asset and a financial asset, depending on how you invest in it. Generally, each asset class has a different level of risk. Increasingly, another group of investments, called derivatives, is being described as a fifth financial asset class.

What is a cash investment?

Cash is purely an interest-earning investment. It provides no capital growth. There are a number of different options for cash investments. The most common is a bank savings account. Cash investments are those where only interest is paid on your money. Other cash investments include the following:

- Term deposits: These are also called fixed deposits. You lend your money to a bank for a fixed period of time at a fixed interest rate, and after, say, six months or two years the bank returns your money with interest.
- Money market accounts: These are accounts, offered mainly by unit trust companies, where your money is pooled together with other small investors and lent to big institutions. This way, you have a better chance of getting a higher interest rate.
- Notional Certificates of Deposit (NCDs): These are fairly substantial amounts of money lent to large institutions like banks and businesses.

Cash investments hold a number of attractions:

- Your capital is normally guaranteed.
- Your rate of interest is often guaranteed.
- You can get access to your money fairly quickly, particularly if it is in a money market account.

The main downside of cash investments is that they seldom keep up with inflation, particularly after tax is taken into account.

What is a property investment?

Property is both an interest-earning investment (rent) and a capital growth investment (its underlying value can increase). A property investment can be a lot more than simply buying your own home. There are plenty of different types of investment in property:

- Residential property: You own a property and someone else pays you rent to live on it.
- Commercial or industrial property: Again, you own the property and a business pays you rent to use the premises.
- Mortgage participation bonds: You lend money to someone else to buy property. A financial services company seeks out people needing money to buy property, and investors to lend the money. The theory is that the borrower pays less interest than on a normal mortgage bond and the investor receives a higher-than-normal interest rate.
- Property syndications: These are investments where you join up with a number of other buyers to purchase a commercial or industrial property. They have proved to be high risk because they have often involved buildings that need significant repair and/or have little tenant demand.
- Property unit trusts (PUTs): These are not normal unit trust funds; they are investments listed on the stock exchange. As with a unit trust fund, you can invest smaller amounts of money in companies that specialise in investing in property. Like unit trusts, these investments are highly regulated.
- Property loan stocks: You invest in a company with a portfolio of properties listed on the JSE Securities Exchange. Unlike PUTs, property loan stocks can borrow money to buy properties and do not require a management company.
- Normal unit trust funds that invest in property companies.
- Life assurance endowments where the underlying investments are in property.

The advantages of property investments are that:

- they can provide an income stream that normally keeps ahead of inflation; and
- you can get capital growth if you buy in the right area.

The disadvantages of property investments include:

- getting it wrong by buying in the wrong area (you need to be extremely careful with property investments, as buying in the wrong area can mean significant losses);
- buying a building with design or other problems;
- putting your income stream at risk because you do not have a tenant paying you rent;
- the fairly large amounts of capital that are needed in most cases;
- the high costs of buying and selling property – with taxes, commissions and legal fees; and
- the difficulty in accessing your money if you need it in a hurry (you have to find a buyer); although you can borrow against the property investment.

What are bond investments?

Do not confuse the bond market with your mortgage bond. A bond investment is simply another way of saying you are lending money to a big institution like a government. Bonds are certificates that are issued when a big institution like the government, your local authority, or Telkom or Eskom or a major company wants to borrow money. They borrow your money and pay you interest.

Bonds are both interest-earning and capital growth investments.

Most bonds have what is called a coupon. The coupon states that you will be paid interest at a fixed rate, normally every six months.

After bonds are issued, investors buy and sell them on what is called the secondary market. The price depends on where they see interest rates in the future. Bonds are strange things in that when interest rates are high no one wants to invest in them. The government has to offer high interest rates to attract investors to lend it money. This means that you can buy a bond cheaply. When interest rates are low many investors want to buy them, so the bonds become expensive.

If interest rates are high, bonds are sold for less than their original value, because investors want to get a better and safer return elsewhere.

If interest rates start dropping, the price of the bond starts going up, because investors want to lend money to the institution. By selling when interest rates are dropping, you can make a profit.

So, you can make money from the interest that is paid as well as from the price of the bonds. If you buy the bond cheaply and sell it when it is expensive you will make what is called a capital gain. In other words, your original investment (your capital) is worth more. If you invest in bonds when they are expensive and sell when they become cheap you suffer a capital loss. The bond market is very complex and bond traders spend many years getting experience in dealing in bonds. Very few individuals invest directly in bonds because of the significant amounts of money required. Bonds are used extensively as the underlying investments in annuities (pension payment investments).

What are shares?

Shares in companies are both income-earning (dividends) and capital growth investments (their underlying value can increase).

When you buy a share, you are buying a part or a share in a company. You become a part owner. As a part owner you expect to get part of the profits. If a company has 10 shares and you buy one share, you can expect to get one-tenth of the profits. When profits are paid out to shareholders (people who own shares) the payment is called a dividend.

Companies sell shares for a number of reasons, including to expand, to buy new machinery or to buy another company.

Once they have sold the shares to investors, the investors can also buy and sell them. There are a number of reasons why you as a shareholder may not want to hold on to the shares you own. You may need the money for something else; or you may not like the way the company is being managed and suspect that profits will drop; or you may feel that the company is out of date (for example, it may still be making typewriters, which no one wants to buy, instead of computers).

The price of a share will go up or down, depending on what investors think about the future profits of the company. If they think a company is going to make great profits many investors will want to buy their shares, and the price of a share will go up. So, as with bonds, you can also make a capital gain (if you buy the share when it is cheap and sell it when it goes up in price), or a capital loss (if shares go down in value).

You can buy shares both in companies listed on a stock exchange and in companies that are not listed. It is better to buy shares in listed companies because you have greater security, as these companies must abide by regulations in order to be listed.

What are derivatives?

Derivatives are mainly capital growth investments. A derivative is not a tangible asset. Its value is derived from another asset such as property, bonds or shares. Most derivatives are based on what you expect a price of an asset to be at some date in the future. This can be a higher or lower price. You invest by taking a bet on what you expect that price to be.

There are many different forms of derivatives. The best known of which are futures, options and warrants. Derivative markets are very complex and need a great deal of investor sophistication. Large amounts of money may be made on derivative markets, but many people also lose vast fortunes.

Hedge funds are the most common way for investors to invest in derivative markets, but they come in many different forms and can be complex. A major advantage of derivative investments is that you can make money in them when the more traditional markets are moving sideways or down.

Understand investment risks

Investment risks are the chances of losing all or part of your money. Risk is not a single-digit affair. There are many different types of investment risk. Some risk factors are greater than others. Risk factors you need to take into account include the following:

- Systemic risk: This is the potential of a system such as the banking system collapsing altogether.
- Prudential risk: This is the risk that an asset manager (someone who manages investments) will not make careful decisions.
- Advice risk: This is the risk of your being misled into buying the wrong product for your needs.
- Market risk: This is the risk of a particular market (e.g. the share market) generally collapsing.
- Market-sector risk: Sectors of markets can move downwards. For example, the entire technology sector of stock markets around the world collapsed in 2000.

- Volatility risk: This is the ability of the value of an investment to go up and down. If the value of the investment is down when you want to sell the investment, you will lose money. The share market is far more volatile than the bond market; in the past it has provided better returns over the longer term.
- Dishonesty: This continues to be a significant risk, particularly with the opening up of foreign investment markets to South Africans. Many scam artists operate in the financial services field, and you need to be constantly on your guard. The best defence is to deal only with companies that are registered to do business in South Africa and have a sound track record.

Generally, the higher the potential income or capital growth, the higher the risk of the product.

The different asset classes have different risk levels attached to them. These can be summarised as being low, medium or high risk.

Asset class	Example	Level of risk
Cash	Bank savings or deposit accounts	Low
Property	Houses, shops and factories	Low to medium
Bonds (gilts)	Loans made to institutions	Low to medium
Shares (equities)	Part ownership of companies	Medium to high
Derivatives	Futures and options	Medium to high

Decide on your risk profile

Your psychological make-up will to a large extent determine your willingness to take risks. For example, if you were in a television game show and you were offered various options, which of the following four things would you do:

A. take R10 000;

B. take a 50:50 chance of turning the R10 000 into R15 000;

C. take a one in five chance of doubling the R10 000 to R20 000; or

D. take a one in 50 chance of turning the R10 000 into R100 000?

Which would you choose? If you selected D you should run off to the closest casino. Investment is not gambling. Taking risk in investment should be a deliberate choice. It is not a game of chance in which you put all your capital at risk with an outside chance of increasing its value.

The most important question you need to ask yourself in considering the risk of investments is: How much can you afford to lose if the investment goes wrong? Don't ask yourself how much you want to make.

Your risk profile is determined by other factors, including the following:

> **Taking risk in investment should be a deliberate choice.**

- How long you are prepared to invest: The longer your investment period, the less likely you are to be subjected to short-term market volatility. Volatility is the movement up or down of an investment. The greater the volatility, the greater the risk. Markets do move up and down, often violently, but the longer the investment term, the more the volatility is removed from the investment. You should not really invest in capital growth investments for periods of less than three years. For short-term investments you should use interest-earning investments. It is preferable to invest for at least 10 years in a capital growth investment, as in the long term most capital growth investments provide consistent growth.
- How much money you have or earn: The more money you have, the more you can afford to take an investment loss.
- Your age: If you are young you can take bigger investment risks because you have time to recover from the losses. Conversely, as you get older you should take fewer risks.
- Your health: If you are unhealthy and suspect that you may not be able to work soon or could die young, you should again have a lower risk profile.
- Your investment knowledge: You should not take high risks if you have little knowledge of investment products. Rather stick to well-known products like life assurance endowments issued by well-known companies, or unit trusts.
- Your investment target: If you are investing for a need, such as the education of your children, the risk profile should be lower than investing for a want, such as a beach cottage.

Any good financial adviser can run you through a risk profiler that can show your mental and financial ability to accept investment risk.

Diversify

Diversifying your investments is important. What this means is that you should spread your investments across the asset classes and over the sectors within asset classes. In other words, don't put all your eggs in one basket. Diversification lowers your risk: you will not lose everything if one investment sector goes wrong, but if one takes off you have a better chance of going along for the ride. Not only can a properly diversified portfolio reduce your risks, it can also increase your potential for better returns.

With the partial lifting of exchange controls, you also need to have investments in foreign markets. South Africa is a very small investment pool, and you do not have access to all the best investments.

Most of us don't have the money to diversify properly by buying bonds and shares directly. You will not be able to get a properly diversified share portfolio for less than about R250 000. But this need not stop you from having a properly diversified investment portfolio. The good news is that you can get the same investment portfolio, with the same share, bond, cash and property profile as any billionaire. You will merely own less of each. This is made possible by what are called pooled or collective investments.

With a pooled investment you and many thousands of other investors put money into a single pool (also called a portfolio or fund). The person managing the portfolio (the asset manager) can then go and buy the same investments as any billionaire. A pooled investment is likely to have at least R100 million in assets (a comparatively small pool), but some can have many billions of rands.

There are four big advantages to pooling investments:

Diversity: You get little bits of the most important investments the world can offer – from computer giant Microsoft to South Africa's own world players, such as mining company Anglo American Corporation or tobacco and luxury goods company Rembrandt.

Expertise: If you went to an investment adviser to handle all your investments you would pay a lot of money for the kind of expertise you would need. In a pooled investment, you along with other investors have access to people who do nothing all day but look for the best investment opportunities. They may not always get it right, but they are more likely to get it right than you are.

Time: You are unlikely to have the time available to watch markets with the attention that is required. By pooling your investments you have more time to get on with earning money in your field of expertise.

Investment amounts: You can invest as little as R100 a month in most pooled investments.

There are three main types of pooled investments. These are:

- life assurance investment products, which are also called endowment policies;
- unit trust funds, which are known overseas as mutual funds; and
- multimanager investments, where asset managers who are experts in specific market sectors are given different parts of an overall portfolio to manage. The asset managers normally work for a number of different companies. A unit trust fund of funds is an example of a multimanager product.

For more on collective investments, see Choose the right product on p. 182.

Understand market sectors

Each financial asset has different underlying sectors. This is important if you are to diversify your investments properly. While diversification of your assets is important, don't over-diversify. If, for example, you bought a number of investments that were all in one sector of the market or if you invested in a number of investments that all had a similar investment pattern, you would be over-diversifying.

The best way to understand market sectors is to look at share price and unit trust performance tables published in newspapers.

In the share price pages you will find categories and subcategories for the JSE Securities Exchange that include:

- mining and resources (with subcategories that include coal, diamonds, gold, platinum, metals and minerals, mining holdings and houses, and mining exploration);
- financial (with subcategories that include investment trusts, private equity funds, banks and financial services); and
- the industrial sector. (This is the biggest sector by number of companies listed on the JSE Securities Exchange. It has 19 subsectors.)

In the unit trust pages you will find four broad categories:

- Domestic funds, which subdivide into the three categories of equity funds (which invest in shares), asset allocation funds (which invest in all the financial asset classes) and fixed interest funds (which invest in bonds and money markets): Each of these divisions has subsectors. In the equity sector there are 14 different sectors, ranging from funds, which invest only in big companies, to those that invest in small companies. Domestic funds invest 85 percent or more of their assets in South African investment markets.

- Worldwide funds, which also divide into the three broad divisions of equity funds, asset allocation funds and fixed interest funds: Worldwide funds invest at least 15 percent of their assets in South African investment markets and a minimum of at least 15 percent in foreign markets.
- Foreign funds, which again divide into the three broad divisions of equity funds, asset allocation funds and fixed interest funds with underlying funds: Foreign funds invest at least 85 percent of their assets in foreign markets.
- Regional funds, which again divide into the three broad divisions of equity funds, asset allocation funds and fixed interest funds: Regional funds invest at least 85 percent of their assets in a single country or region other than South Africa.

As share markets and regions of the world go through cycles, so do underlying sectors. For example, before 1998 small companies were flying high, while investors were ignoring large companies. Everyone was talking about the new-economy and technology stocks. By 2000 investors were scooting back into the old large companies, while the share prices of small companies and technology stocks had collapsed.

The important thing is to get your investments across the different sectors. With unit trust funds you can select specific sectors, or you can have the job of diversification done for you by selecting general equity or asset allocation funds.

Understand investment styles

An investment style is a methodology in selecting shares. The two main styles are value and growth. The world's most successful investor, Warren Buffet, sticks rigidly to an investment style called 'value' investing.

Value

Value investment means identifying companies that are 'undervalued'. There are a number of ways of finding undervalued companies. These include the net asset value test and the price/earnings ratio test.

- The net asset value test: Every company holds assets of one type or another, whether it is intellectual value, such as in computer software companies, or bricks and mortar. If the total value of the assets less the liabilities (the net asset value) is worth more than the total number of shares issued, then the company is undervalued, in other words, if the assets of the company were sold off and provided more money than the shares.
- The price/earnings ratio test: You will often hear of the price/earnings or p/e ratio. It is a calculation that shows you how many years it will take to recover your initial investment from the profits made by the company. To get the p/e ratio, divide the total value of all shares issued by the company by the profit (e.g. total value of shares of R100 million divided by a profit of R10 million equals a p/e of 10). The lower a p/e, the more value it has. Any company with a p/e of less than 15 would be in the range of a value investment. But you need to be careful, as a company with a low p/e may also be in trouble, because there is no demand for the shares, and the share price is low.

Growth

Growth investments are investments in companies that grow or are expected to grow quickly and provide big profits in the future. Growth companies will often have very high p/e ratios, because the extraordinary growth expected in the future will provide extraordinary profits.

You can select investments directly using the different styles; or you can get style-specific unit trust investments, where a style investment manager will do the selections for you. After some of the recent disasters, particularly in the information technology sector where p/e ratios reached totally unrealistic levels before crashing back to earth in 2000, growth asset managers have qualified their position, calling their style GARP, which stands for 'growth at realistic prices'.

Consider liquidity

A major consideration in investing is liquidity or access to your money. If an investment is considered illiquid this means that it could take time to sell. If you attempt to rush a sale you could lose money if there is no demand at the time you want to sell.

Different asset classes have different levels of liquidity. These are:

- high liquidity (e.g. shares and unit trusts);
- medium liquidity (e.g. life assurance products); and
- low liquidity (e.g. most retirement fund products and property).

In considering the liquidity of your investments you must take into account any penalties you may incur for cashing in an investment early. In other words, you may be allowed to cash in the investment, but there could be significant fees, which indirectly make it an illiquid investment.

Consider guarantees

Guarantees can be good if you have a very low-risk appetite. However, you must accept that guarantees cost extra money, and this will be reflected in lower performance.

You need to be very sure about the guarantees you receive and any qualifications to the guarantees. You can get guarantees on your capital investments and your performance. One of the major areas of confusion over the years has been with what are called voluntary annuities, where you invest a lump sum, receive an income at a guaranteed level, and at the end of a specific period receive capital back. Many people assume that they will receive back the same capital. If markets have performed poorly you get back less capital, as any shortfall in investment performance to meet the guaranteed income level comes from your capital.

Many guaranteed products are very complex, such as those called structured products. These products come with so many bells and whistles that they can be very confusing, and you need expert advice to decipher them. Recently, a financial solutions company, ipac, did extensive research into structured products and found that the chances of needing the guarantees provided were about 1 percent – so the costs involved were not worth investing in the products. The reason is that most investments improve with value over time.

The most popular and easy-to-understand guaranteed products are supplied by life assurance companies, mainly through voluntary annuities and smoothed/stable bonus policies.

You need guarantees to secure value when markets are high or when an investment has matured. You should not use guarantees when markets are down – as in most cases the only way is up.

Consider costs

All investment products come with costs. You need to pay reasonable costs, but costs are often one of the most underestimated risks to achieving investment targets. They also come in various forms. Always ask for full disclosure of costs, including commissions. You need to know what commissions are paid, as extraordinarily high commissions often indicate a suspect product.

Costs include initial costs, annual costs, withdrawal (backend) costs, hidden costs and layered costs, where you have a product wrapping underlying investments, which in turn invest in other underlying investments (e.g. wrap funds, which invest in unit trust funds, which in turn invest in shares or bonds).

You also need to be aware that costs can be charged as a percentage of your invested assets as well as fixed rand amount charges.

Plan your tax affairs

Tax is an important issue in investment decisions, but it should never be an overly significant factor in deciding on an investment. People will often turn away from an investment purely because it has a tax consequence.

Investments are affected by a number of different taxes. These are:

- income tax, which you will pay on any interest or rental income, or if you actively trade assets for a profit to generate an income;
- capital gains tax, which you'll pay on capital growth on most investments;
- donations tax, which you will pay on any investment you give away with a value greater than R30 000 in one year; and
- estate duty, which you may pay on investments when you die.

You are entitled to plan your financial affairs in order to minimise the amount of tax you pay. There are various legal ways to do this, using differences between the various types of taxation and exemptions that are allowed by the tax authorities. Tax-planning opportunities include the following:

Deferred income tax: This means delaying the payment of tax until a later date. In the meantime, you can invest the money you would have paid to the SARS to earn more money. A good example of deferred tax is on retirement funding investments. Your contributions to a retirement pension fund or retirement annuity (see Chapter 21) are deductible from your income. You pay tax when you start drawing an income (pension) from your retirement savings.

Preferential tax rates: The SARS sometimes gives you a preferential rate of taxation on certain investments. For example, when you retire and commute one-third of your retirement savings to cash, you are taxed on your average rate of tax, which is lower than your marginal rate of taxation.

Exemptions from tax: The first R10 000 in capital gains every year is exempt from capital gains tax. The first R4 000 (R5 000 if you are older than 65) in interest earnings is exempt from income tax.

Tax arbitrage: Depending on how you invest your money, you can pay lower tax. For example, if you invest through a life assurance investment product the life assurance company pays both income tax and capital gains tax on your behalf. It pays 30 percent tax on interest and rental income arising from investments. So, if you are on a rate of marginal tax higher than 30 percent, you can score. The same applies to capital gains tax. If you are paying the highest effective rate of 10 percent then you could be better off with a life assurance product where a lower 7.5 percent is paid on your behalf.

Converting capital gains to income: If you sell off assets to generate an income then you could pay capital gains tax rather than income tax. However, you must be careful that the SARS does not see this as a tax dodge.

The objective of investment must be to give you a real rate of return after subtracting the effects of inflation and taxation.

Choose the right product

There is a wide array of investment product choice. Having worked through the previous steps you will now have a better idea of the type of investment product you should use. Remember that the simplest products, such as a life assurance endowment or general equity unit trust fund, tend to be among the safer investments providing steady returns.

You should avoid the complex investment products until you really understand investment markets. Some complex products, such as what are called structured, capital-guaranteed, geared, index-linked products, are often mis-sold because investors do not understand the full implications of the product.

Don't fall for the flavour of the month (e.g. hedge funds or small companies).

It is fine to put a small portion of your money into specialist areas, but don't take big bets.

Most people will invest through a pooled investment. You need to be aware of what the main ones – life assurance, unit trust and multimanager – offer. There is also a relatively new type of investment, called an exchange traded fund, which is likely to become increasingly popular. The different structures can suit you for different purposes. It is not that one type of product is necessarily better than another.

Life assurance endowment (investment) policies

These are the main elements of life assurance endowments:

Contract period: There is a minimum contract period of five years, with penalties for cancelling your policy or failing to pay the premiums before its maturity date. You can lose all or part of your investment as a result of the penalties on recurring-premium investments. The downside is that even if the life-assurer or asset manager underperforms you will not be able to change to a better asset manager without incurring substantial costs. However, you are offered some flexibility in switching between the different investment portfolios offered by a particular life assurance company. This includes switching from a market-linked portfolio to a guaranteed portfolio. With the new-generation endowments, fairly extensive switching is permitted.

Disciplined saving: The contractual nature of the investment and the severe penalties for not sticking to the contract help make life assurance investments a very disciplined form of saving and investment.

Premiums: You agree at the start on the minimum amount that you will save as a recurring premium on a regular basis, mainly every month or as a lump sum. You can increase the amount you invest by a maximum of 20 percent in any one year. There are minimum levels of recurring and lump-sum premiums, which vary from policy to policy.

Costs: There are both initial and annual costs:

- Initial costs: On recurring-premium policies these vary between 3 and 12 percent, but they are zero or close to zero on single-premium investments.

Initial costs vary between life assurance companies. These costs cannot be negotiated.

- Annual costs: These vary between 2 and 2.5 percent of the value of your investment, depending on the company. The annual charges are not negotiable. A monthly policy fee is also charged, which varies between R5 and R30 a month.

Transparency: The level of transparency of life assurance products has increased substantially since the introduction in 2001 of the policyholder protection rules issued in terms of the Long-Term Insurance Act. The rules require the disclosure of all important facts, including costs. However, comparative investment performance tables are still not widely available, and this remains a problem.

Guarantees: This is one of the major advantages of a life assurance investment. Guarantees are available on your capital at maturity, on some growth, and on investments that provide an income (annuities).

Investment choices: Investment choices have tended to be fairly limited on traditional endowments, but have increased significantly in recent years. There are two main choices:

- Smoothed bonus investments: These products smooth out investment performance with performance bonuses added on an annual basis. This is an advantage, as you are not subject to vagaries of the market. These products also normally guarantee your capital and some growth, particularly with the introduction of new-generation endowment policies, which allow you a wide selection across the broader financial services industry.
- Market-linked (related) investments: With this choice you take your chances on market conditions when your policy matures. If the market is up you will be fine but if it is down you may have a problem if you want to withdraw the cash at that time.

Investment performance: There are no guarantees on performance with market-linked products. There are portfolios that perform well for short and longer periods, and there are policies that perform badly for both short and long periods. Performance depends on the skill of the asset managers who invest money on your behalf.

Assurance on life and disability: You can combine your investment policy with assurance against dying or disability, paying one premium for both.

On death: If you have named a beneficiary or beneficiaries in your policy, when you die the accumulated value of your investment can be paid directly to your dependants within days of your death. Although the amount is subject to estate duty (death taxes), it is not added to your estate, where it would be subject to executor's fees of 3.5 percent (plus VAT). This is a significant advantage of a life assurance policy, as dependants need money on which to survive after the death of the sole or major provider. Estates can take many months to be finalised, which could leave dependants in dire financial circumstances or having to take loans. If you have not named a beneficiary, the amount will be added to your estate.

Loans: Life assurance companies give loans against endowment policy investments. The amount of the loan will vary from 60 to 90 percent of the value of the investment. In terms of legislation you are allowed only one loan in the first five years of the policy contract. Life assurance policies can be used as collateral against loans from banks and other lenders.

Protection against creditors: If your investment has assurance against dying or disability attached, the first R50 000 in the value of the total policies you own, if you have dependants, is protected against creditors if the policy or policies have not been ceded to someone else.

Investment security: A life assurance company has to keep reserves to ensure that it can meet its commitments (liabilities) to you. However, if a life assurance company goes bankrupt you have no claim on the underlying assets used to make investments with your money. Your claim would be against the bankrupt company.

Fund management restrictions: Life assurance asset managers have wide discretion in selecting underlying investment choices. They can invest any amount in any company, and there is no restriction over what percentage of the shares of a company is bought. Any company in which investments are bought may be listed or not listed on a stock exchange. Investment may also be made directly in residential and commercial property. Unrestricted use may be made of derivative financial instruments. Although this gives greater investment flexibility to fund managers, it may also increase risk for investors.

Unit trust funds

These are the main elements of unit trust funds:

Contract period: There are no minimum investment periods. You can invest and withdraw on the same day if you want, although this is highly inadvisable. Your investments are flexible. Not only can you adjust the amount you invest as and when you want, you can also withdraw your money at any stage. You can switch for free, in most cases, between funds of the same unit trust management company. However, you will pay a new set of initial costs if you switch between funds of different unit trust management companies.

Disciplined saving: There is no enforced discipline to your investment plans, as you can withdraw amounts or stop paying whenever you want. However, by having a debit order for recurring premiums you can maintain some discipline.

Premiums: You can vary the amount you invest in unit trust funds as you please. There are minimum levels of recurring and lump-sum payments, which vary from fund to fund.

Penalties: There are no penalties for withdrawing your money or halting any recurring payment. However, there is an indirect penalty in that if you withdraw your money soon after you have made your investment you may not have recovered the initial costs of the investment, which are up to 7 percent of its value.

Costs: There are both initial and annual costs:

- Initial costs: The maximum initial fee is about 7 percent. You can negotiate the initial costs, depending on the size of your investment and whether you deal directly with a unit trust company (removing the need to pay broker commissions). Initial costs can vary between unit trust funds.

- Annual charges: These average about 1 percent, but on newer funds annual charges have been increased, with some funds charging up to 2.5 percent of the value of your investment every year.

Transparency: The level of transparency is good. Costs, historical performance and information on underlying investments are freely available. The high level of disclosure allows for extensive analysis and comparisons of funds.

Guarantees: There are no guarantees of any kind on unit trust investments. You are entirely vulnerable to market fluctuations.

Investment choices: You have an extensive range of investment choices, from broad-based investments to very narrow options, such as gold funds. You can also choose between active and passive management.

- Actively managed funds: These are unit trust funds where a small army of investment managers and analysts seek out what they believe will be the best-performing investments in a market or sector of a market.
- Passive (index) funds: These are funds where the fund managers do not apply any skill. They merely try to match what is called an index. You get many different indices. An index is a measure of performance of a particular market or sector of a market and replicates the different shares in the market, mainly according to their value. So, if company A represents 10 percent of the value of a sector of a market, it will make up 10 percent of the index. By watching an index you can see if a market or a sector is moving up or down. The most well known is the JSE All Share Index. The fund manager merely buys the shares in the same proportion as the index. On the whole, passive management funds are cheaper than actively managed funds, because there is no need to do any research.

Investment performance: There are no guarantees on performance. There are funds that perform well for shorter and longer periods, and there are funds that perform badly for both short and long periods. Performance depends on the skill of the asset managers who invest money on your behalf.

Comparability: Unit trust prices and performances are comparable on a daily basis, as they are published by most newspapers.

Assurance on life and disability: You cannot combine your unit trust investments with assurance against dying or being disability.

On death: The accumulated investment will be added to your estate and is subject to both estate duty and executor's fees.

Loans: Unit trust companies do not provide loans against unit trust investments, but you can cash them in whenever you want.

Collateral: Banks will accept unit trusts as collateral for loans, but will lend you only about 50 percent of the market value of the unit trusts.

Protection against creditors: There is no protection against creditors. A creditor can lay claim to your unit trust investments.

Investment security: The unit trust management company must hold your money in a trust. If the management company goes bankrupt it has no access to the assets it manages on your behalf.

Fund management restrictions: Unit trust asset managers are generally allowed to buy shares only of companies listed on a stock exchange. Only 5 percent of the shares of a particular company may be owned by any one fund, and a maximum of 5 percent of the assets of a fund may be used for investment in any single company. Only limited use of derivative financial instruments is permitted. Although this curtails investment flexibility, it does reduce the level of risk for unit trust investors.

Multimanager products

These are also known as split investments and they come in a number of different forms. With a multimanager product you are offered access to a number of different asset managers. This can be either direct or through other products, like underlying unit trust funds. The main argument in favour of multimanager investments is that you are seeking out the 'best of breed' asset managers. The asset managers can work for any company. A manager of a multimanager fund will seek out the best managers in various sectors and then blend together the various managers in an attempt to give superior investment performance. The main vehicles are unit trust multimanager funds, unit trust funds of funds, linked investment products and wrap funds. Hedge funds are also included in this section. Although you can invest directly in hedge funds, most people will invest in these funds through a collective investment.

Unit trust multimanager funds

These unit trust funds seek out asset managers who are considered the best in their fields. Apart from not using one dedicated asset manager they are exactly the same as any other unit trust fund. Often, the unit trust management companies of these funds do not have their own associated asset managers.

Unit trust funds of funds

These unit trust funds seek out other unit trust funds (not asset managers), particularly sector-specialist funds, which are considered the best in their fields. Apart from having underlying unit trust funds, they are exactly the same as any other unit trust fund.

Linked investment products

Linked investment product companies came into being as a result of the increasing number of specialist unit trust funds offered. They started off as an administrative platform that enabled you to keep your portfolio or unit trusts under one umbrella and to switch between the various funds. With this the linked product companies offered various legal umbrellas in which to house your investments, such as retirement savings vehicles, including retirement annuity and preservation funds, where the underlying investments were in unit trust funds. However, linked product companies have become increasingly embroiled in controversy because of the manner in which they have limited investment choices, their ever-increasing cost structures and the way they have allowed unskilled advisers to sell their products.

Wrap funds

Wrap funds grew out of the linked investment product industry. With the greater choice and switching ability given to investors, many of them, often acting on the advice of unqualified investment advisers, switched around their investments, chasing the latest top-performing unit trust, mostly shortly before it fell from grace. This saw many people losing considerable amounts.

Most people who made these losses forgot a fundamental rule of investment: 'It is not about timing the market; it is about how long you are in the market.'

As a result, most linked product companies set up subsidiaries to mix and match unit trust funds into risk-profiled wrap funds. However, this created problems of its own. Costs were high, there was little transparency on costs or performance, there was no proper regulation and the wrap fund choices were soon as great as those of unit trust funds. This array of funds defeated one of their main purposes, namely to reduce the number of choices of unit trust funds. Many wrap fund managers have converted to unit trust funds of funds, which are better regulated, cheaper and far more transparent.

Hedge funds

Although hedge funds can be individually accessed by investors, the amounts required are often very large, and selection of the correct hedge fund is extremely difficult. Investment in hedge funds is increasing, particularly with current volatile markets. The attraction of hedge funds is that they have the potential to make money when markets are going up and down. Hedge funds have recently become generally available to South African investors through multimanager options, mainly unit trust funds of funds.

Hedge funds come in many shapes and guises – some low risk and some extremely high risk. There are a number of advantages to using the multi-manager concept. These include:

- Proper selection: Hedge funds vary dramatically – from funds that trade in currencies to something as obscure as trading in distressed municipal debt in the United States. An expert multimanager will know what is available and what to include. As an individual you will find it difficult to find out what is available or how to select a hedge fund.
- Reduction of risk: A multimanager is able to assess the risk of the different funds.
- Investment access: By being able to invest in multimanager funds, hedge funds become affordable to ordinary investors.

How hedge funds work

Most investment managers, particularly those looking after unit trust funds, are limited in the way they can invest. When markets are rising, they must select shares that they expect will perform best. During volatile or shrinking markets, they must try to sell off the shares that their research tells them will perform worse than others. In this way, they try to protect the value of the portfolio. In this scenario – which is known as investing 'long' – profits are derived only if the prices of the shares in the portfolio increase.

As a result, a traditional 'long' manager can at best offer you performance relative to a benchmark, such as the JSE Securities Exchange All Share Index. This means that in bad times you will probably see the value of your investment shrink, even though your manager might be outperforming the benchmark. A traditional manager cannot offer you absolute returns, or an ever-growing investment. Yet this is what hedge fund managers set out to do.

Hedge fund managers use 'long' investments, but also hedge their bets by investing 'short'. This means the investment manager can make profits when share prices are falling.

There are a number of ways to invest 'short', or to 'short the market', on a particular investment. In simple terms, the fund manager will seek out not only investments that are expected to outperform, but also those expected to underperform. To achieve a profit on an investment expected to lose ground, the fund manager will:

- sell a share that he/she does not currently own at its current price (say R100);
- buy the share at its cheaper price after the share price has fallen (to say R50); and
- then deliver the share to the buyer who paid the R100, thereby making a R50 profit for the fund.

There are many variations of this basic tactic using option and futures markets (where you buy an option to buy or sell a share at a certain price at some date in the future). It is in these variations that risk comes into play with hedge fund investing.

The risks of hedge funds

Depending on the investment strategies of the hedge fund manager, these funds – as with any other investment class – can range from comparatively low risk to very high risk.

What increases the risk of investing in hedge funds is the ability to leverage, or gear, a hedge investment. Normally, gearing/leverage means borrowing to buy an investment in the hope of selling the investment for a greater sum before the money must be repaid.

Gearing is a bit more complex with hedge funds. In simple terms, a hedge fund manager uses a comparatively small sum of money that can be put down as a deposit to buy or sell a much larger amount (in value) of shares at some stage in the future. If the bet goes wrong and prices move against the original bet, the fund manager may have to pay out additional large sums of money. If the decision turns out to be right, the returns on the original investment are far greater.

So, whereas a traditional 'long' manager can lose only what is invested, a hedge fund manager, using gearing, can lose a lot more.

The Financial Services Board (FSB) has been careful in allowing hedge funds because it is concerned about the implications of gearing.

Although you get high-risk hedge funds, the funds can also be used to reduce the risk of losing money in volatile markets, because the managers can bet against a fall in the market.

Hedge funds are perceived as high-risk investment strategies because the fund managers use derivatives and options to bet on the movement of stock markets, shares, bonds, currencies and commodities, while accentuating performance through leverage.

Other criticisms of hedge funds include:

- lack of transparency;
- lack of proper risk control;
- lack of regulation;
- lack of knowledge by investors, leading to incorrect investment choices;
- high fees; and
- difficulties in selling the investment.

There are a lot of hedge fund multimanagers out there and you need to exercise caution in selecting the right one. Issues you should take into account include:

- The jurisdiction in which the manager is registered: You should preferably deal with a company registered in South Africa and subject to local regulation.
- The jurisdiction in which the investment product itself is registered: As hedge fund management is mainly an international investment, many products will be registered through offshore centres. These centres have varying levels of regulation. For South Africans, the better bet is usually a European offshore jurisdiction.
- Whether the manager has a track record: This should be at least five years.

- Whether the investment has a minimum of 10 to 15 underlying funds.
- The liquidity of the investment – the ease with which you can buy and sell your investment.
- Transparency – whether you receive regular reports about performance, selection of underlying funds and costs.
- The size of assets under management: A multimanager with more sizeable assets has access to the widest range of funds.

Exchange traded funds

The first exchange traded fund (ETF) in South Africa, the Satrix 40, was launched in 2000. The fund is essentially an index fund, which tracks the top 40 companies listed on the JSE Securities Exchange. These funds, which are sponsored by the stock exchanges on which they are listed, are becoming increasingly popular with investors around the world. The costs of ETFs tend to be lower than unit trust index funds.

Choose the right product provider (company)

After selecting the investment products best suited to your investment needs you should also select the product provider.

There are a number of issues you must take into consideration in selecting a product provider:

- Its legality: Do not deal with a product provider that is not registered with the Financial Services Board. It is easy to check. Go to their website: www.fsb.co.za.
- Its reputation: Deal only with companies that have a sound reputation for good and honest service.
- Investment performance: Although historical performance is no guarantee of future performance, if the company has provided consistent, above-inflation returns in the past, you should be fairly safe. Do not seek out companies that provide stellar performance in one year and are dogs the next.

Measure the results

When you have made your investment choice you must monitor the investment performance. There are a number of ways to do this, most of which involve benchmarks. A benchmark is a pre-selected marker against which you can measure how your investment is doing. The benchmark must, however, be appropriate. It is pointless measuring an investment in a bank account against the JSE All Share Index. Benchmarks include:

- Inflation: This is probably the best benchmark you can use. If you aim at getting the inflation rate plus 3 percent you are doing well. Anything above that should be considered a windfall.
- Indices: A wide range of indices are used to measure performance. You must remember that an index benchmark is relative to the benchmark; it is not a measure of absolute performance. So, when an index is going up you should see if you are doing better or worse than the index; and when the index is dropping check whether you are dropping at a lower or faster rate. On the way up you should outperform an index if the asset manager is worth what you are paying; and on the way down you should not drop as fast.

Revisit your investments

If you have made properly considered investment decisions you should not have to switch them around. Many investors switch or get out of investments at the wrong time, impacting negatively on the value of their investments.

Bad reasons for switching investments include:

- Panic selling during times of market volatility, such as the 1998 market crash in South Africa or the terrorist attack on the financial centre of New York in September 2001.
- Advice from advisers that they can get you a better deal elsewhere: Normally the only person receiving a better deal is the adviser, who is generating a new set of commission.
- Investors hearing about how their dentist or hairdresser is making a fortune out of some other investment.
- Investors urgently needing access to their money: Often the cause of this is initial poor financial planning.

Research, conducted both internationally and locally, has proved that switching investments is generally a bad policy, particularly if you are trying to time your investments with market events. Normally this results in:

- locking in what would have been only a paper loss, as the markets are likely to improve;
- the payment of penalty fees for early withdrawal; and
- the reduced value of your investment because of a new round of costs.

One of the main areas where financial advisers encourage investors to switch has been in life assurance investments. There is a switching agreement in place within the life assurance industry, which forces financial advisers and companies to follow certain steps if they switch you from one assurance product to another. However, you do not have the same protection if you switch to another type of investment product.

What to do when an investment matures

If your investment matures and you do not need the money, it is often best to leave it exactly where it is. This is particularly the case where your investment is directly linked to the market. For example, say you have a general equity life assurance investment with performance linked directly to what is happening in the market sector in which you are invested and the market is down. By withdrawing the money at periods when the market is low, you secure the losses. You should rather extend the period of the contract so that you withdraw only when the market improves. Even where you are doing well and an investment matures, if you do not need the money, you should consider extending the contract. It will save costs.

Reasons for switching or cashing in investments include the following:

- Prolonged poor performance, which is unrelated to underlying investment markets: You should always check the performance against the benchmark that you have set.
- A change in your personal financial position.

The area of investment most often affected by a change of personal fortunes is life assurance. However, you should not merely consider keeping or cashing in the investment. You have other options open to you. These include:

- Making the policy 'paid up': This means leaving the investment where it is but making no further contributions. You can always resume payments at a later date.

- Taking a loan against the policy: Most life assurance companies allow you to do this.

Before you make any decisions to surrender or switch an investment, do the following:

- Revisit your original reasons for making the investment.
- Carefully consider the reasons for the switch or cash-in.
- Consider all the alternatives.
- If you are being encouraged to make the switch by a financial adviser, get the reasons in writing and ask the company that holds the investment what it thinks of the reasons.

20

Foreign Investment

Foreign investment deserves special attention. While the rules for foreign investment are much the same as for local investment, you need to take other factors into account.

On 1 July 1997 exchange controls on South African residents were partially lifted. There are now two ways in which you can legally invest in foreign markets. You can invest directly or indirectly. You invest directly by using foreign currency so that you are paid out, when your investment matures, in foreign currency anywhere in the world. This is called a foreign-currency-denominated foreign investment. You invest indirectly through what is know as the asset-swap mechanism, where you invest through a local financial institution in rands and receive your returns in rands. This is called a rand-denominated foreign investment.

Rand-denominated foreign investment

A rand-denominated (asset-swap) investment has the following characteristics:

- You invest in rands and are repaid your capital and investment growth in rands in South Africa.
- You don't use your foreign currency investment allowance to make rand-denominated foreign investments. With your foreign investment allowance you may invest in whatever you like in any currency, and cash in your investments in any currency anywhere in the world.
- As an investor, you are not limited by the foreign investment limits applied to financial services companies. The only limit on you is that an investment product or product range of a financial services company may be closed for

further investment because the financial services company has reached the limit placed on its foreign investment capacity. You can have 100 percent of your savings invested in foreign markets through rand-denominated foreign investments.

- Your foreign investments are indirect and can be made only through an institution registered with the South African regulatory authorities.
- You are limited in your investment choices to investment product types that are available in South Africa and are regulated by the South African regulatory authorities. You cannot invest directly in other assets such as property, or products such as wrap funds, that are not available on the local investment market.
- The investments are treated in the same way for tax purposes as local investments.

Foreign-currency-denominated foreign investments

As of 2000 you are allowed a R750 000 foreign investment allowance if you are over the age of 18 and are in good standing with the SARS. (You need a tax-clearance certificate from the tax authorities.) The limit has been raised from an initial R200 000 in 1997. A foreign-currency-denominated investment has the following characteristics.

- You purchase foreign currency in which to make your investment.
- You can invest the money in anything you want, including a party for friends at the Savoy Hotel in London.
- When the investment matures you do not have to return the money to South Africa. You can spend or reinvest it as you want.
- For tax purposes, you have to declare both income and capital gains from any foreign source as if you had made the gains in South Africa. Residence-based tax also means that you have to pay some additional tax, such as tax on dividends, which you do not pay on local dividends.

UNDERSTANDING FOREIGN INVESTMENT

There are a number of important issues you must understand when it comes to investing in foreign markets.

ISSUE 1 OFFSHORE INVESTMENT

Foreign investment means investing anywhere in the world. Offshore invest-ment means using investment products that are managed from a foreign tax haven. The term 'offshore' was first used in Britain and the United States to describe investments made 'off the shore' of a jurisdiction or country in which no tax or low tax was levied on companies offering investment products as well as on the returns on investments.

Low or no tax for non-residents is not the only feature of an 'offshore' juris-diction, which are known as 'tax havens' or increasingly nowadays as 'offshore financial centres'.

Other features of an offshore tax haven include the following:

- Minimum complications: Because there is no tax on you directly, it simplifies your tax affairs. If you invested in a non-tax-haven country you would be involved in tax laws and regulations of that jurisdiction, which can complicate your investment affairs. You will still be subject to South African taxation.
- Investment secrecy: Many people who invest offshore do not want their own tax authorities and other regulators (or their creditors or even relatives) to know about their investments. Most tax havens have laws that govern the extent of secrecy, making it a criminal offence to disclose 'secret' infor-mation. However, with the international campaign to halt terrorism, the laundering of money by drug cartels and other international criminals, secrecy is increasingly limited.
- Well-developed legislation and regulation: Regulation is required to protect investors and to ensure the proper functioning of financial services. This is in the best interests of the jurisdiction to ensure that investors are prepared to channel their savings through products provided by companies registered in the jurisdiction. Sophisticated vehicles, such as trusts, need to be established with the proper legal structure. You should be warned that the level of regulation does vary from jurisdiction to jurisdiction.
- No exchange controls: There has to be a free flow of money in and out of the jurisdiction. Investors must have the confidence that they can withdraw their money at any stage.
- Political, economic and social stability: Without all-round stability, foreign investors are hardly likely to have confidence.
- A sound and sophisticated banking and financial services sector: Investors

199

have to know that products and other financial services are competitive, comprehensive, up to date, innovative and secure. It is not sufficient for an offshore financial centre to offer only one or two services, as this can lead to complications, particularly for multinational companies that are increasingly basing themselves in offshore jurisdictions.

- Well-qualified investment managers and advisers: Most of the offshore jurisdictions attract the cream of the financial services community. An outstanding feature is the level of intellectual capital that can be found in the jurisdictions.
- Excellent communications: Markets change in the blink of an eye. This means that the jurisdictions must be able to offer excellent communications – from telecommunications to transport facilities. They must be able to provide immediate and rapid access to the world's investment markets.
- Language: Language skills are important. The most important language internationally is English, because it is the language of international finance.
- Geographical position: Traditionally, the main offshore centres have been small jurisdictions that are either fully independent countries (e.g. Bermuda), principalities (e.g. Liechtenstein), or partly independent jurisdictions (e.g. the Channel Islands). There are offshore jurisdictions spanning the globe from romantic Vanuatua, a Pacific Ocean Island, to Luxembourg, wedged between Germany, Holland and Belgium. Most South African financial services companies, operating offshore and offering offshore investment products, have established bases on the tax-haven islands dotted around Britain (the Isle of Man, Jersey, Guernsey), or at one of the other European havens (such as Ireland, Luxembourg and Gibraltar). The main reason for this is that these offshore centres are in much the same time zone as South Africa, and the regulations in the centres are better known. However, more exotic locations are increasingly being used, such as the Indian Ocean islands, particularly Mauritius.

ISSUE 2 **INVESTING IN A NON-OFFSHORE COUNTRY**

If you decide to invest directly in another country that is not classified as an offshore jurisdiction, you must first be aware of the taxation regime, and particularly whether there is a tax treaty between South Africa and your selected country. Most tax treaties are based on allowing you to claim back any tax you have paid on your investment returns or income earned abroad against any tax you would have to pay in South Africa against the same investment returns or income earned abroad. In other words, you do not face double taxation on the same income. However, there may be taxes, such as capital gains tax, that are not covered in a tax agreement. On top of this, estate duty can be extremely complex. If you are contemplating a direct investment in, say, Britain, it may be in your best interests to do it via a trust or company registered in an offshore jurisdiction.

ISSUE 3 CAUTION

You must take care in your choice of offshore jurisdiction. Not all offshore jurisdictions are equal. Many have far stricter regulations than others. For example, many of the scam artists who have tried (and often succeeded) in interesting South Africans in creative investments operate out of some of the Caribbean islands. Regulations, taxation and conditions can vary dramatically from centre to centre. You should take great care in examining the different offshore centres if you are making investments outside of traditional investment vehicles, such as unit trust funds, particularly if they are not registered in South Africa by the Financial Services Board (FSB). As a general rule, you should not invest through any company that is not registered with the FSB. There are sufficient choices in the number of registered companies, so why take a chance?

ISSUE 4 CURRENCY

Because currencies move up and down, not only against the rand but also against other currencies, you have added a new risk·factor. The choice of currency can be as important as the type of investment and the competence of the fund manager.

You only have to look at the rand that has been on a downward trend since its peak in 1980 when it was worth R1.22 to the US$! Since then it has declined on average by 9 percent a year, and this trend is set to continue for the foreseeable future. This is a strong argument for putting your money in a dollar-, euro- or pound-denominated investment.

ISSUE 5 COUNTRY

Today, there are more than 70 different stock markets from which to choose. They are situated all over the world, each with their own growth patterns and problem areas. While you may want to choose your own investments, global investing is best left to fund managers in offshore jurisdictions who will decide where to invest the fund's money and in what currency.

21

Retirement

This chapter breaks into three parts. Part One is about how women are at a disadvantage when it comes to retirement and what can be done to rectify the situation. Part Two covers investing retirement savings, and Part Three deals with tax and retirement.

PART ONE: BEATING RETIREMENT DISCRIMINATION

The Constitution outlaws discrimination. The law states that everyone should be treated equally, but in reality the retirement cards are solidly stacked against women, making them far more vulnerable than men to living out an impoverished old age. Apart from the general problem of not saving enough for retirement, women are disadvantaged for a number of other reasons.

Retirement disadvantages for women include the following:

- Women generally live longer than men, so they need more funds set aside to ensure a comfortable retirement. At age 60 a woman can, on average, expect to live 3.6 years longer than a man.
- Divorce: Unfortunately some women still go to the marriage altar believing they will live happily ever after and that a doting husband will provide for them. But divorce can end in poverty for a woman. Divorce rates creep ever higher, with it being estimated that one in two marriages now end that way. A woman who has not worked during her married life may find herself destitute at retirement if, at divorce, her income drops substantially, as she cannot find an adequately paid job.
- The various marriage contracts available in South Africa affect how much a woman may have available for retirement funding. This is because assets taken into the marriage and built up during the marriage are valued and

accrued to the different parties in different ways. It is important that you understand the manner in which you are being married, for example in or out of community of property, as well as how assets you have accrued before and during your marriage will be recorded. You should get proper legal advice from a lawyer you know and trust before getting married. It may seem that a marriage contract has nothing to do with retirement when you are thinking more of children and a new home, but it definitely has important repercussions.

- Women most often have custody of children after a divorce, and incur costs that are not covered by alimony payments. What is more, South Africa does not have a very sound record in the enforcement of support payments. This means that a divorced mother often has to use any retirement savings to support her family.
- Women generally earn less than men and are often employed in casual jobs, which do not have retirement schemes. This has a dual negative effect, as most retirement fund contributions are based on the amount employees earn. If you earn less you obviously contribute less, but so does your employer – a double-whammy effect.
- Career breaks to raise a family are still common. This can mean no income and no contributions to retirement funds while not working, unless you are merely taking maternity leave. Career breaks also limit promotion prospects with the knock-on effect on earnings and retirement savings.
- Many women still struggle to break through the glass ceiling on the corporate promotion ladder, again limiting retirement savings.
- The retirement age for women is often younger than that for men. In 1995 legislation was updated and the retirement age for both sexes was made 55 from a tax point of view, but this does not mean all fund rules have also been changed.

THE BUILD-UP OF RETIREMENT CAPITAL

The most damaging impact on women's financial hopes is made by the extra years that they can expect to live, and the average of six years they take off to have a family. The two reasons combined are a poverty trap.

It works like this. Let us take two women (Ms A and Ms B) and assume that they both start working at age 21. Both put an initial R50 a month aside for retirement funding. Ms A continues to work without a break until she retires at age 60. Ms B takes off six years to raise a family at age 28. During these six years she makes no pension fund contributions. Assume that when she resumes work her contributions start at the same level being paid by Ms A at that stage. Using this scenario, Ms B has reduced her working life by 15 percent. (The six years taken off to raise a family is an average arrived at in Britain. Similar figures are not available in South Africa.) These six years could reduce Ms B's retirement capital by a dramatic one-third.

Here are various permutations of annually compounded interest rates and salary inflation.

Scenario One:

Annual compound interest	10%
Salary inflation	10%
Ms A	R917 982
Ms B	R776 754

In this scenario those six years will cost Ms B a total of R141 128 or 18.1 percent in accumulated retirement capital.

Scenario Two:

Annual compound interest	15%
Salary inflation	10%
Ms A	R2 467 934
Ms B	R1 953 865

In this scenario those six years will cost Ms B a total of R514 069 or 26.3 percent in accumulated retirement capital. As far as annual income and salary inflation increases are concerned, this is the more probable scenario.

Scenario Three:

Annual compound interest	10%
Salary inflation	15%
Ms A	R2 413 687
Ms B	R2 197 629

In this scenario those six years will cost Ms B a total of R216 058 or 9.8 percent in accumulated retirement capital. This is the least likely scenario.

THE PENSION

Now comes the next hit. Let us again assume that the two use their entire retirement capital to purchase an annuity (monthly pension). This time we will also bring Mr C into the calculation and assume that he has the same amount of accumulated retirement capital as Ms A in each case. We also assume that all three are in the same state of health, etc.

Annuities* (monthly pension) received

SCENARIO ONE:

Person	Retirement capital	Annuity
Ms A	R917 982	R 8 886
Ms B	R776 754	R 7 517
Mr C	R917 982	R 9 669

SCENARIO TWO:

Person	Retirement Capital	Annuity
Ms A	R2 467 934	R23 911
Ms B	R1 953 865	R18 928
Mr C	R2 467 934	R26 016

SCENARIO THREE:

Person	Retirement capital	Annuity
Ms A	R2 413 687	R23 386
Ms B	R2 197 629	R23 165
Mr C	R2 413 687	R25 444

*The annuity figures were supplied by Old Mutual and were valid on 2 August 2001. The following assumptions were made in all cases: The annuities were single-life compulsory purchase annuities. Retirement age for all three is 61 next birthday.

Taking the most likely scenario (Scenario Two), the result is that those six years that Ms B took off to raise a family have cost her dearly. Mr C will receive 26.3 percent more as a pension than Ms B. The longer you take off to raise a family, the worse the situation.

But even Ms A, who worked for the same number of years as Mr C, now faces the prospect of an income that is 8.1 percent less than the income Mr C will receive, because she is likely to live longer than Mr C.

Life assurance companies argue that they are not discriminating against women. The annuity paid out will be exactly the same amount on average as the total amount paid out to men.

From the above calculations it is clear that a single woman has to put aside more than her male counterpart because of her expected extra years in retirement. Then you still need to take account of other limitations, such as gender discrimination.

The solution: Plan on being single

So what do you do about this state of affairs? If you are married you should still plan on being single, not only because of the possibility of divorce, but also because, even if your marriage does last, you are likely to outlive your husband, unless he is younger or in better health. Consider your position from various viewpoints, such as the breakdown of your marriage, the early death of your husband while he is still working, and his death before yours in your retirement years. Each case has different consequences.

TEN RULES FOR A FINANCIALLY SECURE RETIREMENT

There are some general rules that affect retirement planning for women to a greater or lesser degree. These 10 rules will give you a better chance of avoiding living out your retirement years in penury.

RULE 1 GET THE DETAILS OF RETIREMENT SCHEMES

Get the details of your spouse's employee benefits, including retirement and health benefits. A good starting point is to know his income level, as most retirement and disability benefits are based on this. The reason for knowing the details are not malicious, but so that both you and your partner can judge the total effect that each other's plans will have on the other. Before and during marriage women should, on the same basis as their husbands, assess their retirement and other needs. Don't rely on being catered for as a 'spouse' on your husband's retirement plan.

If your partner is employed in the formal sector you need to know the name of the scheme and the type of scheme, for example whether it is a defined benefit or defined contribution scheme. If he is self-employed you need to know what retirement, disability and life-cover arrangements he has made. Pay particular attention to the benefits you could expect in the event of death or disability.

Various retirement schemes have different rules and, consequently, different benefits. For example, a group life and disability benefit (life and disability assurance provided by a retirement scheme or employer) is normally far larger with a defined contribution retirement scheme than with a defined benefit scheme. Both are based on a multiple of the annual pensionable salary. The multiple can vary from one to eight times the annual pensionable salary.

RULE 2 MAKE NON-NEGOTIABLE RETIREMENT PLANS

From the day you start working you should make plans for retirement, and in any marriage agreement you should make the continuation of those plans non-negotiable. For example, if you agree to stop work to bring up children then contributions should continue to be made to your retirement fund. If you have made your retirement plans from pre-marriage and had them written into a marriage agreement, you will avoid scrabbling to retrieve a position after divorce.

RULE 3 SAVE ALL THE TIME

You should seriously consider a retirement annuity into which you can pay money in differing amounts. You can draw a pension from a retirement annuity only from age 55. This can have a drawback in that you cannot get your hands on the money until the retirement annuity matures – but then nor can anyone else. If your husband is unable to contribute to your retirement funding needs while you are not working, then you must ensure that during the periods that you are working you save additional amounts for your retirement.

RULE 4 NAME THE PEOPLE WHO BENEFIT

Ensure that you are the beneficiary of life assurance policies taken out on your partner's life. It is even better to have the policy ceded to you. If the policy is ceded to you it cannot be ceded to anyone else without your permission. As a beneficiary only, the owner of the policy can remove you without your consent. The life assurance company must be informed in writing that the policy has been ceded. You need to ensure that the premiums on the policy are kept up to date. If, say after divorce, the premiums are not paid by your former spouse, make payments yourself so that the policy does not lapse or lose value.

RULE 5   FIND OUT THE HISTORY

If your spouse has been married before, establish the consequences of the divorce. In particular, find out what rights the previous wife has to accrued retirement savings, and whether you and your spouse will be financially secure when you retire.

RULE 6   WHAT'S MINE IS MINE

Ensure that what is yours remains yours. If you are helping out a spouse, for example in funding a business, make it a repayable loan rather than a gift, particularly when retirement savings are involved. Don't see your accumulated retirement funds as a standby source of family financing, unless in dire need. Cashing in your retirement funds (where this is possible) to fund some venture is dangerous, ill-advised and will have tax consequences.

RULE 7   KEEP ASSETS IN YOUR NAME

If your husband runs his own business, ensure that major assets, such as your home and motor vehicle, are in your name or in the name of a trust of which you are also a trustee. You need to do this to ensure that creditors cannot attach the assets if the business venture falls apart. If your assets are exposed to creditors then you may find you will have to use your retirement savings as a financial lifeline.

RULE 8   GET INDEPENDENT ADVICE

It is preferable for you and your spouse to have different financial planners, as there will then be no conflict of interest.

RULE 9   BE IN CONTROL

Don't have the attitude: 'I am bad with figures. I let my husband do all those things for me.' Stay fully involved in all your family finances. There are still a number of ways that assets can be hidden from spouses through instruments such as trusts and nominee companies. If someone has malicious intent, and you have shown no interest, you will pay a financial penalty.

RULE 10   REMEMBER HEALTHCARE

A couple will often retire with what may seem to be more-than-adequate resources, but their savings are eroded by one of the couple needing intensive medical treatment before dying. As men generally die younger than women, it is usually women who suffer the consequences of insufficient healthcare provisions. Many women have been impoverished because savings have been spent on the medical care of a husband dying of a chronic disease over an extended period. For this reason, it is important to ensure that you and your partner have sufficient health cover. (See Chapter 15 for more information.)

It is also a good idea to take out your own disability assurance while you are working so you are covered in the event of both disability and divorce.

TWO LIFE-CHANGING CIRCUMSTANCES

There are two life-changing circumstances that you must take into account in your retirement planning. These are divorce and widowhood.

Divorce

If you get divorced you are entitled to a share of your husband's retirement savings in a clearly defined retirement savings instrument such as a retirement fund or retirement annuity for the period that you were married. However the entitlement of a married woman covers only the period of actual marriage, with the value normally set at the date of divorce. This has four limitations:

- Inflation could reduce the amount in real terms.
- You do not automatically participate in future growth of the assets in most cases.
- You will not be entitled to a higher portion, even though your earning ability may have been dramatically reduced because of marriage.
- You get the money only when he retires.

These limitations are partially offset by the fact that your entitlement to any alimony does not cease when your husband takes retirement. Your ex-partner may, however, ask the courts to reduce the alimony on the grounds that his income has dropped.

You should deal with the share of retirement savings in the divorce settlement and not pick up merely the minimum entitlement by relying on the law as it stands.

It is essential that you inform your former husband's retirement fund of the terms of the divorce to ensure that you receive the portion to which you are entitled. If the fund does not know about a previous marriage and divorce, it will be unable to pay you out. The fund will also pay out only if it is a court order in terms of the divorce settlement.

Widowhood

As has been pointed out, women live longer than men. This means that many women face the prospect of widowhood. Often, widowhood does not occur when you have reached retirement age. Many women are widowed in their forties or fifties. This creates its own problems, particularly if they have children. In most cases, they are placed in a position of virtual early retirement. Early retirement is not a good idea for three reasons:

- There is what is called an opportunity cost. Income that could be earned is not earned.
- You have to start drawing down earlier on what is likely to be less money than you would have accumulated if you retired at an older age, or the amount you would have accumulated if your spouse had died at normal retirement age.
- The accumulated retirement savings will have to last for a longer period, as you have added more years to the total number of years you will be in retirement.

This means that widows, particularly young widows, must take special care in assessing their financial situation. Here is a course of action:

- Be aware that, in all likelihood, you will be in a highly emotional state and should not try to make all decisions instantly.
- Don't do business with strangers who have not been properly introduced with references. Many opportunist financial advisers scan the obituaries in newspapers looking for vulnerable widows who may have recently received large sums of money. They move in quickly, taking advantage of the widow's emotional state, often hoping that she has no idea of finances – an ideal situation for an adviser who is aiming for self-enrichment.
- You will receive fairly large sums of money, which will have to be invested. Do not make any decisions immediately. Place the money in a money market account until you feel more settled. Your capital will be secure and it will earn a comparatively high rate of interest.
- If you already have a qualified and trusted financial adviser you are in

a stronger position. If not, you must carefully seek out someone who will provide proper advice.

- You must go through the financial planning stages detailed in this book to assess your financial situation properly. The most important question you will have to answer is whether you have sufficient money to continue with your current lifestyle until you die. Make conservative assumptions in making these projections.
- If you do not have sufficient money to last you until you die, you will have to make significant decisions, such as finding a job if you are not working, lowering your standard of living, and/or downsizing your accommodation. (Many widows want to hold on to properties where they have experienced happy times, but this can seriously undermine future financial security.)
- Once you have properly assessed your position make conservative investment decisions. Do not, particularly if you are short of retirement savings, make high-risk investments in the hope that you will improve your financial situation. With every financial decision, you must also consider what will happen if you reduce the value of your capital. This does not mean that you should put all your money into a bank fixed deposit, paying a low interest rate. Your capital will be safe, but inflation will eat into your returns, and you will not have sufficient money to last until you die. You will have to split your money between income-creating investments and capital growth investments to ensure continued growth of your capital.

Retirement funding on the death of a spouse

There are two significant financial consequences when your partner dies:

- Anything left to you by your husband is not subject to either estate duty or capital gains tax.
- If you are a beneficiary of a defined benefit pension fund, your pension is likely to be reduced by at least one-third; and depending on the type of pension your partner may have been receiving from the proceeds of a retirement annuity, you could lose all or part of this pension. (See p. 213 for descriptions of different retirement financial structures.)

To avoid any complications you should ensure that at all times your partner has an up-to-date will, and you are fully aware of all his financial affairs as well as where records are kept.

If your former husband dies before you, he will not be able, by deliberate intent, to leave you destitute. The approval by Parliament in 1990 of the Maintenance of Surviving Spouses Act provided for the protection of surviving spouses as well as divorced spouses. Under the Act a surviving spouse may claim for reasonable maintenance from the estate, irrespective of the provisions of the deceased spouse's will. In other words, leaving a spouse out of a will or disinheriting him or her has no standing in court. A divorced spouse is protected by any maintenance order that is in force. The amount of alimony can continue to be claimed by the divorced spouse from the estate automatically.

Much the same situation applies to any group life policy attached by an employer to a retirement scheme. If your husband or former husband dies while still employed, he cannot preclude benefits being paid to you either as a current or former wife. A former spouse will need to prove that she was in fact a dependant. The person covered by a group life policy can indicate a preference as to how funds should be paid, but it is the trustees of the fund who will make the final decision. The trustees have to follow the guidelines set out in the Pension Funds Act and in the rules of the fund. They are not bound by any will or the naming of any beneficiaries. The Pension Funds Act and the fund rules ensure that the money goes to the dependants rather than the heirs (if they are different) of the member. If you are a dependant of a fund member you need to ensure that the fund is aware of you.

PART TWO: INVESTMENT FOR RETIREMENT

Investing for retirement is not the same as investing for, say, the education of children. The reason is that there are various tax structures in place that affect the build-up of retirement savings. By using various investment products that are designed to take advantage of the tax structures, you can reduce the amount of tax you will pay as well as defer the tax you must pay until a later date. When you defer tax you can earn money on the tax deferred.

The tax structures are in place to encourage you to save for retirement. Because you have been given tax incentives to save for retirement, you can draw a pension from your retirement savings only in particular ways. This is an attempt to ensure that you will have money until the day you die.

THE BUILD-UP OF RETIREMENT SAVINGS

Obviously, any long-term asset you acquire (such as your home) will be used to ensure that you have a financially secure retirement, but there are particular retirements savings vehicles that you can use to get the tax advantages. These are retirement funds and retirement preservation funds.

There are four basic retirement fund vehicles used for the build-up of retirement savings that are recognised in law. These are:

- defined benefit pension funds;
- defined contribution pension funds (also knows as money purchase funds);
- defined contribution provident funds; and
- retirement annuity funds.

Defined benefit pension funds

In a defined benefit retirement scheme both you and your employer contribute, but your employer has to meet a promise to pay you a pension at a predetermined level on retirement. The pension you receive is worked out on a formula that takes account of your salary at retirement (this is often your average salary of your last two or three years of service), the number of years of service and a percentage of your salary. Defined benefit schemes are being phased out by most employers because of the risk they must take to ensure that the investments made with your contributions, and theirs, will be sufficient to provide you with the required pension. For example:

Length of service	30 years
Average monthly salary for past two years	R12 000
Percentage of salary for each year of service	2%

Calculation:

30 × 2 = 60% of final average salary
Pension = R72 000 a year, or R6 000 a month

On retirement you are allowed to take a maximum of one-third of your pension as a cash payment. This is called a commutation. The formula for calculating this one-third commutation varies from fund to fund and takes into account your age at retirement and the average expected date of death of all members. For example:

Annual pension	R72 000
Age at retirement	65
Factor of commutation	9
Therefore, your ⅓ commutation would be	R72 000 × 9 = R216 000

The consequence of withdrawing a lump sum is that your monthly pension is then reduced by one-third. For example:

Annual pension	R72 000
Less ⅓ commutation	R24 000
Remaining annual pension	R48 000
Monthly pension	R 4 000

(The calculations are based on what is called your pensionable salary. This does not normally include things such as car or housing allowances.)

Advantages of a defined benefit scheme include the following:

- You do not take the investment risk. In other words, you know what you will receive when you retire. If there is a collapse in investment markets, your employer has to find the extra money to make up any shortfall to meet your pension.
- If you die or have to take early retirement because of ill health when still employed, particularly when you are younger, your family will probably be better off with a defined benefit scheme. The reason for this is that you or your family will receive a pension based on what you could be expected to earn at your normal retirement age. However, your group life benefits also need to be taken into account.
- Your contributions are tax deductible. Tax is deferred until benefits are received. At retirement the one-third lump sum (after an initial tax-free amount) is taxed at your beneficial average rate of tax rather than the harsher marginal rate. Your monthly pension is taxed at your marginal rate of taxation.

Disadvantages of a defined benefit scheme include:

- There are seldom guarantees that your pension payments on retirement will keep up with inflation. Increases are normally dependent on excess investment income of the fund. The decision to increase pensions is taken by the board of trustees of the fund. It is up to the trustees to decide whether or not to pass on some of the out-performance by way of benefit increases.

- If you change jobs you may not be able to take more than your contributions and a nominal amount of growth on your contributions. With the 'job for life' concept virtually out of existence, this is an important factor.

Defined contribution pension funds

Also known as a money purchase scheme, a defined contribution pension fund is similar to a defined benefit pension fund, with two significant differences:

- You and your employer make predetermined contributions. The contributions to the fund by both your employer and yourself are fixed as a percentage of your pensionable income when you join the fund or when you start employment.
- While your employer guarantees to make a contribution, this does not guarantee a pension. The size of your pension will depend on how much has been contributed by both you and your employer, and on the investment growth on the contributions.

A record is kept by the pension fund of exactly how much you and your employer have paid into the fund, as well as the capital and income growth of the investment made on contributions. If the investments perform poorly, you carry this loss. If they perform well, you pick up the benefit.

When you retire, up to one-third of the benefit may be taken in cash. Unlike the payment of the one-third commutation in a defined benefit fund (where the one-third is calculated according to a formula based on your retirement age and the life expectancy of members – see p. 214), the commutation in a defined contribution scheme is worked on the actual amount you have accumulated in your fund (known as your full or accrued benefit).

For example, if you have accumulated R1 million, you are allowed R333 333 as a lump sum.

The remaining amount after the withdrawal of the lump sum is used to provide a pension (known as a compulsory annuity) for you and your dependants. In cases where a pension is bought for you individually from a life assurance company, you should ask your fund to provide you with quotations from various companies in making a decision on where to buy the annuity.

Advantages of a defined contribution pension scheme include the following:

- You may have the advantage of a higher pension than you would have received from a defined benefit retirement fund as a result of good investment performance.
- If you change jobs, you are normally permitted to take your full benefit after a certain number of years. The rules, however, vary from fund to fund.
- You have a greater say in the investment of your funds, with increasing choices being given to members. Normally, as a minimum choice you get to choose between a market-linked fund, where your investments move up and down directly in relation to the value of the instruments in which your money is invested, or a smoothed portfolio, where the asset management company takes out the ups and downs of investment, giving you the average growth. These choices should be carefully considered. For example, if you choose the market-linked option and the stock markets collapse the day before you retire, you could be in dire financial straits, as you would be paid out your retirement capital on the ruling prices or values. If you were in the smoothed category the bump would have been taken out, as you would have received the average growth of the past number of years. As a general rule, you should consider swapping into the smoothed bonus fund some years before retirement, particularly if you are considering early retirement for reasons of poor health or even if you are considering resigning. Normally, you are allowed to make this choice on an annual basis. Check the rules of your fund.
- Your contributions are tax deductible: Tax is deferred until benefits are received, with the lump sum taxed (after an initial tax-free amount) at your beneficial average rate of tax rather than the harsher marginal rate. The monthly pension is taxed at your marginal rate.

Disadvantages of a defined contribution (money purchase) pension scheme include the following:

- You take the investment risk. In other words, you do not know what you will receive when you go on pension. If there is a collapse in investment markets you have to find the extra money to make up any shortfall required for a pension. However, if markets continue to perform the way they have in recent years then you might very well have a better pension than you would have received from a defined benefit pension scheme.

- There are seldom guarantees that your pension payments will keep up with inflation. If guarantees are provided for annual pension increases, it comes at the cost of a lower benefit, i.e. your pension will start at a lower point but will increase in line with inflation.
- Your family may not be better off if you die, or have to take early retirement because of ill health while still employed, particularly when you are younger. The reason for this is that you and your family receive a pension based on what you have accumulated – not on what you may have received at retirement age. However, group life and disability benefits are normally better than those you receive from a defined benefit scheme. You need to take into account the structure of the group life benefits. If there is a shortfall, particularly when you are younger, you may need to buy additional life and disability assurance for a limited period.
- HIV/AIDS could have a significant impact if your employer is forced to increase payments for group life cover and reduce payments towards your retirement funding.

Defined contribution provident funds

There are two major differences between a defined contribution pension fund and a defined contribution provident fund:

- The tax treatment of your contributions and benefits differs. You cannot claim the contributions you make against tax. At retirement, your tax-free portion is calculated in the same way as for a pension fund, but you can claim only your own contributions. Further tax may be levied on any income generated from your investment, depending on how the income was generated.
- You can take all your retirement savings as a lump sum, with no necessity to take at least two-thirds of your benefits as a monthly pension.

Defined contribution provident funds were created mainly for people in short-term employment who wanted to take all their savings at retirement. This is a big advantage for people living in rural areas who find it difficult to secure their monthly pension, or for people who want to emigrate.

Your should ensure that the defined contribution provident fund is established on what is called a non-contributory basis, i.e. your employer pays all the contributions. The reason for this is that your employer can claim the contributions against tax, but you may not. Most employer-sponsored provident funds are structured in this way, with the contributions paid by the employer being part of your total pay package. This is what is known as a salary sacrifice.

These are the other major features of a defined contribution provident fund:

- The contributions to the fund both by your employer and yourself are fixed when you join the fund or when you start employment. This is done as a percentage of your pensionable salary. Your employer guarantees a contribution but not a pension. The ratios between what you and your employer contribute can vary.
- A record is kept of exactly how much you and your employer have paid into the fund, as well as the capital and income growth of the investment made with the contributions. If the investments perform poorly you carry this loss.
- When you retire, all your benefits (made by yourself and your employer, as well as the capital and income growth, known as your full benefit) are paid to you as a lump sum. You then have to make the investment decisions to provide income for your retirement years. No pension is paid by the fund.
- If you change jobs you are normally permitted to take your full benefit after a certain number of years. The rules, however, vary from fund to fund.

An example of payment on retirement:*

Length of service	30 years
Your total contributions	R 200 000
Plus employer's contributions	R 200 000
Plus income and capital growth	R 600 000
TOTAL	R1 000 000

*Tax is ignored for the purposes of this calculation.

Advantages of defined contribution provident funds include the following:

- You may have the advantage of a higher pension than you would have received from a defined benefit retirement fund as a result of good investment performance.
- If you change jobs, you are normally permitted to take your full benefit after a certain number of years. The rules vary from fund to fund.
- At retirement, you have all the cash available to make greater choices, such as to buy an annuity at your full discretion (both in type and in provider),

to set up a post-retirement business, to invest in a wider range of different investments, and to be able to control your investments yourself.

- If you live in a remote area with little infrastructure where it is difficult to receive pension payments, a lump sum can be preferable.
- As with a defined contribution pension fund, you have greater say in the investments of contributions. However, here again you need to be cautious about how you decide on the option most suitable for you.

Disadvantages of defined contribution provident funds include the following:

- The risk of having sufficient money to see you through retirement is yours. This risk is greatest with a provident fund. Not only do you have the risk in the build-up of the fund where investment returns will determine what you receive at retirement; you also need to ensure that your money will last you through retirement, because you do not have to leave two-thirds of the money in an investment that gives you a monthly pension. If it is poorly invested, you may find yourself destitute, particularly if you live for a long time. It is impossible for you to decide how long your natural life will be, making it very difficult to decide how much money you will need for the rest of your life. As a result, it is best to use at least part of the money to purchase a pension, because then you are at least assured of a certain income until you die.
- Your contributions are not tax deductible.
- Your family may not be better off if you die or you have to take early retirement because of ill health, particularly when you are younger. The reason for this is that you or your family receive a pension based on what you have accumulated. However, group life and disability benefits are normally better than for a defined benefit scheme. You need to take into account the structure of group life benefits. If there is a shortfall, particularly when you are younger, you may need to buy additional personal disability and life assurance for a limited period.
- HIV/AIDS could have a significant impact if your employer is forced to increase payments for group life cover and reduce payments towards your retirement funding.

Retirement annuities

Retirement annuities (normally referred to as RAs) were introduced by the government in 1960 to give self-employed people the same tax advantages in saving for retirement as individuals who belonged to retirement funds offered by employers. However, retirement annuities are not restricted to self-employed people; they can also be used by employed people to top up retirement savings. They are particularly useful for women who move in and out of jobs, or mothers who choose to stay at home to raise children.

An RA is very similar to a defined contribution pension fund. An added advantage is that you can add life assurance and disability cover to the scheme. They are also flexible in that you can increase and decrease the amounts you save.

There are two main advantages of saving for retirement using an RA:

- Tax is deferred until the day you retire. In other words, you deduct your contributions within certain tax limits from your taxable income.
- Money paid into a retirement annuity is not counted as being part of your estate. So, if you go bankrupt, your creditors cannot claim this money.

Other important factors about an RA include the following:

- It cannot be matured before the age of 55.
- You cannot contribute to an RA past the age of 69.

However, there are some issues of which you need to be wary:

- RA contracts should be taken out mostly to mature at 55, irrespective of whether you are going to retire at that age or not. The reason for this is that when you reach that age, you have the flexibility to decide whether to continue the RA or whether you want it to mature. If you commit yourself until age 65 you do not have the flexibility to withdraw. If you have a contract period until age 69 and you do need to take the money out earlier, you could be penalised.
- If you are over 50 and want to take out an RA then you should restrict the term to five years, again to give you some flexibility.
- When you retire you are required to buy a compulsory annuity (a monthly pension) with two-thirds of the capital from the maturing retirement annuity. You do not have to buy the annuity from the company with which you had

the RA. You should shop around for the best annuity rates. Also decide on the underlying type of annuity, e.g. whether you want guarantees, inflation-linked escalation, etc. Your financial adviser will help you with these issues.

- Investment choice: In recent years, far more investment choices have been made available to investors, allowing, among other things, the opportunity to vary the risk factor.

RETIREMENT FUNDS – THE BIG DANGERS

Retirement funds often lull people into a false sense of security. Make sure that you are aware of the dangers.

DANGER 1 THE RETIREMENT GAP

Very few funds will provide the level of pension that will maintain the same standard of living that you now have. This is called the retirement gap. You need to ensure that you top up your retirement savings so that you can maintain your standard of living.

DANGER 2 HEALTH COSTS

Health costs go up dramatically when you get older, and many employers are reducing their commitment to after-retirement healthcare funding. Again, you need to put a top-up savings scheme in place to fund additional costs and medical aid fund contributions.

DANGER 3 NOT PRESERVING RETIREMENT SAVINGS

One of the main reasons that people do not have sufficient money when they retire is that they do not reinvest the money when they resign from a job. If you take the money, you will also lose the benefit of deferring tax until you retire. When you resign from a job, you normally have a number of choices if you want to keep the money until you retire:

- You can leave the money in the retirement fund (if the rules of the fund allow this). The result is that you will receive a deferred pension when you retire. If you are in a defined benefit fund, the pension will be determined by a formula – taking account of how much you earned and your length of service. With a defined benefit fund your pension will be determined by the build-up in the fund as a result of investment returns. Take into account that you will pay no reinvestment costs with this choice.

- You can transfer to the fund of a new employer. Again, this will depend on the rules of the fund, and you are unlikely to pay any reinvestment costs.
- You can transfer the money to a retirement annuity. You will not be able to withdraw the money before you are 55. When you draw the money you can take a maximum of one-third as a lump sum, but must buy a pension with the other two-thirds. You will pay initial investment costs, which could be as high as 6 percent.
- You can transfer the money to a provident fund. You are allowed one withdrawal before retirement from a provident fund, which may be a part or the entire amount. The withdrawal will be subject to tax. The retirement date is the same as the fund from which the money was transferred. Again, you will pay initial investment costs, which could be as high as 6 percent.

INVESTMENT AFTER RETIREMENT

If you are not a member of a defined benefit fund you will probably be given the choice of a tax-structured retirement vehicle to use to invest the minimum of two-thirds of your retirement savings you must use to create a monthly pension. This pension is commonly known as an annuity.

Annuities are investment products that provide you with an income. They are for people who want a regular income from any lump-sum amount they want to invest. An annuity, in dictionary terms, is any payment you receive on an annual basis. The life assurance industry has adapted the word to mean an amount you receive on a regular basis (normally monthly) from an investment. Encompassing all types of annuities are two basic forms called compulsory purchase annuities and voluntary purchase annuities.

Compulsory purchase annuities

These are annuities that must be bought with two-thirds of the benefits you receive from a pension fund (not a provident fund). With a compulsory annuity, you invest in a pension for the rest of your life. You are not permitted to invest for a limited term. The types of retirement funds that require you to buy a compulsory purchase annuity are:

- a defined contribution pension fund or defined benefit pension fund;
- a pension preservation fund into which you have previously transferred funds from another defined contribution or defined benefit pension fund; and
- a retirement annuity (RA). With an RA you are also obliged to buy an annuity with at least two-thirds of the proceeds you receive from a pension fund. You are not obliged, however, to purchase the compulsory annuity from the same company with whom you had the retirement annuity. You should shop around for the best annuity (pension).

Voluntary purchase annuities

This is an annuity of your choice, where you invest a lump sum from any source and from which you can draw a regular income. A voluntary purchase annuity can be bought for any period or can last for life.

Within both these annuity structures there are five basic choices of annuity:

CHOICE 1 A LIFE ANNUITY (BOTH COMPULSORY AND VOLUNTARY)

A life annuity pays you a regular amount until the day you die. When you die, the payments stop. No money is passed on to your heirs, unless you also had life assurance built into the contract. In effect, you bet the life assurance company that you will live for a long time. The life assurance company bets that you will live for a shorter time. If you live for a long time, you win the bet, because the amount you receive will be greater than the amount you invested, even with investment growth. Life assurance companies take three main issues into account when they set the level of an annuity:

- Your age: Your current age is taken into account because this will indicate how long an assurance company expects you to live and draw an annuity. Life assurance companies work on mortality tables, which tell them at what age people, on average, are expected to die.
- Gender: Women generally live longer than men so they receive a lower annuity.
- Interest rates: If long-term interest rates are high when you buy an annuity, you can expect a higher annuity, but expect less if interest rates are low.

CHOICE 2 LIFE ANNUITY STRUCTURES

There are a number of underlying choices you can make with traditional life annuities. The combination of choices you make will affect the size of the annuity you will be paid. These are the choices:

- With-profit annuities: With most annuities you can decide whether you want a non-profit annuity, which will provide you with a predetermined regular payment, or a with-profit annuity, where you participate in the returns of the investment through the declaration of bonuses. A with-profit annuity is similar to a guaranteed, smoothed bonus endowment policy. Every year, depending on the investment returns, you will get a share of the returns (or the investment profits).

- Level annuities: Here you will get the same amount every month for the period of the annuity.

- Inflation-linked annuities: These annuities will increase by a fixed amount each year. With inflation-linked annuities you will receive a lower annuity at the start than with a level annuity, but you will be assured of keeping up the same standard of living for the full duration of the annuity. Most companies will permit increases of no more than 20 percent a year on an annuity with a 10-year income guarantee, and 15 percent a year on a life annuity.

- Joint and survivorship annuities: If you are in a relationship, the annuity continues to be paid until the surviving person in the relationship dies.

- Guaranteed term: You are guaranteed an annuity at a certain level for a fixed period, normally 10 years, after which you can renegotiate the new annuity. Another variation is a 'guaranteed for 10 years and then for life' annuity. This means that your heirs will receive the residual capital by way of an annuity if you die within 10 years. After 10 years, the residual capital reverts to the life assurance company.

- Deferred annuities (applies only to voluntary annuities): You can invest the money, but defer receiving the annuity until a later date when it suits you better. For example, say you retire at the age of 55 and have to take a compulsory annuity but intend to carry on working in another job to give yourself sufficient income; you then defer taking the annuity from your compulsory annuity until a later date. As a result, you will receive a higher annuity for two reasons:

- The lump-sum investment will receive investment returns during the deferred period.
- You will be drawing the annuity for a shorter period.

- Enhanced annuities: These annuities are offered, strangely enough, by a few companies to people who can prove that they are in poor health. In other words, if you are likely to die soon or have habits that are bad for your health, such as being a heavy smoker, the life assurance company will pay you a higher annuity.

CHOICE 3 A TEMPORARY LIFE VOLUNTARY ANNUITY

A temporary life annuity pays out until you die or at an earlier fixed date. In other words, you can purchase a temporary life annuity that pays an annuity for life or for 10 years. This means it will pay out until the first of the two events occur. If you are still alive after 10 years, you will no longer receive an annuity. If you die before the 10 years are up, no more money will be paid out by the life assurance company. As with a life annuity, nothing is left to your heirs. This type of annuity, which is only available as a voluntary purchase annuity, is suitable for people who expect to die soon.

CHOICE 4 A TERM-CERTAIN VOLUNTARY ANNUITY

A term-certain annuity is for a fixed period. With a term-certain annuity you do not lose your investment on death. They are available only for voluntary purchase annuities. The annuity rates (the amount you receive), unlike a life annuity, are determined only by interest rates and not by how long you are expected to live.

Term-certain annuities are structured in various ways:

- An income-only annuity, where you will receive a regular annuity for a fixed term: At the end of the term you will receive no money back and the annuity will stop. In effect, the life assurance company structures the annuity so that both the original capital and the investment growth, less costs, is paid out during the fixed period.
- An income-guaranteed annuity, where the level of the annuity is guaranteed for the full period, but where you will also get some or all of your capital back: There is no guarantee, however, on how much capital you will get back. The amount you receive depends on the investment returns achieved by the

life assurance company on your investment. Many people mistakenly believe that both the capital and the income are guaranteed.

- Capital-guaranteed annuities: Say you invested in a 10-year term-certain annuity, you will receive your original capital back on completion of this period. This product may be combined with an income-guaranteed annuity.

If interest rates are low, then you should take out a term-certain annuity only for a short period, in anticipation of them rising. If interest rates are high, you should consider locking in for a longer period or for life.

CHOICE 5 A LIVING ANNUITY

A living annuity (also called an investment-linked living annuity or ILLA) is a relatively new type of annuity, which, again, you have to take for life. But your annuity (the amount you receive) is tied directly to the value of the investment and its investment growth. You can use living annuities for both compulsory and voluntary annuities.

There are three fundamental differences between a living annuity and a traditional life annuity:

- Variable pension: You must draw a pension of between 5 and 20 percent of the capital amount.
- When you die, the residue of your investment is passed on to your heirs. However, the downside with a living annuity is that you are taking bets against yourself that you will have sufficient money to survive until you die. You are not guaranteed a pension at any level.
- You are in charge of the underlying investments. With a traditional life annuity you have absolutely no say in how the money is invested.

The risks of living annuities

There can be significant risks with living annuities, as you have to make investment choices. If you make bad investment choices you will undermine your retirement capital. If you do not understand investing and the risks of investing properly you should be very cautious about putting your money into a living annuity. Before investing in one, ask yourself three questions:

- What will happen if investment markets stay level (remember that you will still be withdrawing from your capital)?

- What will happen if markets drop by 10 percent?
- What will happen if markets drop by 20 percent?

There has been a great deal of mis-selling of living annuities because the risks have not been properly explained. The reason for this is that commission structures are higher than for traditional life annuities. If you need to draw down more than 5 percent of your retirement savings in the initial years you should be wary, as you face the risk of running out of money before you die.

PART THREE: TAX AND RETIREMENT

Tax plays an important part in your retirement. Tax has different implications in the build-up to retirement and in retirement. Be aware that the government is currently restructuring taxation of retirement savings. Because it is still looking at the overall taxation on retirement savings, there is a three-year moratorium on applying capital gains tax to any retirement savings. (You should also read Chapter 8, which will give you a further understanding of taxation issues.)

With tax before retirement, you can claim retirement fund contributions against tax, but there are limits, and these limits can differ depending on the type of fund and also on whether you are employed or unemployed.

Retirement funds are divided into three categories for tax purposes: tax of the build-up of retirement savings, tax at retirement and tax after retirement.

THE BUILD-UP OF RETIREMENT SAVINGS

Defined contribution provident funds

While your contributions to a defined contribution provident fund are not tax deductible, those of your employer are. Against this, on retirement, your contributions are paid to you free of tax. If you are on a defined contribution fund you should ensure that your employer pays all the contributions directly on your behalf by means of what is called a salary sacrifice. The maximum amount an employer may contribute to an employee's retirement fund for tax-deductible purposes is 20 percent of the employee's pensionable income. The same percentage applies, whether it is a pension or provident fund.

Defined benefit, defined contribution (money purchase) pension funds

With these retirement funds, your contributions can be claimed every year against income, i.e. if you earn R50 000 a year, of which R3 500 goes to pension fund contributions, you will pay tax only on R46 500 (all other tax considerations excluded). The deduction is limited to 7.5 percent of your pensionable income (i.e. things such as car allowances are normally excluded from pensionable income). Employer contributions are not seen as employee income and are not included in your income for tax purposes.

Retirement annuities

Retirement annuity contributions can be claimed both by people who are employed and belong to a retirement fund and self-employed people.

Generally you can claim any of the following:

- A total of 15 percent of non-retirement funding income: If you are employed you must first deduct the portion of your income that is considered pension funding. This is normally your basic salary without any allowances, such as car or telephone allowances. This means that maximum contributions made to defined benefit schemes and/or retirement annuities cannot total more than 15 percent of your income.
- A total of R3 500 less tax-deductible pension fund contributions: This applies mainly to people who have a qualifying income of R23 333 or less, which enables them to contribute more than the 15 percent to retirement funding.
- R1 750.

The limits on retirement annuity contributions are particularly important for women who stop working to rear children. Although you are not earning an income, you can still get tax advantages from contributing to a retirement annuity, particularly if you are receiving an income from part-time work and/or interest on investments.

The R3 500 and R1 750 contribution qualifications allow you to make claims against any income that you may still be receiving.

Any excess in retirement annuity contributions can be carried forward as deductions against income in future years, or can be taken into account when calculating the tax exemption portion of a lump-sum payment on retirement.

It may be pointless taking out a retirement annuity if there are no tax benefits in the contributions. There may, however, be benefits in the tax-free amount you get on retirement. Any amount above the limits should be invested in some other investment vehicle, like a unit trust or endowment policy, which gives capital rather than income growth.

TAX AT RETIREMENT

When you retire you have to make decisions about how you want to receive your money. Different funds are treated differently for tax purposes.

Defined contribution provident funds

Benefits are paid as a lump sum. All member contributions, excluding the growth, are tax free (because you did not use your contributions as a deduction against tax). However, employer contributions and growth are taxable at the highest average rate of the previous two years. A minimum tax-free exemption of R24 000 is allowed for provident funds, and the balance is taxed at your marginal rate of tax.

Defined benefit and defined contribution funds, and retirement annuities

You may take one-third as a lump sum and a minimum of two-thirds to fund a monthly pension. The lump sum is subject to a lower rate of taxation according to various formulas. You receive an initial maximum tax-free amount of R120 000, depending on how long you have been a member of a fund, and then the balance is taxed at your 'average' and not your 'marginal' rate of taxation. It is important to know the difference.

Marginal and average tax rates

Marginal rate of taxation: South Africa has a progressive personal income tax system. In other words, the more you earn, the greater the percentage you pay in tax. As a crude example, if you earn R1 000 you will pay 10 percent in tax (R100). If you earn R3 000 you still pay the 10 percent on the first R1 000 (R100), and 15 percent on the next R2 000 (R300). Your total tax will be R400.

Average rate of taxation: The average taxation rate is the average amount of tax you pay on your income. Taking the above example, your average rate would be:

$$\frac{\text{Total tax paid (R400)}}{\text{Taxable income (R3 000)}} \times 100 = \text{your average tax rate of 13.3\%}$$

The advantage of using your average rate is obvious. In the past, you could manipulate your average rate quite easily by reducing the level of income you receive in the year of retirement to reduce your rate merely by retiring early in the year of retirement.

In 1995 the tax authorities changed the law to prevent people retiring in the new tax year to reduce their average rate of tax to a minimum. The average rate is now based on the higher of your average tax rate in the year in which you retire, or the average rate for the preceding year.

Methods to reduce your average rate

There are four methods to reduce your income to bring down your average rate of tax:

Method One: Retire as early in the tax year as possible. By retiring early in the current tax year you will reduce your taxable income substantially because you will be receiving a pension and not a salary plus perks. You can then concentrate on reducing your non-pensionable income in the tax year before retirement.

Method Two: Reduce your income to a minimum in the year before retirement. Examples of how to reduce your income include the following:

- Do not do overtime or work that results in extra commissions.
- Do not earn unnecessary interest on investments.
- Do not cash in accumulated leave.
- Ensure that your salary is properly structured to reduce your taxable income. For example, ask your employer about salary sacrifice schemes.
- Earn income from non-taxable sources, such as dividends or cashing in investments.
- Consider taking unpaid leave before retiring.

Method Three: Reduce lump sums from sources other than retirement funds. Lump-sum payments from non-retirement-fund sources can play havoc with your average rate of tax, both because of the lump sums and because of taxable income that may be generated from the lump sum. Ways to reduce lump-sum problems include the following:

- Not taking share options or proceeds from a retirement annuity: Keep these until at least another year after retirement, at which point your income level will be lower, as will your tax rate. Again, your highest average rate of the current and the previous year are used to tax any retirement annuity lump sum.
- Invest lump sums in investments that give capital growth rather than taxable income.

Method Four: Use tax deductions such as the following:

- Purchasing a single-premium RA with part of your lump sum or other income: You are allowed to claim an amount equal to 15 percent of your annual non-retirement taxable income if you invest the money in an RA.
- If you need significant medical treatment, such as dental surgery, have it done before you retire. Depending on what you earn, you can claim a portion back against tax. This applies only to amounts not payable by medical aid. If you are 65 when you retire you are entitled to a full tax deduction for all medical expenses not paid by medical aid. This can also reduce your average rate.

Taking the maximum lump sum

The general view is that retirees should take the maximum amount they can as a lump sum payment from pension funds.

There are three reasons for this:

- Investment returns are often better.
- It is best to start your retirement debt-free, using the lump sum to put yourself firmly into the black, paying off all debt, including any outstanding amount on your home loan.
- Taxation is lower on what is called a 'voluntary annuity' than the 'compulsory annuity' you would receive by not taking the lump sum. The reason for this is that you deferred tax until you receive a pension, so you are taxed on both the capital as well as the investment growth portions of the annuity, whereas a voluntary annuity is bought with after-tax money so you pay tax only on the investment growth portion.

A few other issues that must also be taken into account include the following:

- Both a husband and wife are entitled to the tax-free exemptions on lump-sum payments, even when married in community of property. This is particularly useful in retirement planning, as one spouse can make retirement annuity contributions on behalf of the other spouse – either over a number of years or as a lump sum, which can double the exemption.
- You cannot stagger lump-sum benefits to claim the tax exemption more than once. For example, if you received the full tax exemption allowed on a lump-sum benefit when you retired, you cannot again claim that benefit on the maturity of a retirement annuity, say, five years later.
- There can be a strong argument for maturing a retirement annuity early, as the R120 000 exemption applies as soon as you reach age 55. The R120 000 has not been adjusted for inflation for a number of years, so in effect it is dropping in value at the same rate as inflation. The only exception is if you have been a member of a retirement annuity for longer than 26 years and nine months (that is the point at which the R4 500 exemption for each year of membership clicks in and exceeds the R120 000).

In other words, when the capital value of the retirement annuity is R360 000 (of which the one-third lump sum is R120 000) you should mature it, unless the length of membership makes a difference. Added to this is the argument that you are likely to get a better investment return from putting your money into a vehicle like a unit trust. Against this are costs of reinvesting the money.

TAX AFTER RETIREMENT

After retirement you become a normal taxpayer with a few differences:

- A compulsory annuity is fully taxable at your normal marginal rate of tax. Both the investment growth and the capital portion paid to you are taxable.
- A voluntary annuity has only the portion coming from investment taxed, as the capital portion was bought with after-tax money.
- When you turn 65 you receive both the primary abatement and a secondary abatement against how much tax you pay.
- When you turn 65 all your medical expenses that are not covered by a medical aid scheme are tax deductible.

22

Estate Planning

Estate planning means having a financial plan for your death. This may sound a bit macabre, but it is essential, particularly if you have children. You have no way of knowing when you will die, so it is important to start planning for death as soon as you acquire assets, start working or have dependants.

Estate planning is a multi-issue affair, which you need to approach in different ways, depending on whether you are unmarried with minor children, unmarried without children, married with minor children, or married or single with other dependants (such as elderly parents or adult dependants).

You need to plan for the unexpected. Estate planning is one of those issues you cannot afford to leave until tomorrow. There are a number of different factors you need to take into account, including your last will and testament, taxes, the value of your estate, and trusts.

Your last will and testament

Your last will and testament is merely a piece of paper on which you set down your wishes about how your assets should be divided and how your current responsibilities can continue to be met.

Don't die without a will. Dying without a will is called dying intestate. If you die without a will, your estate (i.e. everything you own) is divided up according to a formula that could see relatives you have never known getting a slice of the pie. It could also see an undeserving ex-husband getting a bit. Moreover, dying intestate could result in people who are dependent on you not receiving enough money to live comfortably.

Get advice on how to draw up a will. Although you can draw up a simple will saying 'I leave all my earthly possessions to the Home for Tabby Cats', life is normally a lot more complicated. Get advice and assistance to avoid later problems. Lawyers and banks can both draw up wills. In most cases, you will

Although you can draw up a simple will saying 'I leave all my earthly possessions to the Home for Tabby Cats', life is normally a lot more complicated.

not pay a fee because the lawyer or executor will collect a fee of 3.5 percent of your assets when you die for ensuring that the terms of the will are met.

It is important that your will spells out how, when and under what conditions your assets should be divided after your death. Your estate can be divided in a number of ways. This includes creating an income stream for an heir or merely leaving lump sums. You also have to take account of your personal circumstances.

Single without dependants

If you are single and have absolutely no assets then you need not bother to plan, but it is unlikely that you will have absolutely nothing. You should first of all consider whether it is possible that you will have dependants in the future. These could include elderly parents who do not have sufficient money for a comfortable retirement. You can give instructions in your will that the money be held until they retire, and, after their death, paid to other relatives, such as brothers or sisters.

Single with minor children

This is the most complex situation in which you can find yourself, particularly if you are widowed or divorced, as the father cannot or sometimes will not take responsibility for your children. You have to ensure that your children will be properly cared for after your death and that no one will plunder your estate at their expense.

Here are some issues you must take into account:

- You need to leave specific instructions and make arrangements for somebody to be the guardian of your children after your death.
- You need to create legal and financial structures before you die to ensure that no one can fraudulently or senselessly squander the money you have left for your children. Options include using what is called an asset protection trust. (See p. 237 for more information on trusts.)
- If you are divorced, there may be special problems that will need to be resolved. For example, provision for what happens to your children at

your death should be included in your divorce settlement. Again, you will probably have to establish a trust.

- You need to appoint an executor of your estate or trust who is not the guardian of the children to ensure that your assets are properly allocated.

Married with minor children

Being married with minor children can also create its own problems. For example, you need to plan for both you and your husband dying at the same time. Most married couples leave their assets to each other, but in the event of their simultaneous death, their children become the heirs. Your will must detail what will happen in the event of simultaneous death. So both you and your husband have to spell out details of guardianship and the structure of how your assets should be handled. When one parent dies, the surviving parent has to adjust estate planning to take account of being a single parent.

Married with adult dependants

Adult dependants could include elderly parents or children who are in some way incapacitated and need care for the rest of their lives. Adult dependants also fill a class of their own, as, again, you will probably have to establish a trust and make a decision about what happens to the residue of the trust when those dependants die.

Tax

The taxman follows you to the grave. The introduction of capital gains tax (CGT) has made it even more imperative that you plan properly for what happens after your death. You now potentially pay both estate duty and CGT on the assets you have when you die. (There is one important exemption. When one spouse leaves assets to another spouse no CGT or estate duty is payable.)

The taxman follows you to the grave.

These are the basics of estate duty and CGT:

- Estate duty (death taxes): Your estate, after the payment of debts, is taxed at a rate of 20 percent of everything over R1.5 million. The first R1.5 million of your estate is tax free, but after that you will pay 20 cents of every rand.
- Capital gains tax: Death is counted as a CGT event. This means that 25

percent of all capital gains, apart from the first R50 000, is subject to CGT at the marginal rate of tax you pay in the year of your death. CGT does not apply to assets that are normally exempt from the tax, such as your primary residence, personal effects and, importantly, the proceeds of life assurance policies (both investment and assurance against dying).

The gain is arrived at by subtracting the market value of your taxable assets from the base cost (their value when you acquired them, or their value on 1 October 2001 when CGT was introduced).

Let's look at an example of CGT at death: Jill, who is single, dies with the following assets that are subject to CGT. Her marginal income tax rate in the year of death is 40 percent.

Shares

Market value	R	650 000
Base cost	R	100 000
Capital gain	R	550 000

Unit trusts

Market value	R	250 000
Base cost	R	150 000
Capital gain	R	100 000
Total capital gains	R	650 000

Less capital losses
Industrial property

Base cost	R1	100 000
Market value	R	900 000
Capital loss	R	200 000
Total capital losses	R	200 000
Total capital gain	R	450 000
Less exemption	R	50 000
Net capital gain	R	400 000
Tax on 25% of gain	R	100 000
Tax payable at 40%	R	40 000

The value of your estate

Don't underestimate the value of your estate. Many people, particularly when they first draw up a will, don't believe they will ever have to pay estate duty or capital gains tax, because they underestimate either the current or future value of their estates. There are more millionaires than you think. If you add together the two main assets of most people – their homes and their retirement savings – the amount totals up quickly, particularly when you add any life assurance policies, savings, personal effects, etc.

Until the 2002/3 budget, the exemption had remained at R1 million for many years, meaning that inflation was reducing the value in real terms. In February 2002, it was increased to R1.5 million.

There are three main ways to reduce the tax paid on your estate, including donations, trusts and insurance:

- Donations: While you are still alive you can give away your assets at a tax-free rate of R25 000 a year. If you donate any greater sum, except to registered charitable institutions, you will have to pay donations tax of 20 percent. So, you can start giving away assets to children before you die. There are ways of giving away assets while you are alive but retaining their use. This is called a usufruct. You will, however, have to pay tax on any capital gain made on the asset you are donating, unless it is going to a charitable institution.
- Trusts: This is a way of freezing the value of your assets and removing them from your estate.
- Insurance: You should take out life assurance to cover the estate duty and capital gains tax payable. This is particularly important if your estate is made up of hard assets such as property and motor vehicles. You do not want the assets to be subject to an urgent sale so that the various taxes can be paid.

Trusts

Trusts play an important part in estate planning, particularly if you are wealthy and/or if you have dependants who may not be able to look after their own financial affairs.

A trust comes into existence when the owners of an asset surrender control of the asset or assets to trustees who act in a fiduciary capacity. The trustees (of which you can be one when you are alive) look after the assets for the benefit of beneficiaries (of which you can be one), who are nominated in terms of the trust deed. Among other things, this makes it possible for the assets to be protected after your death.

There are two basic types of trusts: testamentary trusts, which are created when you die, and intervivos (or living) trusts, which come into existence while you are alive.

Testamentary trusts

A testamentary or will trust comes into being when you die. The founding document of the trust is contained in your will. The trust is administered by trustees who are appointed in terms of your will. The driving force and rationale of a testamentary trust is that it allows for better management and control of assets as well as the protection of the beneficiaries of the assets (e.g. where there are minor children) after you die.

The trust can be designed to dissolve at any particular moment, for example when the children reach the age of 21. A testamentary trust can also be set up in terms of a joint and survivorship will, with the trust coming into effect only when the last person dies. This, for example, gives a surviving spouse the right to the assets, without interference, until death.

A testamentary trust is particularly useful for people who will not be subject to large amounts of death taxes but who want to protect the interests of minor children or other dependants who may not be capable of rational decisions.

If professional trustees are appointed (as opposed to the guardians) then you can be assured that the money will not be squandered, and the financial interests of the children will be safeguarded.

An intervivos trust

An intervivos or living trust is established during your lifetime. There are many purposes of an intervivos trust:

- Estate planning: By placing major assets like your home in a trust, you remove it from your estate. A trust is in many ways like another person, but one who need not necessarily ever die. The assets in the trust are owned by the trust and not by you. You can, however, have full use of the assets while you are alive.
- Preservation of assets after death: If you place a business in a trust it can

remove many of the problems of keeping the business going after your death, particularly if there is a partnership.

- Protection from irresponsible or vulnerable heirs: By establishing a trust with independent trustees you can assure the proper administration of your assets after your death. For example, if you have minor children your assets are kept intact and can produce an income stream for your dependants. So, if your children are adults but you feel they would spend your money irresponsibly, you can provide access to an income but not the capital amount.
- Ensuring that a new spouse does not get a claim: Second marriages after the death of a partner sometimes see the assets of one spouse going to the children of a new spouse, rather than to your children. A trust can ensure that you can, in ways, rule from the grave.

The structure of a trust

There are three parties to a trust: the settlor, the trustee and the beneficiary.

- The settlor is the person who makes the initial settlement (provides the initial amount of money, which is nominal) to get the trust going. In most cases, this is not you. The settlor is also called the donor or the founder.
- The trustees administer the trust and are appointed in the trust deed. It is generally accepted that it is best to have at least three trustees – the estate planner (yourself), another family member (e.g. your spouse) and an independent third party, who has the expertise but is independent. This is someone like a lawyer, an accountant or the representatives of a financial institution that does estate planning.
- The beneficiaries are people who are entitled to benefit from the trust administered by the trustees in terms of the trust deed.

Capital gains tax and trusts

CGT has put a different slant on trusts. Trusts have been particularly targeted by the South African Revenue Service, probably because they have increasingly been used, quite legally, as vehicles to reduce income tax and estate duty liabilities. Trusts, with the exception of what are called special trusts, pay the highest effective rate of capital gains tax.

You need to take special care with CGT on both living and testamentary trusts, as different rates of CGT apply.

Trusts are taxed on 50 percent of a capital gain, against 25 percent on an individual. Also, exemptions that apply to individuals do not apply to trusts. This includes the exemption of the first R10 000 in capital gains each year (R50 000 in the year of death) and the first R1 million of a capital gain (profit) on your primary residence. If your primary residence is held in a trust, you will pay CGT on the entire amount. As with an individual, disposal of an asset triggers a CGT event. Every time a property held in a trust is sold, even if it is your primary residence, it becomes a CGT event.

All trusts, with the exception of special trusts and testamentary trusts for minor children, which are taxed at individual income tax rates, pay income tax at the top marginal rate of 40 percent.

The only CGT exemption is on a trust (called a special trust) that is established to preserve assets used for the financial well-being of people who are mentally or physically incapacitated and unable to earn a living. Special trusts are subject to the same CGT rate and exemptions as individuals. In other words, 25 percent of a gain is taxed and not the 50 percent as applies to normal trusts.

Because of the complexities involved you should get proper advice on the impact of CGT on a trust. In essence, you need to balance whether capital gains tax will cost you more or less than estate duty and how this impacts on your other reasons for establishing a trust.

Trusts in South Africa are structured in two ways: as vesting trusts or as discretionary trusts. Vesting trusts are vehicles where the beneficiaries of a trust have an automatic right to both the income and the assets in the trust. Discretionary trusts do not give beneficiaries an automatic right to income and assets. The discretion to distribute either income or assets lies with the trustees.

This difference has an impact on how CGT is levied. A vesting trust is treated as an agent. The capital gain or loss is seen as a gain or loss in the hands of the beneficiary, with the beneficiary being liable for CGT. If an actual asset is distributed the trust will be deemed to have made the distribution at the market value (not the original book value) of the asset and will pay CGT on any gain. The beneficiary's base cost will be the market value.

With a discretionary trust, if a distribution is made by the trustees within the year that a capital gain/loss is made, then the gain/loss is transferred to the beneficiary. If a capital gain is made in a different year from a distribution, the trust is liable for the tax. If an asset is distributed by the trustees to a beneficiary, the disposal creates a CGT event in the hands of the trust. The asset is transferred to the beneficiary at a base cost that is equal to the market value.

As a result of these two legal structures, you can also alter the CGT rate you will pay on the assets housed in the trust. Because an individual pays a lower rate of tax than a trust and qualifies for the R10 000 annual exemption, tax will be saved if an asset is awarded to a beneficiary who is a South African resident. The reason is that any capital gain will be taxed in the hands of the beneficiary at the lower rate.

A trust deed should empower the trustees to vest assets or rights in local beneficiaries at their discretion. The trustees will then have the flexibility to ensure that a beneficiary, rather than the trust, pays the tax.

Other issues you need to take into account in placing assets into a trust include the following:

- The estate duty you will save at death.
- The possibility of creating CGT events, and the subsequent tax these events will generate.
- Income tax planning: These advantages should be secondary and seen as a bonus – not as the primary motive. Alarm bells should ring if tax planning is the primary motive for a trust, as there are many provisions in the Income Tax Act that will deem income to be taxed in your hands if the SARS believes you are avoiding tax.
- Preservation of assets after death.
- The ongoing management of your assets, including contractual arrangements: This is particularly useful in a business arrangement where value could be lost by selling off a business share.
- Protection of assets from creditors: If you are in debt and cannot repay the money, the person or company (creditor) to whom you owe money can apply to court to take possession of any assets you own. If the assets are held in a trust they cannot be claimed by your creditors. However, if it can be proved that you transferred the assets to a trust to prevent payment of debts, the court can order the assets to be taken from the trust.
- Protection from extravagant children, who will not be able to go on a spending spree, reducing the assets to nil.
- Protection of a vulnerable spouse, particularly in the case of a second marriage after your death.

- Protection of minor and/or vulnerable children, particularly if they are disabled in some manner.
- Income tax splitting: Under some circumstances income from a trust can be split between a couple, thereby reducing tax liability. For example, if one spouse has a marginal rate of 40 percent and the other of 30 percent, there is an advantage in the spouse on the lower marginal rate being the recipient of the income from the trust.
- Assuring rapid access to income and capital after your death: Payment to beneficiaries can be delayed for up to a year in the winding up of your estate. A trust avoids many of the complications and delays, with beneficiaries receiving benefits immediately.
- Multi-ownership of assets: It is not easy to divide some assets, such as a business, a farm or other property, between heirs. By placing the asset in a trust, it can be held intact, with your heirs being the beneficiaries to the income generated by the asset.
- Impartiality: You can expect the decisions of a third (professional) trustee to be impartial, not favouring any individual beneficiary, particularly after your death.
- Confidentiality: On your death your will becomes a public document. However, because a trust does not become part of your estate, the assets held in the trust remain confidential.
- Flexibility: Trusts provide wide choices, giving flexibility if the tax, political or economic situation changes significantly.
- Cost saving: The assets in the trust are not subject to any of the fees or costs of winding up an estate.

Select Bibliography

Bruce Cameron, Alide Dasnois, Charlene Clayton and Esann de Kock, *Personal Finance: The Scrapbook Series*. Johannesburg: Worth Publishing.

Bruce Cameron and Magnus Heystek, *Retirement: The Amazing and Scary Truth*. Johannesburg: Worth Publishing. 2000.

A.H. Davey, *Handbook on Estate Planning*. The Life Underwriters Association of South Africa. 1995.

Deloitte & Touche, *Pay Less Tax: The Essential Guide to Practical Tax Planning*, 13th edition. Durban: Butterworths. 2000/01.

C. Divaris and M.L. Stein, *The Old Mutual Income Tax Guide* (various editions). Durban: Butterworths.

James A.B. Downie, *The Essentials of Retirement Fund Management in Southern Africa*. Durban: Butterworths.

Esann de Kock, *60 Minute Guide to Healthcare Finance*. Johannesburg: Worth Publishing. 2000.

M.A. Kourie and S. Keetse, *Tax and Investments Easiguide*. Durban: Butterworths. 1999.

Personal Finance magazine. Various articles by Personal Finance staff. Independent Newspapers.

Personal Finance newspaper. Various articles by Personal Finance staff. Independent Newspapers.

South African Department of Finance, *Budget and Budget review documents*.

Willie van der Westhuizen and Anthony Chiat, *A Practical Approach to Trusts*. Durban: Butterworths. 1996.

Contact Details

The banking adjudicator
Telephone: (011) 838 0035
Fax: (011) 838 0043
Postal address: PO Box 5728, Johannesburg 2000
E-mail: adjudicator@adjudicator.org.za

The Financial Services Board (FSB)
Telephone: (012) 428 8000
Fax: (012) 347 0221
Postal address: PO Box 35655, Menlo Park 0102
E-mail: info@fsb.co.za

The ombudsman for life assurance
Telephone: (021) 674 0330
Fax: (021) 674 0951
Postal address: PO Box 45007, Claremont 7735
E-mail: ombud@mweb.co.za

The ombudsman for short-term insurance
Telephone: (011) 726 8900
Fax: (011) 726 5501
Postal address: PO Box 30619, Braamfontein 2017
E-mail: hendrikv@insuranceombudsman.co.za

The pension fund adjudicator
Telephone: (021) 674 0209
Fax: (021) 674 0185
Postal address: PO Box 23005, Claremont 7735
E-mail: enquiries@pfa.org.za

Index

access bonds *see* variable home loans
accident indemnity assurance 120
ad valorem taxes 65
AIDS *see* HIV/AIDS
alimony 103, 212
    and life assurance 121
amount-based saving 27
antenuptial contracts (ANCs) 100–101, 106
appreciating assets 20
asset allocation funds 177, 178
asset classes 169–73, 174
asset managers 176, 177, 179
asset protection trusts 234
automatic teller machines (ATMs) 32, 33
    and safety 35–6
average tax rates 56, 229–31

balance sheets 4, 7–9, 21
bank accounts 31–3
banking 31–9
banking adjudicator 39, 244
banking security 34–9
benchmarks 191, 193–4
beneficiaries 47, 111, 123–4, 185, 207, 238,
        239
    preferential beneficiaries 47
bond investments 171–2, 174, 176, 181
bond registration 78
budgets 4–7, 21, 111
Buffet, Warren 178

call centres 33
capital gains tax (CGT) 53, 57–63, 116, 211
    base values 60–62
    and estate planning 235–6
    exemptions 57, 59, 62–3
    rollovers 59
car financing 66–73
    cash 67
    and consolidated debt loans 68
    hire purchase 68–9

and home loans 67–8
    residual value financing 69–71
    vehicle leases 69–72
cars 66–73
    Automobile Association (AA) 72, 73
    guarantees for 72
    and maintenance contracts 73
    second-hand vehicles 72
    tax implications 73
    see also car financing
capital growth 168, 171, 172
cash investments 169–70, 174
CCMA *see* Commission for Conciliation,
        Mediation and Arbitration
Certified Financial Analysts (CFAs) 167
Certified Financial Planners (CFPs) 154, 161
cheque accounts 31, 32
cheques 21, 31
    and security 36–7
childbirth 110–11
    and medical aid cover 111
    and employment conditions 110
    and Unemployment Insurance Fund
        (UIF) 48
children x, 110–13
    costs of 110–13
    education of x, 111–12
    and estate planning 112–13
    and life assurance 111, 120–21
    see also childbirth
chronic disease assurance 119
collective investments *see* pooled investments
Commission for Conciliation, Mediation
        and Arbitration (CCMA) 49
compound interest 28–30
compulsory purchase annuities 222–3, 231,
        232
consolidated debt loans 68, 82
consumables 21
convenience stores 42
convertible term assurance 119

coupons
  shopping 43
  bond 171
credit cards 21, 22–3, 24, 32–3, 41–2
  and security 37–8
credit life assurance 43–7
  and add-on investments 46
  and home-loan-linked endowments 46
current accounts *see* cheque accounts
custody 103, 104

death taxes *see* estate duty
debit orders 38–9
debt 5, 7, 20–26
decreasing term life assurance 119
defined benefit pension funds 213–15
  taxation of 228, 229
defined contribution pension funds 215–17
  taxation of 228, 229
defined contribution provident funds 217–19
  taxation of 227, 229
Department of Trade and Industry 94
dependants 112, 115–16, 117
  adult dependants 233, 235, 237
depreciating assets 21, 66
derivatives 169, 173, 174
disability assurance 115, 116, 119, 120, 124–9
  benefits 126
  exclusions 126
  limitations 127–8
  premium payments 128–9
discount stores 42
discretionary trusts 240
diversification 175–7
dividends 168, 172
Division of Pension Interests on Divorce Bill 108
divorce 102–8
  alimony 103
  custody 103, 104
  division of assets 104–5
  legal advice 102–3
  and life assurance 103, 105–6, 121
  maintenance 103, 104
  and medical insurance 103,105

remarrying after 109
and retirement savings 103, 106–8, 209–10
Divorce Act 106
donations tax 53, 64, 181
dread disease assurance 119, 124

effective interest rates 29–30
EFTs *see* exchange traded funds
electronic banking 33–4
emergency fund 5, 25, 111
employment xi–xii, 48–51
  discrimination xi–xii, 48–9
  and labour laws 48
  and retirement 51
Employment Equity Act 49
equities *see* shares
equity markets 163
equity unit trust funds 25, 177, 178
estate agent's fees 80–81
estate duty 53, 64, 116, 181, 211, 235, 237
  and life assurance 123, 185
estate planning 233–42
  and tax 235–6
  and dependants 234–5
exchange controls 176, 197, 199
exchange rates 201
exchange traded funds (EFTs) 193
executor's fees 123, 185

financial advisers 152–7, 161–2, 166–7, 208
  and commission 152, 154, 156, 157, 161, 163, 181
  company agents 154–5
  general agents 155
  independent financial advisors 155–6
Financial Advisory and Intermediary Services Act 153
financial assets 169–73
financial needs analysis 16–18, 111, 117, 120, 158
financial plan 15–19
Financial Planning Institute of South Africa 154, 161
Financial Services Board (FSB) 145, 164, 167, 192, 193, 201, 244
fixed deposit account 160, 169

fixed-level term life assurance 116, 118
foreign investment 176, 197–201
   rand-denominated (asset-swap) foreign
     investment 197
   foreign-currency-denominated foreign
     investment 198
   offshore investment 199–200
   non-offshore investment 200–201
foreign-currency-denominated foreign
     investment 198
freehold title 76
FSB *see* Financial Services Board
fuel levy 65
futures 173, 191

gambling 24, 59, 166, 174
GARP *see* growth at realistic prices
gearing 191–2
gender discrimination ix–xiii, 48–51, 52,
   202–3
gilts *see* bond investments
glass ceiling xii, 203
granny flats 83, 84
group life and disability assurance 105–6,
   118, 207, 217, 219
growth at realistic prices (GARP) 179
growth investment 179
guarantees 40–41
   on motor vehicles 72
   on investments 162, 180, 184, 187
guardianship of children 104, 112

hard assets 169
health assurance 130–39
healthcare 18, 130–39, 208–9, 221
hedge funds 173, 182, 190–93
hire purchase 42, 69
HIV/AIDS 49, 118, 119, 132, 217
   and life assurance 122, 123
   and disability assurance 126
home loan interest rates 78, 82
   variable rates 82
   fixed rates 82
home loans 23–4, 67–8, 81–2, 83
household contents insurance *see* short-term
   insurance

Housing Development Schemes of Retired
   Persons Act 85

import taxes 65
impulse shopping 41, 42
income disability assurance 126
income protection assurance *see* disability
   assurance
income statement 4
income tax 53, 54–6, 181
   rates 55–6
increasing term life assurance 118–19
indices 187, 193–4
   see also benchmarks
indirect taxation 64–5
inflation 159, 182, 194, 237
   push inflation 159
   pull inflation 159
information technology market collapse
   173, 178
interest 168
   see also compound interest
interest rates 20, 29–30, 25, 78, 82, 171–2
Internet 16, 33–4, 37, 167
Internet banking 33–4
Internet shopping 37
intervivos trusts 238–9
investments 158–201
   benchmarks 191, 93–4
   costs of 181
   diversification of 175–7
   guarantees on 162, 180, 184, 187
   income vs capital growth 168
   liquidity 179
   maturation of 195–6
   own portfolios 167
   pooling 167–8, 176, 183
   product providers 193
   and risks 173–5
   switching of 194–5
   taxation of 181
   types of 169–71, 177–9, 183–93
investment markets 163, 163–4,
   173–4, 177
ipac 180

joint bank accounts 11
joint life assurance 119
JSE Securities Exchange All Share Index 187, 191, 194
JSE Securities Exchange 60, 170, 177, 191, 193

Labour Court 49
last will and testament 112, 233–5
leases
    car 69–71
    housing 74–5
lending investments 168
leverage *see* gearing
life assurance 18, 114–29
    capital amount required for 117
    endowments 183–6
    exclusions 123
    premiums 122–3
    types of 118–20
linked investment products 189
liquidity 179–80
live-in relationships 99
long investments 191
Long-Term Insurance Act 184
Lotto 59, 166
luxury taxes 65

maintenance for children 103, 104
maintenance contracts for vehicles 73
Maintenance of Surviving Spouses Act 212
marginal tax rates 55, 159, 229–30
market sectors 177–8
market-linked investments 184, 216
marriage 99–101
    and life assurance 121
    in community of property 100
    out of community of property 100–101
    out of community of property with accrual 101
Masterbond property scam 165
maternity benefits 50
maternity leave 49, 50
medical aid schemes 131–9
    traditional medical aid schemes 132–4
    managed healthcare schemes 143

new-generation schemes 135
    limitations 136
    and retirement 139
    taxation of 137
medical assurance 130, 131
Medical Schemes Act 130, 131, 153
Medical Schemes Council 137
mining 177
minister of finance 53, 153
money market accounts 25, 160, 169
mortgage participation bonds 170
multimanager investments 183, 188–93

NCDs *see* Notional Certificates of Deposit
negative-response selling 45
net asset value test 179
net worth 9, 21
no-claim bonuses 145, 149
nominal interest rates 29–30
non-offshore investments 200–201
Notional Certificates of Deposit (NCDs) 169

offshore investments 199–200
ombudsman for life assurance 244
ombudsman for long-term insurance 153, 155
ombudsman for short-term insurance 151, 153, 244
ombudsmen, role of 153
opportunity costs 210
options 173, 191
overdrafts 31, 32
ownership investments 168

paper loss 163, 195
Parliament 53, 85, 212
Pay As You Earn (PAYE) 54
pension fund adjudicator 153, 244
Pension Funds Act 108, 212
pensions 18, 205–6
personal identification numbers (PINs) 35
policyholder protection regulations 145, 153, 184
pooled investments 167–8, 176, 183
premium waiver life assurance 120
price/earnings (p/e) ratio test 179

property
   buying 74–90
   freehold title 76
   renting 74–6
   sectional title 76–7
   see also property investments
property investments 70–71, 174
   mortgage participation bonds 170
   property loan stocks 170
   property syndications 170
   property unit trusts (PUTs) 170
   see also property
property rates 79
property syndications 170
property transfer tax 53, 64, 78
property unit trusts (PUTs) 170
provisional income tax 54–5
PUTs *see* property unit trusts
PINs *see* personal identification numbers

RAMS *see* Rates of Medical Societies
rand-denominated (asset-swap) foreign
      investment 197
rand-denominated foreign investment 197
rates 53, 79
Rates of Medical Societies (RAMS) 132–3, 136
real growth 159, 182
Receiver of Revenue *see* South African
      Revenue Service
remarriage 109
   and blending families 109
   after divorce 109
   as a widow 109
retirement xii–xiii, 168, 202–32
   beating retirement discrimination 202–12
   capital 203–4
   investment for 212–32
   pensions 205–6
   see also retirement homes
retirement annuities (RAs) 18, 53, 106,
      107, 108, 154, 181, 189, 207, 209,
      211, 213, 220–21, 222, 223, 228,
      229, 231, 232
   taxation of 228, 229
retirement homes 83–90
   see also retirement villages

retirement savings 203–4, 212–32
   defined benefit pension funds 213–15,
      228, 229
   defined contribution pension funds
      215–17, 228, 229
   defined contribution provident funds
      217–19, 227, 229
   taxation of 227–32
retirement villages 84–90
   frail-care facilities 85, 87
   freehold title 88
   lease schemes 90
   levies 86
   life right 89–90
   sectional title 88
   share block schemes 88–9
risk assurance 18
risk profile 174–5
Rule of 72 28

SA Home Loans 81
Satrix 40 193
saving 27–30, 158
savings account 32
savings goals 13–15, 111, 116
   short-term goals 14
   medium-term goals 14
   long-term goals 14
second-hand cars 72
sectional title 76–7
   timeshare schemes 91, 92
secured debt 22
shares 172–3, 174, 176, 181
shorting 191
short-term insurance 140–50
   brokers 144
   excess 141
   exclusions 141
   premiums 141, 143
   types of 142, 144
   valuations 143
single-debt loans *see* consolidated debt
      loans
singlehood 98–9
   and life assurance 120–21
small claims court 149–50

smoothed bonus investments 180, 184, 216
South African Revenue Service (SARS) 51, 53, 54, 55, 107, 181, 182
special trusts 113, 240
spending 40–7
  and credit cards 41–2
  and paying cash 41
stable bonus policies *see* smoothed bonus investments
Standard Income Tax on Employees (SITE) 54
stop orders 39
store cards 21, 22–3, 42
structured investment products 180

taxation 52–65, 159
  arbitrage 182
  deductions 57
  deferral of 53, 181–2
  direct 53–63
  exemptions 182
  and income-shifting 53
  and income-splitting 52–3, 242
  indirect 53, 64–5
  and investment choice 53
  preferential rates 182
  rebates 56
tax havens 199
terminal illness assurance 120
testamentary trusts 238
time-based saving 27
timeshare 91–7
  club schemes 91, 92
  point schemes 91, 92
  RCI rating 95
  sectional title schemes 91, 92
  shareblock schemes 91, 92
Timeshare Institute of South Africa (TISA) 93–4
transfer taxes 53, 64
  see also property transfer taxes
transmission accounts 32
trusts 237–42
  asset protection trusts 234
  and capital gains tax 239–42

discretionary trusts 240
intervivos trusts 238–9
structure of 239
testamentary trusts 238
vesting trusts 240

Unemployment Insurance Fund (UIF) 50–51
  adoption benefits 50
  and dependants 50
  illness benefits 50
  maternity benefits 50
unit trust funds of funds 189
unit trust multimanager funds 189
unit trusts 25, 177–8, 183, 186–93
  actively managed funds 187
  passive (index) funds 187
  types of 177–8
unsecured debt 22

value added tax (VAT) 65, 123, 185
value investment 178–9
variable home loans 23–4, 67–8, 81–2
VAT *see* value added tax
vehicle financing *see* car financing
vehicle insurance *see* short-term insurance
vehicle leases 69–71
vesting trusts 240
voluntary purchase annuities 180, 223–7, 231, 232
  life annuities 223
  life annuity structures 224–5
  living annuities 226–7
  temporary life voluntary annuites 225
  term-certain voluntary annuities 225–6

warranties *see* guarantees
warrants 173
widowhood 109, 210–12
  and capital gains tax 109
  and life assurance policies 109
  and remarrying 109
  and retirement funds 109, 210–12
wills 112, 233–5
wrap funds 181, 189–90